Literary Quotations:

Genre

Compiled, Edited, and Arranged by

Jim Fisher

ISBN: 1515126366
ISBN-13: 978-1515126362

Also by Jim Fisher

Security for Business and Industry

The Lindbergh Case

Fall Guys:
False Confessions and the Politics Of Murder

The Ghosts of Hopewell:
Setting the Record Straight in the Lindbergh Case

Crimson Stain (mass market paperback)

Ten Percent of Nothing:
The Literary Agent From Hell

The Writer's Quotebook:
500 Authors on Creativity, Craft, and the Writing Life

Forensics Under Fire:
Are Bad Science and Dueling Experts Corrupting Criminal Justice?

SWAT Madness and The Militarization of the American Police:
A National Dilemma

Crimson Stain (trade paper edition with Epilogue)

The GE Mound Case:
The Archaeological Disaster and Criminal Persecution of Art Gerber

The Mammoth Book of Murder:
True Stories of Violent Death

The Mammoth Book of True Crime:
True Storied of Bad Behavior

CONTENTS

ACKNOWLEDGEMENTS

Veronica Fisher designed and prepared this book for publication. I am grateful for her invaluable contribution to this project.

1 THE MAINSTREAM NOVEL

The *tone* of a novel may be described in words like comic, wry, reflective, tongue-in-cheek, bittersweet, or in compounds such as incipient fear, sense of lurking evil and sense of unease.

Lesley Grant-Adamson, *Writing Crime and Suspense Fiction*, 1996

Willing suspension of disbelief is a strange state of mine--reading nonfiction does not require it and neither does reading poetry, since both are based on logical argument...The world is full of people who are rather proud that they don't read novels. Publishers often lament that the audience for novels is narrowing, and especially that it is losing men. A literary education not only enlarges a readers' willingness to suspend disbelief by extending her range of pleasures, it also strengthens her ability to enter the meditative state, and to be receptive to the influence of another human mind, because it is a state of contemplation that is essential to the true appreciation of the novel.

Jane Smiley, *13 Ways at Looking at the Novel*, 2005

In any piece of fiction, the writer's first job is to convince the reader that the events he recounts really happened, or to persuade the reader that they might have happened (given small changes in the laws of the universe), or else to engage the reader's interest in the patent absurdity of the lie. The realistic writer's way of making events convincing is verisimilitude. The tale writer, telling stories of ghosts, or shape-shifter, or some character who never sleeps, uses a different approach: By the quality of his voice, and by means of various devices that distract the critical intelligence, he gets what

Coleridge called--in one of the most clumsy famous sentences in all literature--"the willing suspension of disbelief for the moment, which constitutes poetic faith."

John Gardner, *The Art of Fiction*, 1983

I have to drink and gamble to get away from this typewriter. Not that I don't love this old machine when it's working right. But knowing when to go to it and knowing to stay away from it, that's the trick. I really don't want to be a *professional* writer, I wanna write what I wanna write. Else, it's all been wasted...So did Hemingway, until he started talking about "discipline"; Pound also talked about doing one's "work". But I've been luckier than both of them because I've worked the factories and slaughterhouses and I know that work and *discipline* are dirty words. I know what they meant, but for me, it has to be a different game.

Charles Bukowski in *Charles Bukowski: Selected Letters 1965-1970*, edited by Seamus Cooney, 2004

Any novelist who's ever stood in a bookstore, watching as someone picks up a copy of their book and pauses before returning it to the shelf, knows there's no logical explanation for why particular books appeal to particular people. Over time, though, readers do tend to make intuitive decisions. Someone who wants a fast-moving story may seek out what she imagines is a plot-driven novel. Someone who wants to spend time in close quarters, getting to know a person like herself, or perhaps like no one she's ever met, may choose what appears to be a character-driven novel. And someone who tends to pepper margins with exclamation points, who calls a friend to shout, "Listen to this line!," may gravitate to a book preoccupied with language.

Meg Wolitzer, "Life Intervened," (a review of *Clever Girl* by Tessa Hadley), *The New York Times Book Review*, March 16, 2014

Fiction explores how interesting people deal with significant problems at important times in their lives. Stories explore human vulnerabilities and strengths and are usually focused on a character's goals and dilemmas. They inquire into why people act, react, struggle and change as they do. Stories are shaped from techniques that make the narrative lifelike, involved, complicated, and tense...

There are many types of fiction configured into novels, novellas, and short stories. There are comedies, tragedies, happily-ever-after stories, horror stories, historical re-creations, fantasies, young adult stories, and novels that roller coaster along with pathos, black humor, and grim portrayals of humanity. Some novels track the affairs of the heart; others track a murderer to his hideout or a monster to his lair. Fiction can be of a serious or literary bent or can be as fluffy as marshmallows. Short stories come in all sizes, and novels weigh in at 60,000 words or ramble on to 200,000 words.

Jessica Page Morrell, *Between the Lines,* 2006

I like the Randall Jarrell line: "A novel is a prose narration of some length that has something wrong with it." I think that's true. If you're going to write a hundred, a hundred and fifty, two hundred thousand words, perfection is a fantasy.

Salman Rushdie, *The Paris Review,* 2005

In my view, stories and novels consist of three parts: narration, which moves the story from point A to point B and finally to point Z; description, which creates a sensory reality for the reader; and dialogue, which brings characters to life through their speech.

You may wonder where plot is in all of this. The answer--my answer, anyway--is nowhere. I won't try to convince you that I've never plotted any more than I'd try to convince you that I've never told a lie, but I do both as infrequently as possible. I distrust plot for two reasons: first, because our *lives* are largely plotless, even when you add in all our reasonable precautions and careful planning; and second, because I believe plotting and the spontaneity of real creation aren't compatible. It's best that I be as clear about this as I can--I want you to understand that my basic belief about the making of stories is that they pretty much make themselves.

Stephen King, *On Writing,* 2000

If I am to be honest, I must admit that most books disappoint me. Contemporary American fiction in particular. What so many writers seem to have forgotten, or never to have learned in the first place, is that reading should not be a torture. I will also admit that I find whimsy fatiguing.

David Leavitt, *The New York Times Book Review,* June 29, 2014

Novels of Manners emphasize social customs, manners, conventions and mores of a definite social class. Such novels are always realistic, and sometimes they are satiric and comic, as in Henry Fielding's or Jane Austen's work.

Sherri Szeman, *Mastering Point of View*, 2001

Is there a subject too daunting, a perversion too kinky to mention? Show a writer a taboo and we'll turn it into a story. Pedophilia? Nabokov's Humbert Humbert has been there, done that…The recent craze for zombie fiction offered an orgy of the restless undead feasting on human flesh. Genre novels serve up all sorts of grisly horrors and murder, and the popularity of *Fifty Shades of Gray* suggests that readers have no problem with sex beyond the vanilla. Even love between the species finds its expression in fairy tales like *The Frog Prince* and *Beauty and the Beast*.

Francine Prose, *The New York Times Book Review*, July 20, 2014

Many writers distrust fiction that smacks of autobiography. They believe that autobiographical fiction represents in some way a failure of the writer's imagination, or that such writers have only one good book in them and, after they have finished their autobiographical effort, they will have spent their creativity and no more will be heard from them. There's an air of smugness in that kind of attitude. The writer who makes such a claim is, in effect, saying "Autobiographical writing is not *real* writing," and "I'm a real writer and people who want to be real writers should write like me--that is, from the unlimited stores of my superior imagination."…

There might be *some* truth in the fact that writers whose first novels are autobiographical find it more difficult than other writers to write a second novel, but writers of any stripe have a difficult time following a first novel. I've heard that as many as half of all first novelists never write a second.

Robin Hemley, *Turning Life Into Fiction*, 2006

Let us consider the problems of the long novel, in which the heft is apt to come in for almost as much critical examination as the contents. There is, for instance, Jack Beatty's famous critique of James A. Michener's *Chesapeake* (865 pages): "My best advice is don't read it; my second best is don't drop it on your foot." Presumably, Beatty read it--or at least skimmed it--before offering these helpful hints, but you get the idea. In this hurry-scurry age, big books are viewed with suspicion, and sometimes disdain.

The book buyer's suspicions are more justified. The critic, after all, is being paid to read. Consumers must spend their hard-earned cash for the same privilege. Then there's the question of time. Prospective buyers have every right to ask: "Do I really want to give two weeks of my reading life to this novel? Can it possibly be worth it when there are so many others--most a good deal shorter--clamoring for my attention?"

Stephen King, "Flights of Fancy," *The New York Times Book Review,* October 13, 2013

Notoriously, women tolerate qualities in a lover--moodiness, selfishness, unreliability, brutality--that they would never countenance in a husband, in return for excitement, and infusion of intense feeling...Perversity is the muse of modern literature. Today the house of fiction is full of mad lovers, gleeful rapists, castrated sons--but very few husbands.

Susan Sontag, *Against Interpretation,* 1969

Imagine, if you will, a book on trial for being boring...Imagine the arguments: the solid citizens called by the prosecution to testify that this book had bored them senseless. Imagine the authors and hip professors brought in by the defense to assert that the book was not boring at all, but on the contrary a work of great and lasting interest.

James Parker, *The New York Times Book Review,* July 20, 2014

No historical character in a novel should do or say anything that you don't know he said and did. You can't displace him in time, and you can't move him geographically. And you've got to be true to him. If I wrote a novel that included Billy The Kid, it would be the Billy The Kid out of history; in other words, he couldn't be the main character....I would never quote Billy if I didn't have a valid quote. I wouldn't put him in any part of New Mexico that he wasn't in at that date; I believe you owe that to historical characters. Nothing distressed me more than to see an historical character in one of those historical, romance novels take the hero aside and give him a little advice on his love life or something. I don't think you have a right to do that with historical characters.

Shelby Foote (1916-2005), *Conversations with Shelby Foote,* 1989

The line between fiction and nonfiction is more blurry than many people like to admit. Sometimes, political writing that claims to be nonfiction is actually fiction. The political power of such fiction-as-nonfiction is undeniable...

The power of fictions that admit to being fiction, such as novels, may seem to pale in comparison. There are exceptions, of course: In popular lure, Harriet Beecher Stowe's *Uncle Tom's Cabin* is said to have led to slavery's abolition.

Novels aren't directly credited with starting wars, yet fiction still instigates change. Fiction can say publicly what might otherwise appear unsayable, combating the coerced silence that is a favored weapon of those who have power...

Does fiction affect politics? Yes, inevitably. So is all fiction political? To my mind, yes again. Fiction writers who claim their writing is not political are simply writers who seek to dissociate themselves from the politics furthered by their writing. Making up stories is an inherently political act. Like voting is. And like choosing not to vote is, too.

Mohsin Hamid, *The New York Times Book Review*, February 17, 2015

At his sentencing hearing in 1981, after he was convicted of John Lennon's murder, Mark David Chapman read aloud from J.D. Salinger's *The Catcher in the Rye:* I'm standing on the edge of some crazy cliff. What I have to do, I have to catch everybody if they start to go over...I'd just be the catcher in the rye and all."

The Catcher in the Rye was the book Chapman had been reading at the crime scene when he was arrested. It was the book that held, as he claimed, his message for the world. He was standing at the cliff; he was just doing his work.

A few years later, the serial killers Leonard Lake and Charles Ng embarked on what they called "Operation Miranda," a violent spree of torture, rape and murder named for the woman abducted by a deranged butterfly collector in John Fowles' novel *The Collector*, which they cited as their inspiration.

Leslie Jamison, *The New York Times Book Review*, September 14, 2014

Some authors appeal mainly to men: Tom Clancy, Len Deighton, Jack Higgins, Gavin Lyall, Frederick Forsyth, Harlan Coben, Lee Child, Gerald Seymour. This is neither praise nor blame, it's just a fact. I don't think there's a school of writing that's classified as Bloke Lit, not yet. But it may be the next big thing.

Points that come to mind about writing for men are: Men like information and excitement. Men like heroes and heroines who are lookers. Men like shorter books. [Most true crime readers are women. Women like their crime, and they like it real.]

Maeve Binchy, *The Maeve Binchy Writer's Club*, 2008

My own idea is that fiction...falls into three main categories: literature, mainstream fiction, and pulp fiction...To label a novel "pulp" is not the same as saying it's a bad novel, or will give the reader no pleasure...To condemn pulp writing out of hand is like condemning a girl as loose simply because she came from unpleasant family circumstances.

Stephen King, *Secret Windows*, 2002

One learns most clearly what not to do by reading bad prose. Reading *Valley of the Dolls* and *Bridges of Madison County* is worth a semester at a good writing school, even with the superstar guest lecturers thrown in.

Good writing, on the other hand, teaches the learning writer about style, graceful narration, plot development, the creation of believable characters and truth-telling. A novel like *The Grapes of Wrath* may fill a new writer with feelings of despair and good old-fashioned jealousy--"I'll never be able to write anything that good, not if I live to be a thousand"--but such feelings can also serve as a spur, goading the writer to work harder and aim higher.

Stephen King, *On Writing*, 2000

Many people have written thinly veiled tell-all books disguised as fiction. They're called romans a`clef. In the late 1970s, Truman Capote was working on one about Hollywood called *Answered Prayers*, and an excerpt was published in *Esquire*. Half of his friends disowned him because he'd told a lot of secrets about their lives. He uncovered a lot of dirt. His defense was pretty valid: His former friends told him these stories freely at parties, in the presence of others, knowing all along he was a writer. "What did they think I was?" he asked with a mixture of hurt and acidity, "the court jester?"

Robin Hemley, *Turning Life Into Fiction*, 2006

It's more interesting to read about something being wrong than everything being right. Happiness threatens the things that every writing workshop demands: suspense, conflict, desire. It also threatens particularity. Happiness collapses characters into people who look just like everyone else, without the sharper contours of pathos to mark their edges and render them distinct. As Tolstoy famously tells us at the beginning of *Anna Karenina*: "All happy families are alike; each unhappy family is unhappy in its own way."

Leslie Jamison, "Bookends," *The New York Times Book Review,* March 16, 2014

Movies have always seemed to me a much tighter form of storytelling than novels, requiring greater compression, and in that sense falling somewhere between the short story and the novel in scale. To watch a feature film is to be immersed in its world for an hour and a half, or maybe two, or exceptionally three. A novel that takes only three hours to read would be a short novel indeed, and novels that last five times as long are commonplace.

Television is more capacious. Episode after episode, and season after season, a serial drama can uncoil for dozens of hours before reaching its end. Along the way, its characters and plot have room to develop, to change course, to congeal. In its near limitlessness, TV rivals the novel...

Mohsin Hamid, *The New York Times Book Review,* March 2, 2014

The 1960s were when the demise of fiction became something to crow about. Philip Roth told us that life in America had become so barbaric and bizarre that no fiction could hold a candle to the grotesque truth. Truman Capote allowed as how he had invented a new kind of narrative treat, the nonfiction novel that made the un-non kind as obsolete as hand-churned ice cream. Tom Wolfe let us know that his new journalism was zippier, grabbier, funnier, wilder, and truer-to-life than any old wistful bit of fiction published, say, by those tiny giants over at *The New Yorker*.

John Updike in *Handbook of Short Story Writing,* Jean M. Fredette, editor, 1988

In our time, the only type of fiction that shows definite signs of fading from our culture is the traditional, unclassifiable story variously identified as literary, academic, and mainstream. If your writing cannot conveniently be defined as suspense, romance, western, or science fiction, your chances of publishing under a major imprint are about as likely as being struck by lightening while being kidnapped by terrorists on your way to claim your million-dollar lottery check.

As with all trends, this one is governed by the laws of commerce. General fiction is a hard sell.

Loren D. Estleman, *Writing the Popular Novel,* 2004

Television was so bad for so long, it's no surprise that the arrival of good television has caused the culture to lose its head a bit. Since the debut of "The Sopranos" in 1999, we have been living, so we are regularly informed, in a "golden age" of television. And over the last few years, it's become common to hear variations on the idea that quality cable TV shows are the new novels....

To liken TV shows to novels suggests an odd ambivalence toward both genres. Clearly, the comparison is intended to honor TV, by associating it with the prestige and complexity that traditionally belong to literature. But at the same time, it is covertly a form of aggression against literature, suggesting that novels have ceded their role to a younger, more popular, more dynamic art form. Mixed feelings about literature--the desire to annex its virtues while simultaneously belittling them--are typical of our culture today, which doesn't know quite how to deal with an art form, like the novel, that is both democratic and demanding. [I don't know about democratic, but demanding, yes. Instead of demanding, I would use the term pretentious and unreadable other than to English lit professors who force this crap on their students who will someday be doing the same to their students.]...

Spectacle and melodrama remain at the heart of TV, as they do with all arts that must reach a large audience in order to be economically viable. But it is voice, tone, the sense of the author's mind at work, that are the essence of literature, and the exist in language, not in images. This doesn't mean we shouldn't be grateful for our good TV shows; but let's not fool ourselves into thinking that they give us what only literature can....

Adam Kirsch, "Are the New 'Golden Age' TV Shows the New Novels?" *The New York Times,* February 25, 2014

You've seen the movie, now read the book. The movie came from an original screenplay, but several weeks before the film comes out, there's a book on the stands. Novelizations, they're called...

The authors of these books are usually paid a bit more up front than the average first novel advance--but their percentage of royalties is far lower, so that a box office hit won't mean that much more money to the novelizer than a complete failure. Also, writing a novelization can be a frustrating experience, since you almost always have to work from the screenplay, turning in your manuscript before the filming has been competed. Often the whole plot of the movie will be changed in filming or editing, and there sits the book, with the old "wrong" version firmly enshrined.

Novelizations can be fine pieces of work, but in most cases very few readers and no critics will notice or care. There's little joy in the work, it does nothing for your career, and whether the money is worth it to you is for you to answer.

Orson Scott Card, *How to Write Science Fiction and Fantasy*, 1990

2 THE LITERARY NOVEL

A novel is the literary equivalent of a symphony, the big, ambitious form of fiction. Novels aren't just longer than other forms of fiction, they generally have more of everything: more characters, more scenes, more developments, and more *heft*. They may have a central story, but the story is usually surrounded by a whole swirling world of activity. Someone once told me she could tell if a work was a novel or short story simply by reading the first sentence.

Alexander Steele, *Fiction*, 2003

"Genre fiction" is a nasty phrase--when did genre turn into an adjective? But I object to the term for a different reason. It was clever marketing by publishers to set certain contemporary fiction apart and declare it Literature--and therefore important art and somehow better than genre writing.

The term sneaks back into the past in an anachronistic way, so that, for example, Jane Austen's works are described as literary fiction. This is nonsense. Can anyone think for a moment that were she writing today she'd be published as literary fiction? No, and not because she'd end up under romance, but because she writes comedy, and literary fiction, with rare exception, does not include comedy. [Literary novels are humorless. Perhaps that's why they call it "serious fiction."]

Jane Austen never for a moment imagined she was writing literature. Posterity decided that, not her. She wrote fiction to entertain and to make money which is what we novelists have been doing ever since. Perhaps in our serious and solemn way, we ask fiction to bear a burden it was never intended to carry.

Elizabeth Edmondson, *The Guardian*, April 21, 2014

"Serious fiction" is not necessarily great and not even necessarily literature, because the talents of its practitioners may not be as dependable as their intentions. But a literature, including the great, will be written in this spirit.

The difference between the writer of serious fiction and the writer of escape entertainment is the clear difference between the artist and the craftsman. The one has the privilege and the faculty of original design; the other does not. The man who works from blueprints is a thoroughly respectable character, but he is of another order from the man who makes the blueprints in the first place.

Wallace Stegner, *On Teaching and Writing Fiction*, 2002

In general, fiction is divided into literary fiction and commercial fiction. Nobody can definitively say what separates one from the other, but that doesn't stop everybody from trying…

Literary fiction pays more attention to style than does commercial fiction. It also probes characterization more deeply. It's often slower paced than commercial fiction because added description and character development take up many words. The typical worldview implied by literary fiction is complex and ambiguous, trying to be faithful to the complexity and ambiguity of life. A traditional "happy ending" is possible but not common.

Commercial fiction can be just as well written, but in an entirely different way. It's usually faster paced with a stronger plot line: more events, higher stakes, more danger. Characterization can range from good to practically nonexistent. The style is usually transparent, which means the writer wants to tell the story in words that don't call attention to themselves, so the story itself--and not the style--receives the attention.

Nancy Kress in *Novel Writing*, 2002, Meg Leder and Jack Heffron, Editors

I'm reminded of a few serious novelists I know who have consciously set out to write best-sellers, often under pseudonyms. They've become veritable students of commercial fiction, reading everything by Danielle Steele or Tom Clancy, but when they actually write such a book themselves, it almost never works. The novel is rejected by publishers who say that the manuscript is lacking something basic, although they can't put their finger on what it is. I think what these novels are lacking is conviction. The difference between a writer of literary fiction attempting one of those books and Danielle Steele doing so is that Danielle Steele actually believes in her stories and her characters.

Meg Wolitzer, *Fitzgerald Did It*, 1999

There is something dreary about wanting fiction writing to be a real job. The sense of inner purpose, so often unmentionable in a society enamored of professionalism, distinguishes a writer from a hack. Emily Dickinson didn't turn her calling into a job, and neither did Franz Kafka, or Fernando Pessoa, or Wallace Stevens, or any of the millions of writers who have never earned a penny for their thoughts. A defrocked priest forever remains a priest, and a writer--independent of publication or readership or "career"-- is always a writer. Writing, after all, is something one does. A writer is something one is.

Benjamin Moser, *The New York Times,* January 27, 2015

You've got to start with a certain amount of talent, the sine qua non. Very occasionally, a literary gift shows up that is vast, awe-inspiring, as it was in Tolstoy, Proust, or Dickens, compared to whom even big talents seem small. Yet many fine, even famous, careers have been built on making the most of relatively ordinary gifts. Be it modest or magnificent, you got to have some talent. It may be latent; it may be undeveloped; it may be neglected. But it must be there.

What is literary talent? A nimble fluency. A way with words. An imagination that's easily aroused, quick to see, to hear, and to feel. An ear for the music of the language and a tendency to become absorbed in the mysterious movements of its significance and sound. A sense of audience. Skill at organizing verbal concepts solidly, effectively, and fairly swiftly. An aptitude for catching the elusive forms and figures of a vivid imagination and a knack for pinning them down on the page.

Stephen Koch, *Writers Workshop,* 2003

There is a tendency to categorize writers of fiction as either literary or commercial. The implication is that either a writer chooses to write for the masses or the discerning few, for money or critical acclaim, for the here and now or the ages. There isn't always a clear delineation between the one and the other, and sometimes a book will achieve recognition both as commercial and literary fiction, but mostly not. Basically, this is how fiction writers are grouped.

But I don't believe writers choose their material based on how they think it is going to be received. I don't even believe that they make a conscious decision to write in a certain fashion. Rather, I think that writers just try to do the best they can with what skills they possess. I think they are imbued with a desire to write about certain subjects, and mostly that is what they do. It isn't a matter of sitting down and saying, "Okay, I think I'll write the next Stephen King thriller and get on all the best-seller lists and make millions." Writing requires passion and commitment in order to come alive. Writers write about what intrigues and compels them, what speaks to them in the same way it will speak to their readers once they find the right way to set it all down.

Terry Brooks, *Sometimes the Magic Works*, 2005

It's quite true that fiction writing can't be taught; but the teacher can pass along a few shortcuts and get students interested in the craft of it. I don't think any student wastes his time in a good fiction workshop, not even the talentless ones. By the end of the semester they'll have developed their critical skills to some extent, will respond more deeply to literature, will know a bit more about human nature than they did at the start. It may not be much, but how many other English courses achieve more?

Martin Russ, *Showdown Semester*, 1980

For many years now, literary academics high and low have preempted serious criticism, have been riding hard on students who are so unused to general reading that they have little taste of their own and are glad to be told how to read. This supposedly will get these students closer and closer to the work of art. What nonsense. What gets us closer to a work of art is not instruction but another work of art.

Alfred Kazin, *Writing Was Everything*, 1995

I think literary fiction has fallen prey to campus navel gazing and has lost touch with ordinary humanity. And it has the audience to prove it.

Jack Hart in *Telling the Story* by Peter Rubie, 2003

During the late 1990s, we saw the rise of a new literary subject: the postcolonial immigrant. In the metro centers of the North Atlantic--in London and New York, Paris and Toronto--the protagonist emerged: a parvenu, an outsider with a sturdy work ethic, a grocer or taxi driver seeking to make it in his or her new home. There were geographical variations, but central to these narratives was the direction of movement. The postcolonial subject moved from the outside in, from the former colony to the city, from beyond to the imperial center. Gatsby-like, he or she often tested the outer limits of the American dream--that still regnant myth about capitalist self-making. The narrative arc was that of the arriviste: a story not only of assimilation and the arduous passage toward citizenship but also of accumulation and the trials of "making it."

David Marcus, "Dangling Man," *Bookforum,* Dec/Jan, 2015

In a detective story, the hero often has no development. Hercule Poirot [Agatha Christie] is pretty much the same from beginning to end of a particular novel; he merely changes in the way he perceives things. Popular action heroes such as James Bond, Dirk Pitt, or Captain Kirk don't develop much either; they are pretty much the same beginning to end, from book to book. [The same is true of Sherlock Holmes.] But in a more serious work of dramatic fiction, the characters do change, often profoundly.

Scrooge in *A Christmas Carol* turns from unrepentant miser to generous celebrant; Charles Allnut in *The African Queen* changes from a drunken sot to a responsible husband. Fred C. Dobbs in B. Traven's *The Treasure of the Sierra Madre* is changed from a rather likable, down-and-out tramp to a greedy paranoiac by his lust for gold.

Well-plotted, serious dramatic fiction is transformational by its very nature. The vicarious experience of this transformation is the most important reason people read serious fiction. A plot isn't just a matter of one thing happening after another; it's the progress toward the resolution of a predicament that transforms the character.

James N. Frey in *Novel Writing,* 2002 edited by Meg Leder and Jack Heffron

When I flick through my old copies of J. D. Salinger's stories, I see that all the passages my teenage self has identified as especially moving and wonderful are precisely those that now make me frown and recoil. Where once the angst and alienation of Salinger's heroes--their hypersensitivity to "phoniness"--filled me with awe and some sheepishness about my own capacity for compromise, I am now inclined to feel that phoniness, as much as any other human weakness, deserves a bit of sympathy. I can still enjoy the *Catcher in the*

Rye if I read it with a sort of squint, maintaining the illusion of some separation between Holden's disaffected worldview and Salinger's. But by the time I get to the Glass stories, wherein the preternaturally brilliant and morally fine Glass children struggle to bear a world filled with second-rate English professors and inadequately nuanced productions of Chekhov, I have to give up. [When I discovered *Catcher in the Rye* as a seventh grader, I felt I was reading the best novel ever written. This book, among others, inspired me to be a writer. Last year, when I reread *Catcher in the Rye* for the first time, I found the novel a bit puerile, and forced.]

Zoe Heller, "Bookends," *The New York Times Book Review,* April 30, 2014

Whitney Balliett reviewed a novel for *The New Yorker* in 1961, saying, "[The author] wallows in his own laughter and finally drowns in it. What remains is a debris of sour jokes, stage anger, dirty words, synthetic looniness, and the sort of antic behavior that children fall into when they know they are losing our attention." The book was *Catch-22* by Joseph Heller.

James Charlton and Lisbeth Mark, *The Writer's Home Companion,* 1987

In later 1999 I wrote a short book called *Gorgons in the Pool.* Quoting lengthy passages from prize-winning novels, I argued that some of the most acclaimed contemporary prose is the product of mediocre writers availing themselves of trendy stylistic gimmicks. The greater point was that we readers should trust our own taste and perception instead of deferring to received opinion....A thriller must thrill or it is worthless; this is as true now as it ever was. Today's "literary" novel, on the other hand, need only evince a few quotable passages to be guaranteed at least a lukewarm review. It is no surprise, therefore, that the "literary" camp now attracts a type of writer who, under different circumstances would never have strayed from the safest crime-novel formulae, and that so many critically acclaimed novels today are really mediocre "genre" stories told in an amalgam of trendy stylistic tics.

B. R. Myers, *A Reader's Manifesto,* 2002

Now it is the unassuming storyteller who is reviled, while mediocrities who puff themselves up to produce gabby "literary" fiction are guaranteed a certain respect, presumably for aiming high.

B.R. Myers, *Reader's Manifesto,* 2002

I love words. Most writers love words....When a writer has given new life to words you've heard a million times or used words you don't use or ordinarily think of, but love, it's inspiring.

I love reading novels that send me to the dictionary to look up words. Jonathan Franzen's *The Corrections* did this. So did Don DeLillo's *Underworld.* I pulled out the Webster's to look up *crepuscular.* "Of relating to, or resembling twilight: active during twilight, insects." I can never look at fireflies, now, without thinking of them as crepuscular. [Come on. Comments like this set off my crap detector. No wonder nobody reads "literary fiction."]

Ann Patchett's *Bel Canto* yielded the word *sangfroid:* "self-possession or imperturbability esp. under strain." So I have sangfroid when I don't stress out if I'm late getting somewhere. [I avoid pretentious novelists who show off by using arcane words for simple things and ideas. This is *bad* writing.]

Barbara DeMarco-Barrett, *Pen on Fire,* 2004

Sometimes it takes courage to drop our pretensions, to choose *use* instead of *utilize, rain* instead of *precipitation, arithmetic* instead of *computational skills.* An idea expressed in simple English has to stand on its own, naked and unadorned, while ostentatious words sound impressive even when they mean nothing.

Not all pompous writers are showing off or covering up their ignorance. Some are just timid, imagining that their ideas are flimsy or flawed or silly, even when they aren't. If you've done your homework, you shouldn't have to disguise your ideas with showy language. Be brave. Write plainly.

The truth about big, ostentatious words is that they don't work as well as simple ones.

Patricia T. O'Conner, *Words Fail Me,* 1999

1. *Be Writerly:* Read aloud what you have written. If it sounds clear and natural, strike it out.
2. *Play the Part:* Take yourself seriously. Practice before the mirror until you can say things like this with a straight face:

"It's because I want every little surface to shimmer and gyrate that I haven't patience for those lax transitional devices of plot, setting, character, and so on, that characterize a lot of traditional fiction."
(Mark Leyner)

B. R. Myers, *A Reader's Manifesto,* 2002

As one reads contemporary novelists, one can't shake the feeling that they write for one another rather than for some more or less common reader. Their prose shares a showiness that speaks of solidarity and competition-- the exaggerated panache with which teenaged boys shoot hoops in their driveways while pretending they don't notice their neighbor watching from across the street.

Dale Peck, *Hatchet Jobs*, 2004

All of the most prestigious awards for fiction each year are given to the works of literary fiction, which makes it sometimes easy to say that writers who write literary novels are *better* writers.

In reality, neither of the two categories of writers necessarily deserve the distinction of being better writers. *Different* writers is a better word choice…

Is essence, the best genre fiction contains great writing, with the goal of telling a captivating story to *escape from reality*. Literary fiction is comprised of the heart and soul of a writer's being, and is experienced as an *emotional journey* through the symphony of words, leading to a stronger grasp of the universe and of ourselves.

Steven Petite, huffingtonpost.com, April 28, 2014

Literary prizes sometimes seem to function like parents whose approval we crave as well as spurn. The complaints are as common as they are contradictory: Prizes are awarded to tepid, undemanding best sellers everyone reads; prizes are awarded to obscure, abstruse books no one reads. They are awarded to the right authors, but for the wrong work (Hemingway for "The Old Man and the Sea," Faulkner for "A Fable"). They are awarded to the wrong authors for the wrong work (Margaret Mitchell for "Gone With the Wind"). They are withheld from the right authors for the right work (Gravity's Rainbow," by Thomas Pynchon, won jury approval for the Pulitzer Price in 1974 but was overruled by a board that deemed the novel "turgid," and "obscene"). Sometimes the grousing has the whiff of sour grapes. "Prize X has never been awarded to Philip Roth." Prize Y has never been awarded to me."

Jennifer Szalai, "Bookends," *The New York Times Book Review*, November 24, 2013

The good ship Literary Fiction has run aground and the survivors are frantically paddling toward the islands of genre. Okay, maybe that's a little dramatic, but there does seem to be a definite trend of literary/mainstream writers turning to romance, thrillers, fantasy, mystery, and young adult...

What is going on? Is it a mass sellout, a belated and half-hearted attempt by writers to chase the market? Are they pushed into genre by their agents and publishers? Are the literary novelists simply ready for a change, perhaps because even the most exalted among them have a tiny readership compared to genre superstars? Or are the two worlds finally merging?

Once upon a time, genre was treated as almost a different industry from literary fiction, ignored by critics, sneered at by literary writers, relegated by publishers to imprint ghettos. But the dirty little and not particularly well-kept secret was that, thanks to the loyalty of their fans and the relatively rapid production of their authors, these genre books were the ones who kept the entire operation in business. All those snobbish literary writers had better have hoped like hell that their publishers had enough genre moneymakers in house to finance the advance for their latest beautifully rendered and experimentally structured observations of upper class angst.

But while genre authors were always the workhorses of publishing, lately they've broken out as stars and are belatedly receiving real recognition. In 2010 there were 358 fantasy titles on the best seller lists, more than double the number in 2006. Publishers, always the last to recognize a literary trend, are pursuing top genre writers who, for the first time, have not only bigger paychecks but genuine clout...

A lot of literary writers actually support themselves through other jobs, such as teaching, and they may be prepared to wait out the change and hope that literary fiction returns.

Kim Wright, "Why So Many Literary Writers Are Leaving the Genre," themillions.com, September 2, 2011

3 THE FIRST NOVEL

As a first novelist I learned about the odds I was facing. They were, shall we say, long. It has been estimated that the number of novel manuscripts each year to be in excess of 100,000. The number of first novels published annually by major houses? Three to four hundred.

Stephen White in *How I Got Published*, edited by Ray White and Duane Lindsay, 2007

If you do not seek to publish what you have written, then you are not a novelist and you never will be.

George V. Higgins, *On Writing*, 1990

I wrote my first novel when I was nineteen. It was bad, the kind of mystery they call "cozy" these days, but with added pretensions to high literary values. I had never taken a creative writing class and knew nothing of plot, character, or pace except for what I had gleaned from my random reading habits. It took me about a year to finish it, and the moment it was done I set about mailing it out to whatever big, famous publishers seemed most likely to back a dump truck full of money up to my parents' front door. It was, I figured, no more than I deserved.

No one bought it. No one so much as nibbled. I'd be astonished to learn that anyone read more than a few pages of the thing before mailing out the obligatory polite rejection. Over the years I accumulated quite a stack of polite rejections.

A. J. Hartley in *How I Got Published, edited by Ray White and Duane Lindsay, 2007*
I completed my first novel on July 29, 2012 and spent the next two months sending it out to hundreds of agents and any publisher I could find that

accepted unsolicited manuscripts. Dropping over a grand on ink, paper, and postage, my days consisted of checking my email, walking to the post office, and scanning the Internet for details of any literary agency that had an address, never mind a respectable client list.

I received dozens of rejection slips but mainly non-replies. Those that did get back to me all said the same thing: love it, but can't see it selling. After a few months I was forced to admit that my novel wasn't going to be bought for $500,000 or even for the price of a battered second-hand paperback. I was devastated. What would become of me now?

James Nolan, vice.com, April 29, 2014

I always wanted to be a novelist, from the time that I was a little kid and first learned that such a job existed. I decided to attempt my first novel when I was a teenager, and I thought it was going to be easy--that I'd no doubt be published before I graduated from high school. It obviously didn't work that way. It would be ten years of learning the craft and abandoning novels that weren't working before I had my first novel published.

Marissa Meyer in *Children's Writer's and Illustrator's Market,* edited by Chuck Sambuchino, 2013

When I was writing my first novel, I had no serious hopes of publishing it. I was sophisticated enough to know that twenty-year-olds don't publish novels. I was writing it because I enjoyed writing and because it was cathartic. Some people release their pain and anxiety through, oh, I don't know, playing sports, or a hobby, or through sex or drugs. Writing
for me was always a great stress reliever. It was Joe McGinness who thought the book had commercial potential, so he showed it to his agent. *Less Than Zero* was published in May 1985.

Bret Easton Ellis, *Paris Review,* Spring 2012

New novels fare poorly for one simple reason. Nobody knows them. With few exceptions, big fiction sales only come about through recognition of an author's previous work. Thus, most authors must crank out several novels before they become trusted by a large enough universe of book buyers to generate respectable word-of-mouth sales.

Marc McCutcheon, *Damn! Why Didn't I Write That?* 2001

First novels are unpredictable. For one author it's the best thing he will do in his career, something into which he empties so much of his heart and talent and experience that he's left with too little fuel to light much of a fire under future work.

For another the first novel sets the course for an entire career: He's found the key in which his voice is most comfortable and he sticks to it.

For some writers that first novel gives no hint as to what is to come. Every new work is a departure from the last.

F. Paul Wilson in *How I Got Published,* edited by Ray White and Duane Lindsay, 2007

Highly autobiographical first novels are out of fashion. Budding writers are expected to cast their eyes away from themselves. And yet in our culture of instant gratification and celebrity, a writer's reputation can depend almost exclusively on the critical reception of a first novel. The problem is twofold: we expect first novels to be works of non-autobiographical genius well before a writer has time to mature.

Rosalind Porter, findarticles.com, 2005

The first novel is a good place to put in things that would be awkward to use elsewhere. No one requires much fiction from a first novel.

Peter S. Prescott, *Never in Doubt,* 1986

Usually the first novel of a young writer is a book of discovery. From his meager experience, accentuated by his youth, comes a knowledge so new and startling and so wonderful that its pain is almost beyond bearing. Mellow, many-faceted understanding is not for now; understanding is the hard reward of decades of summers. Youth's knowledge, youth's discoveries, are as sure as an April dawn. [This man was a great writer but a bit of a mental case.]

Thomas Wolfe in *Wolfe* by Richard Walser, 1961

Examining the first copy of your novel is a mixed experience. On the one hand, proof now rests in your hand that you indeed wrote a book. This exciting thought lasts for about six seconds then the mind turns elsewhere: couldn't my publisher have found a better typeface for the jacket? Next time, I'm going to hire a professional photographer to take a good author picture. I wonder how long it will take before my novel shows up on remainder tables. I wonder if it's going to get panned. I wonder if anyone will read it at all.

Ralph Keyes, *The Courage to Write*, 1995

I believed, before I sold my first novel, that the publication would be instantly and automatically gratifying, an affirming and romantic experience, a Hallmark commercial where one runs and leaps in slow motion across a meadow filled with wildflowers into the arms of acclaim and self-esteem. This did not happen for me. As a result, I try to warn writers who hope to get published that publication is not all it is cracked up to be. The act of writing turns out to be its own reward.

Anne Lamott, *Bird By Bird*, 1995

What do we imagine our published novel will bring us? In part it is a trophy we want. Not entirely, of course, for we want all the pleasures of writing and we want the pleasure of knowing that someone else may read our words and savor a story that once existed only in our heads--and yet in part there is a yearning for a trophy. But a trophy of what?

Bonnie Friedman, *Writing Past Dark*, 1994

Some of the American writers are said, particularly by European and British critics, to be one-book writers. They produce one good novel and never again produce anything to equal it, apparently because their first book was so heavily autobiographical.

Mary McCarthy in *Conversations with Mary McCarthy*, Carol Gilderman, editor, 1991

There will always be that flash in the pan, that one-off novel that strikes the fancy of publishers, sells a few million copies, and gets made into a successful--or unsuccessful--film before the person who wrote it fades into permanent obscurity, laughing, as they say, all the way to the bank. These types of writers have always existed.

    The creators of those largely forgettable and sometimes laughable pieces of prose bang them out, often with nothing more to recommend their work than a fairly decent idea badly realized, a fairly bad idea decently realized, or a schtick of some sort--author as former policewoman, forensic pathologist, weight lifter, beauty queen, seriously abused child, seriously abusive adult come to the Lord or an excellent publicity campaign that worked like a charm.

What these creators of fiction have in common tends to be that they got lucky. They wrote their novels without an idea in the world what they were doing and the managed to pull it off. Problem was, though, they could not do it again.

Elizabeth George in *Sometimes the Magic Works* by Terry Brooks, 2005

When you have a first novel [*Fear of Flying*] that sells 6 million copies, anything you do after it has to be a disappointment. You set a standard that you cannot compete with, and the pressure it puts on you is almost unreal.

Erica Jong in *On Being a Writer*, Bill Strickland, editor, 1989

Writing the second novel does feel different. I'm more confident and enjoying it more because I feel less anxious about the time I am spending on it. A first novel is such an exercise in hope and obsession, early mornings and late nights, trying to justify your time to your family and yourself. Now there's none of that. I also know so much more about the craft of writing and how to accomplish my goals.

Tara Conklin, npr.org, May 16, 2014

Now that I had written one novel and they, the actual readers and the critics who had read it, were looking for a second, I was up against it. I was not up against it in the way I dreaded, I was up against it cold and hard as one comes up against a wall. I was a writer. I had made the writer's life my life; there was no going back; I had to go on. What could I do? After the first book there had to be a second book. What was the second book to be about? Where would it come from?

Thomas Wolfe in *The Golden Age*, Richard L. Tobin, editor, 1974
I wrote my first novel when I was a freshman in college and submitted it to a first-novel competition--I believe it was the Bennett Cerf competition. I thought the book had an outside chance, and I was enormously proud to have fathered such a wonderful creation at the age of nineteen. It was

rejected with a short "Dear contributor" note, and I was too crushed to show that book to any publisher in New York.

Stephen King, *Secret Windows*, 2002

Ignoring the hot MFA [Masters of Fine Arts] grad you read about in *Publishers Weekly* whose novel starts a big publishing house bidding war, literary first novels are almost impossible to introduce into the marketplace. Bookstores will only order them in small quantities, if at all, and it is difficult to get reviews, especially in places that really matter. Additionally, getting a bookstore reading for a first fiction author is an effort that would make Sisyphus proud. A well-established independent bookseller once told me flat out that he would never book a first fiction author into his store.

Robert Lasner, mobylives.com, 2005

4 WRITING THE NOVEL GENERALLY

All my life as a writer I have been committed to the idea that in fiction the story holds value over every other facet of the writer's craft; characterization, theme, mood, none of those things is anything if the story is dull. And if the story does hold you, all else can be forgiven....

I'm not any big-deal fancy writer. If I have any virtue it's that I know that. I don't have the ability to write the dazzling prose line. All I can do is entertain people. I think of myself as an American writer....

My greatest virtue is that I know better than to evade my responsibilities by the useless exercise of trying to write fancy prose. I entertain people by giving them good stories dealing with the content of ordinary American lives, which is the best, truest tradition of American fiction.

Stephen King, *Windows: Essays and Fiction on the Craft of Writing,* 2000

Fiction, first of all, involves the invention of a world. Here the writer needs, not only the gift of writing, but the ability to create scenes, particulars and persons--to make imaginary lives and objects.

William H. Gass in *Afterwords,* edited by Thomas McCormack, 1988

I've been drinking too much lately and have made plans to cut it down somewhat. Also there have been some rough seas on the home front. Everything seems to get in the way of the writing but maybe it creates it too.

Charles Bukowski in *Charles Bukowski: Selected Letters 1971-1986,* edited by Seamus Cooney, 2004

The fact that nobody has even been able to reduce the elements that go into the fashioning of a predictable best-seller has long been illustrated by the classic story of an expensive book-business survey that produced the three kinds of books that had always proved most popular: books about Abraham Lincoln, books about doctors, and books about dogs. The only thing predictable about the survey was that some publisher was bound to act on it, and not long after the survey some publisher did. He brought out a book called *Lincoln's Doctor's Dog.* It was--predictably--a disaster.

Jerome Weidman, *Praying For Rain,* 1986

I think that over-ambition kills. I think that *trying* to be a writer kills. Writing simply has to be a sickness, a drug. It doesn't *have* to be, it just is. When one thing or another cures your sickness, that's it. And, of course, there are no guidelines.

I've been lucky. For decades now I haven't had to force myself to write anything in any particular way...If you slant your writing it means you want to make money, you want to get famous, you want to get published for the sake of getting published. I think that only works for a while. The gods are watching us. And they extract their toll. Without fail.

Charles Bukowski in *Charles Bukowski: Selected Letters 1987-1994,* edited by Seamus Cooney, 2004

What is literary talent? A nimble fluency. A way with words. An imagination that's easily aroused, quick to see, to hear, and to feel. An ear for the music of the language and a tendency to become absorbed in the mysterious movements of its significance and sound. A sense of audience. Skill at organizing verbal concepts solidly, effectively, and fairly swiftly. An aptitude for catching the elusive forms and figures of a vivid imagination and a knack for pinning them down on a page.

Stephen Koch, *Writer's Workshop,* 2003

What are the hallmarks of a competent writer of fiction? The first, it seems to me, is that he should be immensely interested in human beings, and have an eye sharp enough to see into them, and a hand clever enough to draw them as they are.

H. L. Mencken in *H. L. Mencken on American Literature,* edited by H. L. Mencken and S. T. Joshi, 2002

Getting ideas is the least difficult part of the fiction writing process. What's hard, really hard, is making those ideas come together in a well-conceived, compelling story. So many of these ideas that seem wonderful at first blush end up leading nowhere. They won't sustain the weight of a story. They won't spin out past a few pages. They won't lead to something insightful and true.

Terry Brooks, *Sometimes the Magic Works*, 2005

The term "creative writing" offends some people; they think it has something affected or precious about it. Actually it is an innocent phrase developed in American schools and colleges sometime between the two world wars [1920-1940] to designate that kind of writing *course* which is not Freshman English or Report Writing for Engineers. One suspects that "creative writing" courses grew up partly because ordinary courses in composition had got bogged down in "correctness," gentility, and the handbook-and-exercise method, and some means had to be found to free students for the development of their natural interest and delight in language.

Creative writing means imaginative writing, writing as an art, what the French call *belles lettres*. It has nothing to do with information or the more routine forms of communication, though it uses the same skills...

Like all other forms of creative writing, it is written to produce in its reader the pleasure of aesthetic experience, to offer him an imaginative recreation or reflection or imitation of action, thought, and feeling. It attempts to uncover form and meaning in the welter of love, hate, violence, tedium, habit, and brute fact that we flounder through from day to day.

Wallace Stegner, *On Teaching and Writing Fiction*, 2002

Writing a novel doesn't get any easier the second or the eleventh time you do it. And unfortunately, you won't have fans in your writing room to urge you on. There'll be no applause. Just month after month of putting it down and crossing it out and recasting the sentence once again. Everyone who has a life thinks he has a novel to write. And he or she may. But very few people understand that the life is not the novel, that chronology is not plot....

Writing isn't easy. Simply because you have access to a pen, some paper, and a dictionary does not mean that you can write a novel any more than having access to a piano means you can play the Goldberg Variations. Anyone can make noise. It's music we're after. Anyone can write on and on indefinitely. We're after the definite article.

John Dufresne, *Is Life Like This?* 2010

Never ever read a powerful novel when you're trying to write a novel of your own.

Richard Price, *The New York Times Book Review*, February 22, 2015

Novel writing is considered a profession and I don't think it is a profession. I think that everyone who does not *need* to be a writer, who thinks he can do something else, ought to do something else. Writing is not a profession but a vocation of unhappiness. I don't think that an artist can ever be happy.

Georges Simenon, *Paris Review*, Summer, 1955

This writing game is more desperate than holding up liquor stores, yet I'm snared in now and there's no out. A man finally gets lazy, too lazy and the mind gets too lazy to do any damned job. Now I'm almost too lazy to write. An empty belly and rent due might stove that up, though.

Charles Bukowski in *Charles Bukowski: Selected Letters 1971-1986*, edited by Seamus Cooney, 2004

When it comes to the novel you have to work long and hard even to produce a bad one. This may help explain why there are so many more bad amateur poets around than there are bad amateur novelists. Writing a good poem may be as difficult as writing a good novel. It may even be harder. But any clown with a sharp pencil can write out a dozen lines of verse and call it a poem. Not just any clown can fill 200 pages with prose and call it a novel. Only the more determined clowns can get the job done.

Lawrence Block, *Writing the Novel*, 1979

If you want to write a novel, the best thing you can do is take two aspirins, lie down in a dark room, and wait for the feeling to pass.

Lawrence Block, *Writing the Novel*, 1985

What follows is the process I use when I'm writing a novel. These are the essential steps that I've developed for myself over the creation of twelve books.

I don't begin until I have an idea. But this idea is more than just a glimmer, more than a potentially evanescent wisp of inspiration. For me, what the idea is is a complete thought that contains one of three elements: the primary event that will get the ball rolling in the novel, the arc of the story containing the beginning, the middle, and they ending *or* an intriguing situation that immediately suggests a cast of characters in conflict. If I have one of those three elements, I have enough to begin.

Elizabeth George, *Write Away*, 2004

Ideas are not the best *subject matter* for fiction. They do not dramatize well. They are, rather, a by-product, something the reader himself is led to formulate after watching the story unfold. The ideas ought to be implicit in the selection and arrangement of the people and places and actions. They ought to haunt a piece of fiction as a ghost flits past an attic window after dark.

Wallace Stegner, *On Teaching and Writing Fiction*, 2002

Someone will always ask, "How long does it take you to write a novel?" I hardly ever give them the real answer. "It depends," I will say. "A year. Sometimes three or four." The real answer, of course, is that it takes your entire life. I am forty-four, and it took me forty-four years to get this novel finished. You don't mention this to too many people, because it can fill their hearts with sadness, looking at you and thinking, Jesus, forty-four years to come up with *this*? But it's always the truest answer. You could not have written it any sooner. You write the book when its time has come, and you bring your lifetime to the task, however few or many years you have behind you.

James D. Houston in *The Writer's Life*, Carol Edgarian and Tom Jenks, editors, 1997

Novelists are and always have been split between, on the one hand, a desire to claim an imaginative and representative truth for their stories, and on the other hand, a conviction that the best way to secure and guarantee that truthfulness is by a scrupulous respect for empirical fact...Novels burn facts as engines burn fuel, and the facts can come only from the novelist's own experience or acquired knowledge.

David Lodge, *The Practice of Writing*, 1996

One of the most difficult things is the first paragraph. I have spent months on a first paragraph, and once I get it, the rest comes out very easily.

Gabriel Garcia Marquez in *For Writer's Only* (1994) by Sophy Burnham

After twenty years and a hundred books, I...realize that I don't *know* how to write a novel, that nobody does, that there *is* no right way to do it. Whatever method works--for you, for me, for whoever's sitting in the chair and poking away at the typewriter [now computer] keys--is the right way to do it.

Lawrence Block, *Writing the Novel,* 1979

Though everybody is talented and original, often it does not break through for a long time. People are too scared, too self-conscious, too proud, too shy. They have been taught too many things about construction, plot, unity, mass and coherence....

Another trouble with writers in the first twenty years is an anxiety to be effective, to impress people. They write pretentiously. It is so hard not to do this. That was my trouble.

For many years it puzzled me why so many things I wrote were pretentious, high-sounding, and in consequence utterly dull and uninteresting. It was a regular horror to read them again. Of course they did not sell either, not one of them.

Brenda Ueland, *If You Want to Write,* originally published in 1938

You've always wanted to write a novel, but you haven't been able to. Not yet, you haven't. Perhaps you've been too intimidated to even begin. (Who do I think I am?) Or you've started writing several novels over the years, each with abundant hope and enthusiasm, but you soon become discouraged when the characters in your head did not breathe on the page. Or maybe you keep pulling the same novel out of the desk drawer whenever you have some downtime, and you work on it again for a week or a month--you feel a feverish sense or urgency--and the novel keeps growing, year after year, but seems unwilling to resolve itself, and then, alas, the so-called real world summons you, or you lose confidence in your creative or organizational abilities, and you shove the manuscript back into the drawer and push your chair away from the annoying desk. Well, you should know that you are not alone. We've all done the same thing. Writing is hard, and it's harder for the writer than it is for anyone else.

John Dufresne, *Is Life Like This?* 2010

American novelists, more than others, are haunted by the fear of failure, because it's such a common pattern in America. The ghost of Fitzgerald, dying in Hollywood, with his comeback book unfinished, and his best book, *Tender Is The Night,* scorned. His ghost hangs over every American novelist's typewriter.

Irwin Shaw in *Writers at Work, Fifth Series,* edited by George Plimpton, 1981

The most common reason for writer's block is problems with the storyline. There are no hard and fast rules as to overcome this, but without swift attention, an acute attack can turn into a chronic condition. Start by revisiting the storyline. Have you introduced new elements, and are the characters true to your original outline? If you have veered from your original plan then you have to decide whether to rewrite the outline, and potentially the plot line of the story, or rewrite chapters. Both are painful decisions to make, but remember that writing is a work in progress, so revisiting your ideas is an essential element of writing successfully. By focusing on the bigger picture (the framework, context, plot and characters) the details often become clearer.

Maeve Binchy, *The Maeve Binchy Writer's Club*, 2008

All working writers devise their own program for keeping fear at bay. Although writing nerves never vanish, they do become more manageable over time. No magic strategy exists that will turn an anxious novice into a self-assured veteran. Since courage points vary so much from writer to writer, there is no one-size fits-all program to recommend. Developing writing courage involves learning about one's working style and how it's best manipulated.

Ralph Keyes, *The Courage to Write*, 1995

Before the days of word processing, how did authors keep track of their various drafts and revisions? Purple prose writer Jacqueline Susann [*Valley of the Dolls,* 1966; *The Love Machine,* 1969; and *Once Is Not Enough,* 1773] typed each draft on different colors of paper: yellow for the first draft, then blue, pink, and finally white. [It's hard to believe she wrote four drafts of these dreadful novels.]

Erin Barrett and Jack Mingo, *It Takes a Certain Type To Be A Writer,* 2003

The study I've made of the writing methods of others has led me to the belief that everybody in this business spends a lifetime finding the method that suits him best, changing it over the years as he himself evolves, adapting it again and again to suit the special requirements of each particular book. What works with one person won't necessarily work for another; what works for one book won't necessarily work with another.

Some novelists outline briefly, some in great detail, and a few produce full-fledged treatments that run half the length of the final book itself. Others don't outline at all. Some of us revise as we go along. Others do separate drafts. Some of us write sprawling first drafts and wind up cutting them to the bone. Others rarely cut three paragraphs overall.

Lawrence Block, *Writing the Novel,* 1979

I find it helps a lot to talk to friends or editors immediately after I return from a reporting trip. It puts me in a storytelling mode. Even though I'm less preoccupied with producing a seamless narrative then I used to be, I do feel that narrative energy is crucial to distinguishing a *story* from a research report. When you are telling a story to a live human being [as apposed to a reader] you get a sense, immediately, of what people respond to. It gets you outside of your own head. And often people ask questions that I haven't thought of--questions that force me to look at the reporting in a new way.

Ron Rosenbaum, in Robert S. Boynton's *The New Journalism,* 2005 [Most writers of fiction do *not* discuss works-in-progress.]

We're now past the halfway point of National Novel Writing Month [November]--or, as it's inelegantly shortened online, NaNoWriMo--when aspiring authors aim to produce 50,000 words during November. More than 277,000 writers signed up for the sprint this year. Erin Morgenstern, whose best-selling novel *The Night Circus* originated as part of the exercise, once advised: "Don't delete anything. Just keep writing. And if you don't want to look at it, change the font to white."

Communal support is an important part of the endeavor, with participants sharing daily word counts and inspirational exhortations on Twitter and Facebook. The forums on the project's official website offer a cascade of advice. One writer asked the crowd: "How old must a child be to survive in the Nordic forest?" Another solicited "favorite literary quotes that a guy might not mind having as a tattoo."

John Williams, "Open Book," *The New York Times Book Review*, November 17, 2013

People want to know what I think about writing critique groups. I belonged to one briefly, but I didn't use it much. I prefer now to use the services of a cold reader when the book is done. But if you're going to belong to a group, check it out carefully before you commit yourself to joining. If there's someone in there with an ax to grind, don't become a member. If the group isn't solution-oriented, just saying things like, "I have a problem with X" (your character, your plot, your scene, or whatever) without proposing a solution to the problem or a way to approach developing a solution, just pass them by. If you don't feel good about the group dynamic, trust yourself and don't join up.

Elizabeth George, *Write Away*, 2004

We start out in our lives as little children, full of light and the clearest vision...Then we go to school and then comes on the great Army of school teachers with their critical pencils, and parents and older brothers (the greatest sneerers of all) and cantankerous friends, and finally that Great Murderer of the Imagination--a world of unceasing, unkind, dinky, prissy Criticalness.

Brenda Ueland, *If You Want to Write*, 1938 in the Preface to the Second Edition, 1983

The one drawback to writing a novel is the being alone. In people's imagination, that's the difference between a novelist and a journalist. The journalist, the newspaper reporter, is always rushing, hunting, meeting people, digging up facts. Cooking a story. The journalist writes surrounded by people, and always on deadline, crowded and hurried. It's exciting and fun. The journalist researches a story. The novelist imagines it.

Chuck Palahnuik, *Stranger Than Fiction*, 2004

For public figures who walk away from the source of their fame, the question of what comes next may be treated lightly. A retired athlete can become a sportscaster or investor; the TV actor whose hit show comes to an end can mull over movie scripts. But when a successful novelist retires, it feels somehow different: writing novels is less a job one can leave than proof that one sees the world in a certain way. There's something that seems illogical about a writer declaring that he or she is done. Where, then, do all of the observations channeled into metaphor go?

Daniel D'Addario, *Time*, November 24, 2014

5 THE CRAFT OF NOVEL WRITING

Unlike bombastic journalism that relies on opening with a bang, a novel can open less loudly. Here's an example of a bang opening by Truman Capote in "Children on Their Birthdays": "Yesterday afternoon the six o'clock bus ran over Miss Bobbitt." Yes, this catches our interest, but what next? It'll be hard to match the intensity of the beginning with what follows. The story starts with a climax rather than working toward one; instead of looking forward, we look backward, and the whole story might be an anticlimax.

Josip Novakovich, *Fiction Writer's Workshop*, 1995

My favorite struggling writer is the Billy Crystal character in the movie *Throw Momma From the Train* who spends much of the film trying to write the first line of the book that will free him from his crippling writer's block. "The night was," he writes over and over, never getting beyond those first three words. In the end, comic and harrowing events in his life cause him to throw away the line and just start writing. The lesson is, there is no magic opening line. The magic is what creates the line in the first place.

Loren D. Estleman, *Writing the Popular Novel*, 2004

When I asked an agent recently how she decided whether or not to take on a manuscript, she told me she asked for the first fifty pages and read the first sentence. If she liked the first sentence, she read the second. If she liked that one, she read the third, and so on. If she reached the end of the first fifty pages without putting the manuscript down, she signed it up.

Granted, most readers are willing to read your second sentence even if the first one isn't brilliant, but the agent's answer shows the importance of "hook." If you don't grab your readers with, say, your first fifty pages, you won't have them at all. So If you've been gleaning compliments from your writers group and good responses to your query letters, but your first fifty pages keep coming back with polite rejections, then you may have a good story that doesn't get started soon enough. If so, it's time to go back to the beginning and start looking for trouble.

David King, "The Fifty-Page Dash," in *The Complete Handbook of Novel Writing*, Meg Leder and Jack Hefferon, editors, 2002

Some first lines are so powerful that you absolutely have to keep on reading. This is known as a "hook." Nearly all the great writers employ hooks in one form or another....

Despite popular misconception, though, the hook is more than a marketing tool. At its best, it can be not only a propellant but also a statement of what you might expect from the text to come. It can establish a character, narrator, or setting, convey a shocking piece of information. The irony is there is only so much you can do with one line; thus it is a game: the less space you have to work with, the more creative you must become. It is not surprising then that hooks comprise some of the most memorable lines in literature.

What is rarely discussed is the importance of the hook not only as an opening line but as an opening *paragraph*, not only an opening paragraph but as an opening *page*, not only as an opening page but as an opening *chapter*. In other words, the same intensity of thought applied to the opening line should not be confined to the opening line--a common malady--but rather applied to the text in its entirety. This takes endurance, focus and concentration; with this level of intensity, it might take several days to complete even one paragraph.

Look at your first or last line and think of the agonizing effort you put into it. You knew you were in the spotlight, that it had to be good. How many times did you rewrite that one line? What would the rest of your manuscript be like if you agonized over each line the same way? *It would take forever* is probably your first thought....

I am often amazed by how many manuscripts begin with good first lines--and good openings in general--and then fall apart; it is actually rare to see the intensity found in a first line (or last) maintained throughout a manuscript.

Noah Lukeman, *The First Five Pages*, 2000

A prologue to a novel is introductory material apart in time, space, or viewpoint (or all three) from the main story that creates intrigue for upcoming events. To qualify as a prologue, the information or events must exist outside of the framework of the main story. This stand-alone device must be absorbing, distinct, and beguiling in its own right. Often, an effective prologue will contain drama and dialogue so that it is immediate rather than reportorial. Prologues are always loaded with specific and sensory details.

A prologue's job is to provide a potent insight into the world of the story that cannot be provided through the unfolding of events. It can also be information that cannot be discovered by the protagonist, but is still necessary to the story.

Prologues can take place five years or five centuries before the drama begins, but somehow the gap of time between the prologue time and story time must be bridged. But not all prologues are written strictly from the past. Sometimes they stem from the future or are told from a viewpoint that will not be heard from again.

Although the prologue exists outside the flow of the narrative, it is always linked to the story events, characters, and themes. There are no hard and fast rules for length, but most prologues are at least several paragraphs and can run to twenty or more pages. However, try to keep prologues brief and vital, and no longer than a chapter.

Jessica Page Morrell, *Between The Lines,* 2006

Third-person narrators are identified by the degree and manner of access the reader is afforded to the hearts and minds of the characters....You should decide, for example, that your narrator will not get into the consciousness of any of the characters. [In other words, does not know what they are thinking.]...That's called *third-person objective* or dramatic point of view or fly-on-the-wall point of view....

Or you might decide that your narrator will get into the mind of the central character only. This is called *third-person limited.* We get the thoughts and feelings of the central character, but no one else's. Or you might shift points of view from character to character in what's called *multiple selective omniscience.* Or go all the way and use an *omniscient* narrator who knows all, but can't tell all....

John Dufresne, *Is Life Like This?* 2010

Little nuggets of economy and compression, interpolated stories--anecdotes that one character tells another within the body of a narrative--change the pace of that narrative and illuminate a character who is revealed by the content of the story, by the manner of its telling, and finally by what the reader concludes about the purpose that the anecdote is intended to serve.

Francine Prose, *Reading Like a Writer,* 2006

I can always tell when a writer has rushed through a scene or written around it in order to get to the good stuff. The dialogue is hurried, like the wedding vows in a tired old comedy where the bride's in labor. Descriptions are sketchy or nonexistent. Too often, the scene isn't even there; the novelist has lifted it out and thrown it away, or not written it at all. At best, this leaves an annoying gap. At worst, the "good" scene has not been set up and so it falls in like a cake because someone skimped on the eggs. In between is a lost opportunity, because sometimes the scene you dreaded most turns out to be the best in the book.

Loren D. Estleman, *Writing the Popular Novel,* 2004

I try to make my books linear, which means that the starting point is at the beginning and it travels along a chronological line toward the end, with no flashbacks. I do this because it makes for an easier read.

Janet Evanovich, *How I Write,* 2006

Flashbacks are not designed for the writer's amusement, but rather the reader's education. If your flashback is *not* going to elucidate, illuminate, or provide context, then you probably don't need it.

It is also advisable not to use a flashback in a novel-length manuscript when you only have one or two flashbacks to insert. You're better off setting up a pattern of at least half a dozen flashbacks at fairly regular intervals, rather than taking one or two lonely excursions into the past. If there are only two flashbacks, the reader will be jarred by the digressions and they will stand out as an abnormality.

Jessica Page Morrell, *Between the Lines,* 2006

Every scene in your novel must pertain to your plot. Every single one. Even if a character muses or meanders, that activity must be plot-related. A character under suspicion of murder may drift off into thought, but those thoughts had better be about why he's been wrongfully accused, how he's going to prove his innocence, or who the true murderer is, not random memories of whale-watching or hiking.

Jordan E. Rosenfeld, *Make a Scene*, 2008

As novelists we all know that the ending is the hardest part. Getting it right. If editors interfere, it is likely to be there, at the ending. If we are unsatisfied with a narrative it is likely to be there, at the ending. We wish for happy endings but sometimes we reject them as unrealistic, therefore trashy, and we feel cheated and pandered to. Stern, sadistic endings may not please us either.

Diane Johnson in *The Writer's Life*, Carol Edgarian and Tom Jenks, editors, 1997

One of the main pitfalls to avoid when writing your novel's ending is what I call The Horse Nearing the Barn Syndrome. Writing fiction is satisfying but hard work, and the tendency is to hurry things along when you know you're approaching the end. You want that feeling of accomplishment, and the sooner you type "The End" the sooner you will experience it. But you haven't done your job if the reader senses this impatience in the work. The story's pacing should remain firmly under your control, so that the ending seems a natural outcome of what went before. No inconsistency should jar the reader from your fictional world, or put him or her outside the story looking in, rather than experiencing on a vicarious level what your characters are experiencing. It's comforting to know the reader's cooperating with you in achieving this mesmerizing effect. Even rooting for you. Nobody begins reading a novel wanting to be disappointed.

John Lutz in *Writing Mysteries*, Sue Grafton, editor, 2001

Let us define a plot. We have defined a story as a narrative of events arranged in their time-sequence. A plot is also a narrative of events, the emphasis falling on causality. "The king died and then the queen died" is a story. "The king died, and then the queen died of grief" is a plot. The time-sequence is preserved, but the sense of causality overshadows it. Or again:

"The queen died, no one knew why, until it was discovered that it was through grief at the death of the king." This is a plot with a mystery in it, a form capable of high development. It suspends the time-sequence, it moves as far away from the story as its limitations will allow. Consider the death of the queen. If it is a story we say, "and then?" If it is a plot we ask "why?" That is the fundamental difference between these to aspects of the novel.

E. M. Forster (1879-1970) *Aspects of the Novel,* 1927

There's a difference between an emotional plot and an action plot. If you write stories with emotional plots, it's really hard to get the other. But you've got to have both. The reader gets attached to all the characters, so there's emotional growth and inner turmoil. But it's triggered by something with such great dramatic possibilities. You have to have that outer tension of some kind. It doesn't have to be something cliché, like a car chase. But you need something on the outside. You can't just have inner tension.

Patricia Henley in *Novel Ideas,* Barbara Shoup and Margaret Love Denman, editors, 2001

Settings are as varied in fiction as they are in the world: A humid southern bayou; icy Norwegian fords; a crumbling Victorian mansion; a stable, pungent with the stench of animals. These are just a few of the infinite number of places in which you might set your characters. Though they may seem like merely the backdrop to the action and drama of your narrative, they are more like the rich soil in which you plant your seeds. Do not forget to set the scene. Unless you have a good reason to set your novel or story in a vacuum, establishing a physical setting is one of the most important and literal ways to ground the reader and keep characters from being floating heads.

Jordan E. Rosenfeld, *Make a Scene,* 2008

Many novelists avoid laying out the setting because they fear boring their readers, but the lack of vivid setting may in turn cause boredom. Without a strong sense of place, it's hard to achieve suspense and excitement--which depend on the reader's sensation of being right there, where the action takes place. When descriptions of places drag, the problem usually lies not in the setting, but in presenting the setting too slowly. Make your descriptions dynamic and quick; give bits of setting concurrently with character and action.

Josip Novakovich, *Fiction Writer's Workshop*, 1995

Setting your story or novel in a particular historical time frame allows you to intertwine your story with concurrent events. The Great Depression, the Roaring Twenties, World War II--virtually any time period can provide a rich historical context with real individuals and events you can use as part of your story...

Set your story in the present and you can include current events. The downside is that current events can make your story seem dated. Remember, even for published writers cranking out a book a year, it usually takes two years between when a book is started and when it's published. In addition, most of us lack perspective on current events. What seems like a major news story when you're writing your novel may be a big yawn a year later. So only include current events that matter to your story.

Hallie Ephron, *Writing and Selling Your Mystery Novel*, 2005

The beginning mood in a piece of writing could be compared with the background music you hear at the start of a movie. That music--whether ominous, offbeat, or cheerful--gives you a pretty accurate idea of what kind of movie you'll be watching.

Many books begin with a description of a place that sets the mood for what is to follow. A lead like this can be a sly way of introducing one of the themes in a book. [Truman Capote opens *In Cold Blood* by describing rural Kansas, the site of the Clutter family murders.]

Ralph Fletcher, *Live Writing*, 1999

I hate synopses, and I've never managed to write one. How the hell can you boil down a novel from 400 pages to three?

And what does the reader of a synopsis expect to learn from it, anyway? I'm not nearly good enough a writer to convey tone, voice, and character and summarize a 90,000-word plot in five paragraphs. Someone who writes in romance told me that the synopsis is used to prove you understand the expectations of the genre. Well, okay, I guess. But I've never heard another good reason, and even that sounds weak to me.

If the publisher's demand for a synopsis in nonnegotiable, do the best you can. Otherwise, just skip it--attach Chapter One, or a list of writing credits, instead. For me, the whole point of the game is to get them to read the first few pages. After that, it's all about the writing, as it should be.

Michael Wiecek, in *The 101 Habits of Highly Successful Novelists,* Andrew McLeer, editor, 2008

DIALOGUE

If you need proof that dialogue and spoken words are not the same, go to a supermarket. Eavesdrop. Much of what you'll hear in the aisles sounds like idiot talk. People won't buy your novel to hear idiot talk. They get that free from relatives, friends, and at the supermarket.

Sol Stein, *Stein on Writing,* 1995

Among the things I remember hearing when I was beginning to write was: You shouldn't make fictional dialogue--conversation on the page--sound like actual speech. The repetitions, meaningless expressions, stammers, and nonsensical monosyllables with which we express hesitation, along with the cliché's and banalities that constitute so much of everyday conversation, cannot and should not be used when our characters are talking. Rather, they should speak more fluently than we do, with greater economy and certitude. Unlike us, they should say what they mean, get to the point, avoid circumlocution and digression. The idea, presumably, is that fictional dialogue should be an improved, cleaned-up, smoothed-out version of the way people talk.

Then why is so much written dialogue *less* colorful and interesting than what we can overhear daily...Many writers have a gift for language that flows when they are talking and dries up when they are confronted with the blank page, or when they are trying to make characters speak?

When we speak, we are not merely communicating information but attempting to make an impression and achieve a goal. And sometimes we are hoping to prevent the listener from noticing what we are *not* saying, which is often not merely distracting but, we fear, as audible as what we *are* saying. As a result, dialogue usually contains as much or even more subtext than it does text. More is going on under the surface than on it. One mark of badly written dialogue is that it is only doing one thing at once.

Francine Prose, *Reading Like a Writer,* 2006

Dialogue not only creates space on the page, which is visually appealing, it's also what brings characters to life in a story, which is emotionally appealing. We're much more interested in a story's setting when it comes through a scene of dialogue. Our characters' tense words let readers know where our characters are internally and create suspense for what's ahead in the story. The onset of a dialogue scene immediately propels the story into high gear. [Not necessarily. It depends on the conversation. I've read a lot of boring dialogue created by so-called "literary" novelists.] Through dialogue, we can give readers a very real sense of a story's setting. If done well, dialogue can even communicate the story's theme. [My advice to aspiring novelists-- forget *theme* and focus on story.] Effective dialogue delivers all of these things to eager readers. This is the kind of dialogue we, as writers, want to create.

Gloria Kempton, *Dialogue*, 2004

Naturalistic or "kitchen sink" dialogue involves people expressing themselves informally. The hell with grammar, if the characters knew it to begin with. *Realistic* dialogue, while appearing deceptively natural, is more organized. The vast bulk of modern plays and fiction employ this style combined with naturalistic. Pitfalls in realistic lines are the lack of accurate ear and the old bugaboo of educational freeze-up. One can be so organized, correct and formal that the lines go flat and lose the sound of people talking to each other.

Parke Goodwin in *The Portable Writers' Conference*, edited by Stephen Blake Mettee, 1997

We introduce our characters to our readers through dialogue. Dialogue combined with facial expression and body language indicates to readers who our characters are. In real life, this is how we get to know one another. We start interacting. Sometimes this goes well, sometimes it doesn't. Through dialogue, we decide if we like someone or not. This is also how our readers decide if they like our characters. As they listen to them and watch them interact with each other, they decide if these are good guys or bad guys or a combination. It's in our power to evoke positive or negative feelings in our readers for our characters through the dialogue we create for them.

Gloria Kempton, *Dialogue*, 2004

A writer who overuses dialogue doesn't have an acute sense of pacing, doesn't realize that a work can progress too fast. He relies heavily on dialogue, which means he's also using it poorly, since overuse comes hand in hand with misuse. He might, for instance, be using dialogue as a means of conveying information. He is more likely a beginner, plot oriented, and anxious for a fast pace. Alternately, he might be a playwright or screenwriter turned-author, stuck in the remnants of his previous form. In either case, he is more likely to neglect setting and character development. He is impatient, believes too much in the power of speech, and not enough in the power of silence. And since dialogue rates fairly high on the drama scale, this writer is likely to be overdramatic.

Noah Lukeman, *A Dash of Style*, 2006

Film and television have convinced too many writers that heaps of dialogue make novels more like movies and therefore good. This is an amateur's fantasy, and it has induced some writers to surrender the few advantages they have over cinematic storytelling.

The movie maker is stuck with what the camera can see and the microphone can hear. You have more freedom. You can summarize situations. You can forthrightly give us people's histories. You can concentrate ten years into ten words. You can move anywhere you like outside real time. You can tell us--just tell us--what people are thinking and feeling.

Yes, abundant dialogue can lighten a story, make it more readable and sparkle with wonders. But it is pitiably inadequate before what it is not suited to do. Exposition, for example: the "five w's"--the who, what, when, where, and why of a given situation. Jimmying this information into a visual background through performance and dialogue is cumbersome stuff.

Stephen Koch, *Writer's Workshop*, 2003

Letting a scene drag is one of the worst mistakes a writer can make. [Unless he is an established "literary" novelist.] Bringing two or more characters together and letting them chat on and on about nothing is inexcusable. The problem is many writers aren't even aware that their characters are doing this, even when it's in front of their noses. They're sitting right there writing the story and fail to see they're boring their reader to death with going-nowhere-fast dialogue.

There are many reasons dialogue scenes bog down. The main one is that we clutter them with so much added narrative and action that the reader has to muddle his way through and the going becomes a little clunky. Sometimes, the scene is weak when it comes to tension and suspense, and the reader is yawning.

Gloria Kempton, *Dialogue*, 2004

Exciting dialogue is spoken by smart characters saying important things. Beware of small talk, especially greetings, partings, and politesse. Avoid banter unless it has a clear and significant purpose in the story and suits the mood of what is happening between the speaking characters.

Alice Orr, *No More Rejections*, 2004

CHARACTERIZATION

Where do all the characters in a novel come from? They come from inside the novelist's head. The novelist is a role-player, an actor, and he's got all these different characters he wants to invent…It's not about putting on someone else's clothes, it's putting on someone else's skin, their mind and their body.

Ian Rankin, "On Writing: Writers Reveal the Secrets of Their Craft," theguardian.com, March 25, 2011

If you can't create characters that are vivid in the reader's imagination, you can't create a good novel. Characters are to a novelist what lumber is to a carpenter and what bricks are to a bricklayer. Characters are the *stuff* out of which a novel is constructed.

James N. Frey, *How to Write a Damn Good Novel, II*, 1994

[The novelist] E. M. Forster introduced the term *flat character* to refer to characters who have no hidden complexity. In this sense, they have no depth (hence the word "flat"). Frequently found in comedy, satire, and melodrama, flat characters are limited to a narrow range of predictable behaviors….

Forster's counter term to flat characters was *round characters*. Round characters have varying degrees of depth and complexity and therefore, in Forster's words, they "cannot be summed up in a single phrase."

H. Porter Abbott, *The Cambridge Guide to Narrative*, 2002

If you were to examine the surviving novels of this century, you would find that a majority of the most memorable characters in fiction are to some degree eccentric. Eccentricity has frequently been at the heart of strong characterization for good reason. Ordinariness is what readers have enough of in real life.

Sol Stein, *Stein on Writing*, 1995

In fiction, let your characters look like real people. Let them have bad tastes in their mouths and big moles on their arms and cellulite and dark circles under their eyes and real, beating hearts. Let them be beautiful, if the story calls for it, but let their beauty be unique, not carbon copy beauty. Writing is more vivid when it includes the rough patches of skin, not just satin fantasy flesh.

Gayle Brandeis, *Fruitfish*, 2002

Novice writers continue to make the mistake of choosing as the main character people who don't--or shouldn't--have enough freedom to be interesting. If the story is about a great war, they assume their hero must be the commanding general or the king, when in fact the story might be more powerfully told if the main character is a sergeant or a common soldier-- someone who is making choices and then carrying out those choices *himself*. Or the main character might even be a civilian, whose life is transformed as the great events flow over and around him...

As a main character, only use people in positions of highest authority when you are forced to because the story can't be told any other way. And then be very sure that you understand how people in such positions make their decisions, how power actually works.

Orson Scott Card, *How to Write Science Fiction and Fantasy*, 1990

Who should narrate (or be your viewpoint character) in fiction? A major character? A minor one? A few characters? What difference does it make? How will it impact the work as a whole?

Choosing a narrator is not a choice to be made lightly, yet unfortunately many writers make the choice without giving it much thought. Generally, they automatically assign the task to the protagonist. There is nothing necessarily wrong with this choice--in fact, most often, it is the correct one--but problems can arise if the decision was made without taking to time to consider why this person has merit as a narrator, what perspective he has to offer, what he brings to (or how he detracts from) the telling of the story, and how his perspective might differ from others'.

Noah Lukeman, *The Plot Thickens*, 2002

The very first rule of writing fiction rejects the basic truth of life: Characters must be consistent. If the matriarch of a powerful family of soda pop manufacturers has been established through three hundred pages as obsessively well organized, she cannot meet her end by getting her feet tangled on one of her own discarded sweaters and falling out her bedroom window. This kind of thing happens to people every day in the world we inhabit, despite evidence of past behavior, but we have left that world for a better one. If it happens here, we will throw the novel or short story out the window after the old lady, and good riddance to them both. In a pilotless universe, we accept confusion because there is no place to file a complaint. In a story, plotted and executed by an individual or individuals in collaboration, we know whom to blame.

Loren D. Estleman, *Writing the Popular Novel*, 2004

I should say that the practice of drawing characters from actual models is not only universal but necessary. I do not see why any novelist should be ashamed to acknowledge it. [Perhaps one who is afraid of being sued.]

W. Somerset Maugham in *Writers on Writing*, edited by Walter Allen, 1948

Readers tend to prefer characters who are at least somewhat sympathetic. In the case of villains, sympathetic is perhaps the wrong word: Understandable is better. Interesting is best of all. The bad guy whose sole reason for blowing up the galaxy is because that's what bad guys do won't be around for a sequel. Even Darth Vader needs motivation. It changes him from a cardboard cutout villain to a three-dimensional character, and three dimensions are far more interesting than two.

Ester M. Friesner in *How to Write Funny,* John B. Kachuba, editor, 2001

The 1955 novel *Lolita* stirred a lot of controversy when it was published and Vladimir Nabokov spent quite a bit of time insisting that his own knowledge of nymphets was purely scholarly, unlike the fictional Humbert Humbert, who molested young girls. In *Lolita*, Nabokov committed one of the toughest acts of the fiction writer: staying true to the humanness of a reprehensible character. Humbert Humbert is as disgusting and deplorable as a character as any ever written and it would be easy to cast him in a light that shows him as only horrid. Yet Nabokov allows him some appealing traits: decided charm, dazzling intelligence, a sense of shame for his weakness, and, ultimately, a genuine love for Lolita.

Brandi Reissenweber, *Writing Fiction,* Alexander Steele, editor, 2003

The defining characteristic of a contemplative scene is that your character spends more time thinking than he does in action or speech. These passages of thought are referred to as interior monologue and are meant to reveal something to the reader. These thoughts will be overheard by the reader, and therefore have a bearing on plot and character in each scene.

While the old convention was to set off thoughts by putting them into italics, I'm more of a fan of embedding thoughts within the narrative voice as simple, elegant exposition.

Jordane Rosenfeld, *Make a Scene,* 2008

If you're writing a novel where you are not springing an actual physical trap on your protagonist, think about other less dangerous entrapments. They can be benign, like staging a surprise party for a notoriously shy protagonist; sending a character who is inappropriately dressed to a fancy party or dangerously cold environment; or sending him into a room where another character is fuming with anger. Or it can be a situation in which an antagonist wrests information, a promise, or a concession from your protagonist, who gives in against his better judgment.

Jessica Page Morrell, *Between the Lines,* 2006

If it is true that no two writers get aesthetic interest from exactly the same materials, yet true that all writers, given adequate technique, can stir interest in their special subject matter--since all human beings have the same root experience (we're born, we suffer, we die, to put it grimly), so that all we need for our sympathy to be roused is that the writer communicate with power and conviction the similarities in his characters' experience and our own--then it must follow that the first business of the writer must be to make us see and feel vividly what his characters see and feel. However odd, however wildly unfamiliar the fictional world--odd as hog-farming to a fourth-generation Parisian designer, or Wall Street to an unemployed tuba player--we must be drawn into the characters' world as if we were born to it.

John Gardner, *The Art of Fiction*, originally published in 1983

STYLE

Those who *tell* stories better than they write them are the bane of editors. Editors dread wasting time on captivating talkers whose words lose their fizz on the page. Obviously, writing skills transcend conversational skills. But the drama and flair we bring to *telling* stories is too often lost once our words are nailed down on paper.

Most of us converse better than we write because we feel so much less vulnerable when addressing a limited number of ears. While talking, we can alter material or adjust our delivery in response to cues from others. If things get out of hand, we can change the subject altogether. Even when they bomb, spoken words float off into space. They can always be denied. "That's what I said?" is a great court of last resort. But words we've committed to paper can be held in evidence against us as long as that paper exists. Is it any wonder that we're scared to make this commitment?

Ralph Keyes, *The Courage to Write*, 1995

Though still revered, the classic text, *The Elements of Style* [by Will Strunk and E.B. White] is a little dated now, and just plain wrong about some things. Strunk and White are famously clueless for example, about what constitutes the passive voice. Their book also has some of the hectoring, preachy tone that creeps into so many of the discussions about writing, though it's not as extreme as Lynne Truss's *Eats, Shoots & Leaves,* which declares that people who misuse apostrophes "deserve to be struck by lightening, hacked up on the spot and buried in an unmarked grave."

Charles McGrath, "Omit Needless Rules," *The New York Times Book Review,* October 19, 2014

The really popular novels are full of clichés, people "flushing with anger" or "going pale with fear." Popular novelists bring nothing new to their readers, and I have no wish to belong to that type of popular writer.

Graham Greene in *Conversations with Graham Greene,* edited by Marie-Francoise Allain, 1991

Essentially I think of myself as a stylist, and stylists can become notoriously obsessed with the placing of a comma, the weight of a semicolon. Obsession of this sort, and the time it takes, irritates me beyond endurance.

Truman Capote in *Truman Capote,* edited by George Plimpton, 1997

Style is the relationship between writer and reader, and it is the vehicle through which you say whatever you have to say. It is the way you get your story told, and therefore consists of all your language and the whole manner you bring to its use. Style is always much more than decor or ornament, and it is always more than the way you dress up your story. It is the complete sound of what you write....

Writers often talk about "finding their voice," and that is indeed just what it feels like. In fact, most writers have to "find their voice" many times over, since each new project, with its changed subject and set of demands, will call for some change in manner and inflection.

Stephen Koch, *Writer's Workshop,* 2003

The main thing I try to do is write as clearly as I can. Because I have the greatest respect for the reader, and if he's going to the trouble of reading what I've written--I'm a slow reader myself and I guess that most people are--why, the least I can do is make it as easy as possible for him to find out what I'm trying to say, trying to get at. I rewrite a good deal to make it clear.

E. B. White (1899-1985), the author of the classic book, *The Elements of Style*, in *For Writer's Only* (1994) by Sophy Burnham

Insecure novelists want to show off their vocabulary out of fear of sounding ignorant. If I don't use obscure words, they seem to think, how will readers know that I have a college degree? If I use simple words, won't people think I'm a simpleton? Such attitudes make for deadly writing.

Ralph Keyes, *Courage to Write*, 1995

I've always been a sucker for the simple, bare line because I've always had this feeling that Literature, that of now and the centuries, was largely a put-on, you know, like pro wrestling matches. Even those who have lasted the centuries (with few exceptions) gave me the odd feeling that they were screwing me over. Basically, I feel that with the bare line it could be harder to get the lie across; besides it reads easier, and what's easy is good and what's hard to read is a pain in the ass.

So John Fante gave me the bare line with feeling; Hemingway the line that did not beg; Thurber the line that laughed at what the mind did and couldn't help doing; Saroyan the line that loved itself; Celine the line that cut the page like a knife; Sherwood Anderson the line that said beyond the line. I think I have borrowed from all of these writers and I am not ashamed to admit it. I only hope that I have added, what? If I knew what I were doing I could no longer do it.

Charles Bukowski in *Charles Bukowski: Selected Letters 1987-1994*, edited by Seamus Cooney, 2004

Great Writing was done in a language that had nothing to do with the way one spoke. The words were similar, but arranged more cleverly, less directly. A good literary sentence was like a floor with a hole hidden in it. You got to the end and thought: "Why'd he say it that way? He must really be a great writer." Plain English language was a degraded thing, good only for getting around your dopey miniature world, cashing checks and finding restaurants and talking about television and so on.

George Saunders, amazon.com, 2004

If a novelist cares more for his language than for other elements of fiction, if he continually calls our attention away from the story to himself, we call him "mannered" and eventually we tire of him.

John Gardner, *On Becoming a Novelist,* 1983

Fiction writers tend to fall into two broad camps: those who overwrite and those who underwrite. And, while a novelist may be able to get away with writing a *spare* story, a *thin* story will never ignite the reader's imagination. A spare story is one in which the writer deliberately chooses to pare down every element, using a small cast of characters, only one or two subplots, and little exposition and description. A well-crafted, yet spare story can work when every word counts and there is enough information to take the reader on a fictional journey. Ernest Hemingway usually wrote spare stories, but readers still feel immersed in his stories and understand the ramifications of the plot on the lives of his characters.

A thin story, on the other hand, is not based on deliberate choices, but rather on inexperience. In a thin story, the writer does not supply enough sensory data, creating a story line that can't be followed with confidence because of a lack of needed information. Spare stories spark the reader's imagination, but thin stories do not have enough data to do so, leaving the reader confused. In these anemic offerings, the reader is often adrift, longing for detail to place him in the scene, a hint about the themes or deeper meanings, or any doorway into the writer's intentions.

Jessica Page Morrell, *Between the Lines,* 2006

The term "purple prose" describes prose that is heightened, flowery, and overdone. The culprits of purple prose are usually modifiers that make your writing wordy, overwrought, distracting, and even silly. You might say that Hemingway's prose is the opposite of purple prose.

Jessica Page Morrell, *Between the Lines,* 2006

The one-sentence paragraph is a great device. You can italicize with it, vary your pace with it, lighten your voice with it, signpost your argument with it. But it's potentially dangerous. Don't overdo your dramatics. And be sure your sentence is strong enough to withstand the extra attention it's bound to receive when set off by itself. Houseplants wilt in direct sun. Many sentences do as well.

John R. Trimble, *Writing With Style*, 2000

There is a kind of writing that sounds so relaxed that you think you hear the author talking to you. E. B. White was probably its best practitioner, though many other masters of the style--James Thurber, V. S. Pritchett, Lewis Thomas--come to mind. I'm partial to it because it's a style that I've always tried to write myself. The common assumption is that the style is effortless. In fact the opposite is true: the effortless style is achieved by strenuous effort and constant refining. The nails of grammar and syntax [word order] are in place and the English is as good as the writer can make it.

William Zinsser, *On Writing Well*, 1976

The writer's personality and his personality on the page are not necessarily identical, but often there is a resemblance, not unlike that between an owner and his dog. A writer's work emanates from his personality, ego, sensitivities, and blind spots, his projections and unconscious wishes. All these contribute to what we eventually call style. Not everyone can arrive at a party and command the room; most writers are more inwardly focused. But even for those whose personal style attracts attention, the proof is always, finally, on the page. [This begs the question: can a reader tell if a novelist is a jerk by reading his fiction?]

Betsy Lerner, *The Forest for the Trees*, 2000

The overall effect of a manuscript encumbered with adjectives, adverbs and the inevitable commas in between makes for slow, awkward reading--which these writers would find out for themselves if they only took the time to read their own work aloud.

Manuscripts heavy on adjectives and adverbs can be spotted by an agent or editor immediately--sometimes even in the first few sentences--by looking for a plethora of commas (which inevitably separate a string of adjectives), or in the case of a writer who doesn't even know how to use commas, by looking to the nouns and verbs and then looking to see if adjectives or adverbs precede (or succeed) them.

Noah Lukeman, *The First Five Pages*, 2000

A novelist is revealed in his style, the language which he has created for himself.

Henry Miller in *Henry Miller on Writing,* edited by Thomas H. Moore, 1964

6 THE NOVELIST

When I began to write stories and novels I did so as though it were the most natural thing in the world. I took to it as a duck takes to water. I have never quite got over my astonishment at being a writer. My language was commonplace, my vocabulary limited, my grammar shaky and my phrases hackneyed. But to write was an instinct that seemed as natural to me as to breathe, and I did not stop to consider if I wrote well or badly.

W. Somerset Maugham, *Summing Up*, 1938

I cannot remember a time when I didn't want to be a writer, and specifically a novelist; I can't remember ever wanting to do anything else. I never wanted to be a sportsman, I never wanted to be a musician. I never had the slightest bit of interest in music. When other boys had pictures of footballers [soccer players] on their walls or they had pictures of musicians on their walls, I had pictures of Jane Austen and Ben Johnson. I only wanted to be a writer and I only ever valued writers. And it hasn't changed; I only value writers.

Howard Jacobson, "On Writing: Authors Reveal the Secrets of Their Craft," theguardian.com, March 25, 2011

What kind of an emotion is the desire to write? It is not a core emotion like joy or fear. Nor is it a biological drive in the sense that hunger or sexual desire is. But there are secondary emotions and secondary drives, made up of a mixture of core emotions or drives, often in combination with certain beliefs. Secondary emotions include complicated states such as guilt, hope, and smugness. Secondary drives might include the urge to buy a house or to gamble. It is in this secondary category that the drive to write best fits.

Alice W. Flaherty, *The Midnight Disease*, 2004

Most literary callings announce themselves early. John Dos Passos did not discover his call to write until after graduate school, but the obsession hit Truman Capote around age eleven; William Styron at thirteen. Susan Sontag was nine. Even though she did not publish her first book until she was forty-two, P. D. James always knew she wanted to write. "I think I was born knowing it...I think writing was what I wanted to do, almost as soon as I knew what a book was."

Stephen Koch, *The Modern Library Writer's Workshop*, 2003

You might want to become a nonfiction writer, and yet at every turn you distort things, exaggerate and embellish them, and even introduce characters, places and events that had nothing to do with the original material. In that case, you are a born fiction writer, which is much nicer than saying you are a born liar.

Josip Novakovich in *Fiction Writer's Workshop*, edited by Josip Novakovich, 1995

Do you have a new idea almost every day for a writing project? Do you either start them all and don't see them to fruition or think about starting but never actually get going? Do your begin sentences in your head while walking to work or picking up the dry cleaning? Do you blab about your project to loved ones, coworkers or strangers before the idea is fully formed, let alone partially executed? Have you ever been diagnosed with any combination of bipolar disorder, alcoholism, or skin diseases such as eczema or psoriasis? Do you snap at people who ask how your writing is going? *What is it to them?* Do you fear that you will someday wonder where the years went? How is it that some no-talent you went to high school with is being published everywhere you look?

　　If you can relate to the above, you certainly have the obsessive qualities--along with the self-aggrandizement and concurrent feelings of worthlessness--that are part of the novelist's makeup.

Betsy Lerner, *Forest For The Trees*, 2001

I think aspiring novelists need as much *dis*couragement as we can muster. Nobody should undertake the life of a fiction writer--so monetarily unrewarding, so maddeningly beset by career vagaries--who has any other choice in the matter. Learn a trade! Flannery O'Connor said it best: "People are always asking me if the university stifles writers. I reply that it hasn't stifled enough of them."

Gerald Howard in *Advice To Writers*, edited by Jon Winokur, 1999

I read the essays George Plimpton had done for *Paris Review* about how Hemingway and other great ones got their paragraphs hung together, and I tried to diagnose my own talents, and lack of them. I decided I was adept at description, good at moving narration along, and dialogue was no problem. I had no idea whether I could develop a plot or how I could shape chapters.

Tony Hellerman, *Seldom Disappointed*, 2001

We are not geniuses, most of us who write novels, but we are, many of us, people who have chosen to live the surrogate life of the imagination. We have perhaps settled for that state which Wallace Stevens speaks of. "The final belief," he said, "is to believe in a fiction that you know to be a fiction, there being nothing else."

Brian Moore in *Agony and the Ego*, edited by Clare Boylan, 1994

The phrase "writer's block" was coined by an American, a psychiatrist named Edmund Bergler...In other ages and cultures, writers were not thought to be blocked but straightforwardly dried up. One literary critic pointed out that the concept of writer's block is peculiarly American in its optimism that we all have creativity just waiting to be unlocked. By contrast, Milton, when he could not write, felt that he was empty, that there was no creativity left untapped.

If writer's block is more common in the United States, it would not be the first weakness that is peculiar to our culture. The modern American idea of the literary writer is so shaped by the towering images of Ernest Hemingway and F. Scott Fitzgerald struggling with every word, that there is a paradoxical sense in which suffering from writer's block is necessary to be an American novelist. Without block once in a while, if a writer is too prolific, he or she is suspected by other novelists as being a hack.

Alice W. Flaherty, *The Midnight Disease*, 2004

Blocked writers are now being treated with antidepressants such as Prozac, though some report that the drugs tend to eliminate the writer's desire to write altogether along with his regret over not doing so. Other blocked writers are being given Ritalin and other stimulants on the theory that their problems may be due to the condition of Attention Deficit Disorder.

Joan Acocella, *The New Yorker, June 21, 2004*

The novelist's life is inherently an insecure one. Each project is a new start and may be a failure. The fact that a previous item has been successful is not a guard against failure this time. It's no wonder fiction writers so often turn misanthropic or are driven to drink to dull the agony.

Isaac Asimov, *I Asimov*, 1995

Unless the novelist has the good luck to visit the bestseller lists or wallow in unusual critical adulation, fiction writing often seems an exercise in futility. After a short burst of reviews [Most novelists don't even get that anymore], the comments of one's close friends and a smattering of letters from strangers who care enough to write, a disturbing silence descends. It is like a small death. Something that has long been alive in us struggling to breathe is suddenly without discernible pulse. Nothing looks quite so dusty and dead as yesterday's book on the shelf. The novelist will likely begin to brood that the months or years invested in his work have gone for naught. It is at this point that writers become difficult to live with. They may take up drink, flirt with Godless religion or seek to run away with blondes. One's worth and how one has chosen to spend one's day are called into question.

Larry L. King, *The Night Hank Williams Died*, 1989

Many novelists use alcohol to help themselves write--to calm their anxiety, lift their inhibitions. This may work for awhile, but eventually the writing suffers. The unhappy writer then drinks more; the writing then suffers more, and so on.

Joan Acocella, *The New Yorker*, June 21, 2004

A surprising proportion of novelists are manic-depressive. The psychologist Kay Redfield Jamison, one of the foremost experts on manic-depression, has explored this phenomenon in depth…The work of Jamison and others shows that novelists are ten times more likely to be manic-depressive than the rest of the population, and poets are a remarkably forty times more likely to suffer from this condition...

Although most writers who have been successfully treated for depression find that their work begins to flow again as their mood improves, paradoxically, a few writers have linked their desire to write to their depression...

One justification for such a position is that an artist must suffer to create, and what more effective way to suffer than through mental illness?..

Other writers argue that depression is not necessary for creativity directly, but is an inevitable side effect of the mechanism that produces elated creative states...Several more writers have described how their desire to write disappeared as their depressions lifted, but blame the antidepressant--not the loss of their depression--for their decreased creativity.

Alice W. Flaherty, *The Midnight Disease*, 2004

It's unfortunate that I learned something through booze. Everybody does, but ultimately on the level I was using, it was sickness. Jail, hospitals, DUIs. Briefly it worked, to be frank, but that was on three beers and exactly where, if I were to appear on television today as a spokesperson for anti-alcohol, I'd say: Listen, if you need more than three beers, worry.

Barry Hannah, *Paris Review,* Winter 2004

American novelists, more than others, are haunted by the fear of failure, because it's such a common pattern in America. The ghost of Fitzgerald, dying in Hollywood, with his comeback book unfinished, and his best book, *Tender Is The Night*, scorned. His ghost hangs over every American novelist's typewriter.

Irwin Shaw in *Writers at Work, Fifth Series*, edited by George Plimpton, 1981

Novelists when they're writing live in a spooky, clamorous silence, a state somewhat like the advanced stages of prayer but without prayer's calming benefits. A writer turns his back on the day and the night and its large and little beauties, and tries to fashion other days and nights with words. It's absurd. Oh, it's silly, dangerous work indeed.

Joy Williams in *Why I Write*, edited by William Blythe, 1998

I can go three or four months without having a drink. And then suddenly I'm walking down the street and I feel that I'm going to die, that I can't put one foot in front of the other unless I have a drink. So I step into a bar. Someone who's not an alcoholic couldn't understand. But suddenly I feel so tired. I've had this problem with alcoholism for about fifteen years. I've gone to hospitals, I tried Anatabuse, I've done everything. But nothing seems to work.

Truman Capote in *Capote* by Gerald Clarke, 1988

Novel writing, like other creative and artistic pursuits, tends to be romanticized by many and vilified by some. Novelists in America are seen as special, peculiar but mythical people whose lives have a certain magical charm, or, alternatively, as drunken, neurotic wastrels who sponge off the government and do no work. Sometimes writers themselves perpetrate these myths.

Judith Barrington, *Writing The Memoir*, 2002

The most serious problem a writer can face is "writer's block." This is a serious disease and when a writer has it he finds himself staring at a blank sheet of paper in the typewriter (or blank screen on the word processor) and can't do anything to unblank it. The words don't come. Or if they do, they are clearly unsuitable and are quickly torn up or erased. What's more, the disease is progressive, for the longer the inability to write continues, the more certain it is that it will continue to continue....

A writer can't put anything on paper when there's nothing left (at least temporarily) in his mind. It may be, therefore, that writer's block is unavoidable and that at best a writer must pause every once in a while, for a shorter or longer interval, to let his mind fill up again.

Isaac Asimov, *I. Asimov: A Memoir*, 1994

And there was Aaron Klopstein. Who ever heard of him? He committed suicide at the age of 33 in Greenwich Village by shooting himself with an Amazonian blow gun, having published two novels, two volumes of poetry, one book of short stories and a book of critical essays.

Raymond Chandler in *Raymond Chandler Speaking*, edited by Dorothy Gardiner and Kathleen Sorley Walker, 1962

The best way of all for dealing with writer's block is never to get it. Some novelists never do. Theoretically there's no reason one should get it, if one understands that writing, after all, is only writing, neither something one ought to feel deeply guilty about nor something one ought to be inordinately proud of. The very qualities that make one a novelist in the first place contribute to block: hypersensitivity, stubbornness, insatiability, and so on. Given the general oddity of novelists, no wonder there are no sure cures.

John Gardner, *On Becoming A Novelist*, 1983

I get moments of gloom and pessimism when it seems as nobody could ever like my kind of writing again [social-comedy novels]. I get depressed about my writing, and feel that however good it was it still wouldn't be acceptable to any publisher.

Barbara Pym in *Lot to Ask* by Hazel Holt, 1991

My interest is in solving problems presented by writing a novel. That's what stops my brain spinning like a car wheel in the snow, obsessing about nothing. Some people do crossword puzzles to satisfy their need to keep their mind engaged. For me, the absolutely demanding mental test is the desire to get the work right. The crude cliché is that the novelist is solving the problem of his life in his books. Not at all. What he's doing is taking something that interests him in life and then solving the problem of the book--which is, how do you write about this?

Philip Roth, *The Guardian*, September 11, 2004

Stephen King's First Rule of Writers and Agents, learned by bitter personal experience: You don't need an agent until you're making enough money for someone to steal, and if you're making that much, you'll be able to take your pick of good agents.

Stephen King, *On Writing*, 2000

I spent a hell of a lot of time killing animals and fish so I wouldn't kill myself. When a man is in rebellion against death, as I am in rebellion against death, he gets pleasure out of taking to himself one of the god-like attributes; that of giving it.

Ernest Hemingway in *Papa Hemingway* by A. E. Hotchner, 1966

The first time we heard of Ernest Hemingway's death [1958] was a call from the *London Daily Mail.* I found it shocking. He had only one theme-- only one. A man contends with the forces of the world, called fate, and meets them with courage. Surely a man has a right to remove his own life but you'll find no such possibility in any of Hemingway's heroes. The sad thing is that I think he would have hated accident much more than suicide. He was an incredibly vain man.

John Steinbeck in *Writers At Work, Fourth Series,* edited by George Plimpton, 1976

My theory is that novelists don't much like each other. Their relationships with each other are too complicated. I can't understand how two writers can be married to each other any more than I can fathom how two actors can be. It seems to me that the more contact writers have with other writers, the more vitriolic they are on the subject of one another. If a writer is only known from afar, through his or her written word or an occasional meeting at a writers' conference, the observations about that person are more restrained. It is daily contact, like stone rubbing stone, that most often produces sparks.

James Charlton, *Fighting Words,* 1994

I'm always quite nervous at the beginning of my workday. It takes me a great deal of time to get started. Once I get started, it gradually calms down a bit, but I'll do anything to keep postponing...Anyway, one way or another, I manage to write about four hours a day.

Truman Capote in *Conversations With Capote,* edited by Lawrence Grobel, 1985

I have just spent a good week, alone like a hermit. I abandoned myself to a frenzy of literature; I got up at midday, I went to bed at four in the morning. I smoked fifteen pipes in a day; I have written *eight* pages.

Gustave Flaubert in *Writer's On Writing*, edited by Walter Allen, 1948

I work almost constantly. For a novelist without hobbies, weekends don't make much difference. Most people don't enjoy weekends anyway; they don't know what to do with Sundays.

Joseph Heller in *Fiction Writer's Market*, edited by Jean M. Fredette, 1985

I think it has to be faced: There's something in writing, in being a writer, that is inimical to family life. Or vice versa. P. G. Wodehouse made the point with his usual levity and grace by dedicating *The Heart of a Goof* to "my daughter Leonora, without whose never-failing sympathy and encouragement this book would have been finished in half the time." A priest friend of mine pointed out to me that all the great works of mysticism were written by celibates: "If they'd had kids, they'd all have been too tired to pray." The writer is a solitary person, immersed in moods. The defect, the brain splinter that makes a person a writer is anti-domestic. He or she waits, yearning, for the moment when the imagination goes rogue and love and duty go out the window. Writers are not easy to live with. Children need, require, and deserve attention. So what's the answer? If you happen to find out, do me a favor and let me know.

James Parker, *The New York Times Book Review*, June 15, 2014

I don't think people become novelists for the most part, unless they have experienced a peculiar distancing, which generally occurs in childhood or youth and makes the direct satisfactions of living unsatisfactory, so that they have to seek basic satisfactions indirectly through what we can loosely call art. What makes the verbal artist is some kind of shock or crippling or injury which puts the world once removed from him. He writes about it to take possession of it. We start out thinking we're writing about other people and end up realizing we're writing about ourselves.

Ross McDonald in *Shoptalk*, edited by Donald M. Murray, 1990

There are much easier, more pleasant ways to pass the time than writing, though few so rewarding intellectually and spiritually. But it's no sin to be honest and admit it if you'd rather garden, fish, or socialize with friends than go it alone as a novelist, with no guarantee of success. If you aren't sure you're up to all that writing demands of a person, go no further.

John Jakes in *Writer's Handbook*, edited by Sylvia K. Burack, 1988

One of the cruelest remarks in the language is: Those who can, do; those who can't, teach. The parallel must be: Those who meet experience, learn to live; those who don't, write.

The second remark has as much truth as the first--which is to say, some truth. Of course, many a young man has put himself in danger to pick up material for his writing, but as a matter to make one wistful, not one major American athlete, CEO, politician, engineer, trade-union official, surgeon, airline pilot, chess master, call girl, sea captain, teacher, bureaucrat, Mafioso, pimp, recidivist, physicist, rabbi, movie star, clergyman, or priest or nun has also emerged as a major novelist since the Second World War.

Norman Mailer, *The Spooky Art*, 2003

I get many of my letters from people in madhouses and jails and some from strange people out of them. What they say, mainly, is that I have given them a reason for going on: "Since you are so screwed-up, Bukowski, and still around, there is a chance for me." But I don't write to save people; I dislike most of them. I feel best when I am totally alone. I've tried to answer most of my letters, especially from people in the madhouses but I found that an answer just brings another letter, a longer one and a stranger one.

Charles Bukowski in *Charles Bukowski: Selected Letters 1971-1986*, edited by Seamus Cooney, 2004

Writing a novel is an endurance contest and a war fought against yourself, because writing is beastly hard work which one would just as soon not do. It's also a job, however, and if you want to get paid, you have to work. Life is cruel that way.

Tom Clancy in *Complete Handbook of Novel Writing*, edited by Meg Leder and Jack Heffron, 2002

I just got rid of a short story called "The Other." *Arete* took it. They pay a grand. Then they asked that I might illustrate the story. I sat down and flipped out three or four drawings, took me maybe five minutes. They accepted--$400. Everything is very strange. From a total bum to all this. But something is watching me. I am always being tested. There is always the next day, the next night. I began late and I'm going to have to keep pounding. I missed a hell of a lot of years. But the luckiest thing that ever happened to me is that I didn't get lucky early.

Charles Bukowski in *Charles Bukowski: Selected Letters 1987-1994*, edited by Seamus Cooney, 2004

I don't feel very rapid or prolific to myself. Looking back on the alleged 50 books that I've written, many of them are quite short, some are children's books, some are collections of material that appear in other books, so in a way it's a fraudulent appearance of muchness. Some of the books are sequels, which again is a kind of cheating.

John Updike in *Writer's Handbook*, edited by Elfrieda Abbe, 2002

When I was younger, the main struggle was to be a "good writer." Now, I more or less take my writing for granted, although that doesn't mean I always write well.

Jonathan Franzen, *Paris Review*, Winter 2010

Many novelists peter out. They die with a whimper. They begin to write thin versions of what they wrote when they were young. I don't want that to happen to me.

Anne Rice in *Conversations with Anne Rice* (1996) by Michael Riley

I enjoy the dubious distinction of being known among lawyers as a writer, and among writers as a lawyer.

Arthur Train (1875-1945), *My Day in Court*, 1939.

[Other lawyers who became successful novelists include: Erle Stanley Gardner, Scott Turow, John Mortimer, Louis Auchincloss, John Grisham, and Richard North Patterson.]

Early in his career, John Cheever put on his business suit, then went from his apartment to a room in the basement where he hung his suit on a hanger and wrote in his underwear. Victor Hugo's servant took away his clothes for the duration of the author's writing day. James Whitcomb Riley had a friend lock him in a hotel room without clothes so that he couldn't go out for a drink until he had finished writing. [How do you lock someone in a hotel room?] Jessamyn West wrote in bed without getting dressed for what she thought were two compelling reasons: "One, you have on your nightgown or pajamas and can't go running to the door at the knock of strangers. Also, once you're up and dressed, you see ten thousand things that need doing."

Ralph Keyes, *The Courage to Write*, 1995

Male novelists don't slug and insult each other the way they used to, since they aren't a bunch of drunks any more. They would be drinking less even if it weren't for the sudden humorlessness of the judiciary with respect to driving while under the influence. Not just male writers, but male artists of every sort, are no longer pressured to prove that they are real men, even though they have artistic sensibilities. As I've said elsewhere, my father was a gun nut like Ernest Hemingway, mainly to prove that he wasn't effeminate, even though he was an architect and a painter. He didn't get drunk and slug people. Shooting animals was enough. But male American artists don't even bother to shoot off guns anymore. This is good.

Kurt Vonnegut in *Kurt Vonnegut: Letters,* edited by Dan Wakefield, 2012

Writers published by the biggest New York houses get [blurb] requests all the time. Typically they come from the editors at these publishing houses. It will be an email, or an actual book in the mail with a note attached that says something like this: "Jane Doe's first novel is an exciting new take on an old story and we'd be so pleased if you'd give it a look. And if you deem it worthy, a few words of support on Jane's behalf, sent to us by such and such a date, would give her novel a tremendous lift!"

The more famous and respected the writer, the more of these blurb requests he or she will get. They might come from friends of the famous writer, too, or from his or her editor or agent and their friends. One imagines that Jonathan Franzen, for example, could spend hours and hours responding to the blurb requests he gets. Some writers are famous in the book trade for blurbing a lot (too much), and others for never blurbing at all.

Hector Tobar, *Los Angeles Times*, November 6, 2013

My biggest struggle as a novelist is to put my own story on paper--not to be influenced by what I think my editor, my publisher, my friends, or the reader wants to see on the page. I need to get these people out of my writing space and focus on writing *my* story. If it resonates for me, it will resonate for my readers.

Joan Johnston in *The 101 Habits of Highly Successful Novelists*, edited by Andrew McLeer, 2008

In wanting to be a novelist, there must be something beyond rationality at work. Call it love or obsession, a need to express or a need for attention, an ability to communicate or an inability to shut up, but writers are clearly a little bit insane.

Erin Barratte and Jack Mingo, *It Takes a Certain Type To Be A Writer*, 2003

The novelist has a grudge against society, which he documents with accounts of unsatisfying sex, unrealized ambition, unmitigated loneliness, and a sense of local and global distress. The square, overpopulation, the bourgeois, the bomb, and the cocktail party are variously identified as sources of the grudge. [Today it would be global warming, consumerism, terrorism, and flag-waving yahoos.] There follows a little obscenity here, a dash of philosophy there, considerable whining overall, and the modern novel is born.

Renata Adler, *Toward a Radical Middle, 1969*

It may be that writers are actually happier living in their books than they are in the real world. There is evidence of this in the way writers immerse themselves in their fiction. How many times have you heard it said about someone that they are happiest at their work? Writers are like that, whether they admit it or not. But while most jobs fall into the nine-to-five category, fiction writing is a twenty-four-hours-a-day occupation. You never leave your work behind. It is always with you, and to some extent, you are always thinking about it. You don't take your work home; your work never leaves home. It lives inside you. It resides and grows and comes alive in your mind.

Terry Brooks, *Sometimes the Magic Works,* 2005

Writing a novel is a very hard thing to do because it covers so long a space of time, and if you get discouraged it is not a bad sign, but a good one. If you think you are not doing it well, you're thinking the way real novelists do. I never knew a writer who did not feel greatly discouraged at times, and some get desperate, and I have always found that to be a good symptom.

Maxwell Perkins in *Max Perkins,* A. Scott Berg, 1978

Early in "Limitless" (2011), moviegoers see Bradley Cooper leaning over a keyboard, hands pressed prayerfully to face, waiting in agony for the words. Salvation arrives in the form of a pill that allows Cooper's character, the writer Eddie Morra, to use 100 percent of his brain instead of just 20. The words start coming, clear and fast; indeed, Eddie becomes so lucid that he gives up authorship for day trading.

Because no one wants to watch somebody typing, Hollywood often makes movies about writers who stop writing. It's easier, and more entertaining, to show them being...destroyed by fame or drink or premature success....

On film, authorship is mostly a matter of occupational hazard. Woody Allen's "Deconstructing Harry" (1997) offers a...look at a novelist who writes from his own life, infuriating lovers and family members...."Wonder Boys"(2000), made from Michael Chabon's novel, combines New York trade publishing...with the provincial world of a M.F.A. [Masters of Fine Arts] workshops....

The hard part is always trying to show writers doing what they actually do. The Michael Douglas character occasionally sits at his Selectric wearing a woman's bathrobe, like a pitcher's lucky underwear, trying to summon more phrases for his already overlong, inert manuscript....

Martin Amis once observed that "a writer is, on the whole, most alive when alone." That's when he gets "on with the business of imagining other people." And that's why movies do a much better job of admiring authorship rather than conveying it....

Thomas Mallon, "Why Is It So Hard to Capture the Writer on Film?" *The New York Times Book Review*, May 4, 2014

One of the most public and wholesale rejections of a writer occurred in 1975, when *Esquire* published "La Cote Basque," an early chapter from Truman Capote's novel-in-progress *Answered Prayers*. Capote's women friends from New York's cafe society were horrified by the exposure of their secrets and promptly banished him from their inner circle. According to his editor, Joe Fox at Random House, "Virtually every friend he had in this world ostracized him for telling thinly disguised tales out of school, and many of them never spoke to him again." Their little writer friend, the elfin troublemaker, had taken things just a little too far. Capote crossed a line he claimed he hadn't known existed, though he confessed to a certain amount of delicious anticipation before the piece ran, and he agreed to be photographed for the magazine's cover with a fedora wickedly tilted atop his head while he pared his fingernails with a very long blade.

Betsy Lerner, *The Forest For the Trees*, 2000

I try to work every day. I start around ten in the morning and write until dinnertime, most days. Sometimes it's not productive, and there's a lot of downtime. Sometimes I fall asleep in my chair, but I feel that if I'm in the room all day, something's going to get done. I treat it like a desk job.

Jeffrey Eugenides, *Paris Review*, Winter 2011

It is true that some writers have kept themselves more or less innocent of education, that some, like Jack London, were more or less self-made men; that is, people who scratched out an education by reading books between work-shifts on boats, in logging camps or gold camps, on farms or in factories. It is true that university education is in many ways inimical to the work of the artist: Rarely do painters have much good to say of history-of-art professors, and it's equally uncommon for even the most serious, "academic" writers to look with fond admiration at "the profession of English." And it's true that life in the university has almost never produced subject matter for really good fiction. The life has too much trivia, too much mediocrity, too much soap opera, but consider:

No ignoramus--no writer who has kept himself innocent of education--has ever produced great art.

John Gardner, *The Art of Fiction*, 1983.

I'm egocentric in the sense that I live inside my own head most of the time, and I'm fascinated by my own thoughts. Nothing has ever happened to me in any real sense. I haven't met famous people. I haven't been involved in world-shaking events. I haven't done unusual things like climb Mount Everest. I've led a very quiet life.

Isaac Asimov in *The Writer as Celebrity*, edited by Maralyn Lois Polak, 1986

The most intense relationship anybody can have with a writer is by reading their work, alone, in silence. Yet readers seek writers in search of something additional. It was J.D. Salinger's hero, Holden Caufield, who said that what really knocked him out was a book that when you're done reading it, you wish the author that wrote it was a terrific friend of yours and you could call him up on the telephone whenever you felt like it. It was also J.D. Salinger who, when *Catcher in the Rye* achieved its enormous success, made himself as inaccessible to his readers as any living author has ever been.

Sean French in *The Faber Book of Writers on Writers*, edited by Sean French

The literary bad boy lives today…in the mind of the writer. He is a legend only, a creature of folk memory. Which isn't to say that there aren't plenty of traditionally chaotic real-life writers out there, right now, staying the course, crashing about and appalling their spouses [Norman Mailer knifed one of his wives]. What's changed, for us, is that the media is no longer interested….

In 2014 we have bad-boy chefs (Bourdain, Ramsay), bad-boy comedians (Russell Brand), bad-boy athletes (the demonic Uruguayan soccer player Luis Suarez). And it's possible, I suppose, that some young word-slinger could come along and wring a new twist from the tired repertoire of writerly naughtiness--be a postmodern literary bad boy. But in the end, who cares? Drink, divorce, insanity, firearms: all beside the point. The work is what counts....[If you like bad boy writers, try Charles Bukowski. He was very bad but his writing is good.]

James Parker, "What's Become of the So-Called Literary Bad Boy?" *The New York Times*, February 18, 2014

The literary thesis writers are after me. They demand that I have some sort of "plan" to my work. Actually, I write without calculation. If you write in a complicated way, you can't think you mustn't write in the complicated way because it encourages academics who would be better occupied ranking leaves.

John Fowles in *People, Books & Book People*, edited by David W. McCullough, 1981

When I'm in a writing mode for a novel, I get up at 4:00 AM and work for five to six hours. In the afternoon, I run for 10km or swim for 1500m (or do both) then read a bit and listen to some music. I go to bed at 9:00 PM. I keep to this routine every day without variation.

Haruki Murakami, *Paris Review*, Summer 2004

Maxwell Perkins, dead these many years after he by Herculean effort transformed Thomas Wolfe's undisciplined outpourings into actual novels, did a disservice to novelists today who believe in the notion that all they need to do is get something on paper and some editor somewhere, most likely wearing a green eyeshade, will toil upon the novel until it is fit to print. They are mistaken,

George V. Higgins, *On Writing*, 1990

7 THE SHORT STORY

The novel differs from the short story in more than just length, but they both share the dynamic quality of character-moved-by-plot. But the difference is, that on the long trip the novel provides, there is space and time for a quantity of incidents and effects. Edgar Allan Poe spoke of the short story as providing "a single and unique effect" toward which every word contributes: "If the author's initial sentence tend not to the bring out this effect, then he has failed in his first step. In the whole composition there should be no word written, of which the tendency, direct or indirect, is not to the one pre-established design." Poe's famous "unique effect" dictum can of course be taken too strictly, but it does seem to be the case that there is a degree of unity in a well-wrought short story--what we call an "harmonious relationship of all its aspects"--that isn't necessarily found in a good novel, that isn't perhaps even desirable in a novel.

Rust Hills, *Writing in General and The Short Story in Particular,* 1987

It is not hard to state what Edgar Allan Poe meant by a good short story; it is a piece of fiction, dealing with a single incident...that can be read at a setting. It is original, it must sparkle, excite or impress; and it must have unity of effect or impression. It should move in an even line from its exposition to its close.

W. Somerset Maugham, *Points of View,* 1961

Samuel Langhorne Clements [Mark Twain], Jack London, F. Scott Fitzgerald, Ernest Hemingway, John Steinbeck and dozens of other novelists whose flames burn only slightly less luminously in the history of literature had one thing in common: They learned their craft by writing

75

short stories. Only when they had mastered that form did they undertake the long trek of the novel. The short story, in its heyday, was the universal school for novelists.

Jon Franklin, *Writing For Story*, 1994

The ending of the modern short story doesn't require a long summary of what happened "afterwards." The novel, though, presents a slightly different case. After having spent so long with the characters, the reader of a novel has become so interested in them, almost fond of them as acquaintances, that he is not adverse to a long "afterward" or "conclusion" that tells how they married, settled down and raised children and grew old together.

Rust Hills, *Writing in General And The Short Story In Particular*, 1987

Short-story writing, as I saw it, was estimable. One required skill and cleverness to carry it off. But to have written a novel was to have achieved something of substance. You could swing a short story on a cute idea backed up by a modicum of verbal agility. You could, when the creative juices were flowing, knock it off start-to-finish on a slow afternoon.

A novel, on the other hand, took real work. You had to spend months on the thing, fighting it out in the trenches, line-by-line and page by page and chapter by chapter. It had to have plot and characters of sufficient depth and complexity to support a structure of sixty or a hundred thousand words. It wasn't an anecdote, or a finger exercise, or a trip to the moon on gossamer wings. It was a *book*.

The short-story writer, as I saw it, was a sprinter; he deserved praise to the extent that his stories were meritorious. But the novelist was a long-distant runner, and you don't have to come in first in a marathon in order to deserve the plaudits of the crowd. It is enough merely to have finished on one's feet.

Lawrence Block, *Writing a Novel*, 1979

A novel is so much more difficult than a short story. If you run, it's almost like you can think through your whole short story before you finish running. With a novel, it's almost impossible to do that.

Joyce Carol Oates, *Where I've Been, And Where I'm going*, 1999

The relationship of the short story to the novel amounts to nothing at all. The novel is a distinct form of art having a pedigree and practice of hardly more than a couple of hundred years; the short story, so far from being its offspring, is an ancient art originating in the folk tale, which was a thing of joy even before writing, not to mention printing, was invented.

E. Coppard, *The Collected Tales Of A. E. Coppard*, 1951

Short stories are wonderful and extremely challenging, and the joy of them-- because it only takes me three or four months to write--is that I can take more risks with them. It's just less of your life invested. That's great. But the challenge of a novel is so rewarding--there's so much more you can cram into them. Maybe the metaphor is: With a short story, you're building a table, you have four legs, you're trying to make it as beautiful and as functional as you can. With a novel, you're building not just a table but a whole house--you're building all the furniture inside it. It's more challenging, and then when you finish, it's more rewarding. I do think it's a richer experience.

Carole Burns, *Off The Page*, 2008

When I sit down to write a new piece, I find myself more apprehensive about the idea of writing a short story than embarking on a new novel. A novel doesn't rush me. It gives me time and room to feel out what the story is about…

Short stories are not like that. It takes little skill to ramble on and on and put all you mind's wanderings out there for the world to see. But try turning a page into three sentences, or three minutes of verbosities into a 30-second spiel. It takes effort to transfer great meaning to small places…

Short stories are like messages in bottles. They are adventures wrapped up in small packages.

Justin C. Key, scribophile.com, April 15, 2010

Short stories are gratifying and fun and not the kind of heavy lifting involved with a novel. I used to frequently write them in one sitting. Now it's usually several days. Whatever it is, it's a cheap investment in time. Plus, you can take the amount of chances you can't with a novel because if you waste three days, what do you care?

Lawrence Block, *Writing the Novel*, 1985

The short story form is like a hundred-yard dash, compared to a cross-country race. There's no time for pacing, strategy, getting a second wind. In a short flash you go flat out, and that's all.

Ben Bova, *Notes to a Science Fiction Writer*, 1975

Unlike most novels, great short stories make us marvel at their integrity, their economy. If we went at them with our red pencils, we might find we had nothing to do. We would discover there was nothing that the story could afford to lose without the whole delicate structure collapsing like a meringue. And yet we are left with a feeling of completeness, a conviction that we know exactly as much as we need to know, that all of our questions have been answered.

Francine Prose in *On Writing Short Stories,* edited by Tom Bailey, 2000

There is something about the pace of the short story that catches the tempo of this country. If it is written with sincerity and skill it portrays a mood, a character, a background, or a situation. Sometimes it is not only typically American, it is universal in its feeling; sometimes its inherent truth is not a thing of the month, but of the years. When this is true, that short story is genuinely a classic as any novel or play.

Edna Ferber, *One Basket,* 1964

Deliberately puzzling or confusing a short story reader may keep him reading for a while, but at too great an expense. Even just an "aura" of mystery in a short story is usually just a lot of baloney. Who *are* these people? What are they up to? Provoking such questions from a reader can be a writer's way of deferring exposition until he feels the reader is ready for the explanation of it all. But more likely it's just fogging things up. A lot of beginning writers' fiction is like of beginners' poetry: deliberately unintelligible as to make the shallow seem deep.

Rust Hills, *Writing in General and The Short Story in Particular,* 1987

A basic distinction between an episode in real life and a short story is that the story does have an author, who *creates* his characters, *selects* his actions, and *directs* them in the exploration of some meaningful idea. Any episode in life is filled with irrelevancies of many kinds which confuse our understanding; in the story only those elements are included which serve to focus the overall effect, which is the story. The helpful author is present, then, in the creating selecting, and focusing of the materials of his story.

Jarvis A. Thurston in *Reading Modern Short Stories,* edited by Jarvis A. Thurston, 1955

A young fiction writer should try everything, but some literary forms will come more naturally to him than others. Short stories are more within his scope than longer forms, and he will learn most by making many beginnings and endings--the hardest parts of any piece of writing.

Wallace Stegner, *On Teaching and Writing Fiction,* 2002

I've written about 2,000 short stories; I've only published about 300 and I feel I am still learning. Any man who keeps working is not a failure. He may not be a great novelist, but if he applies the old-fashioned virtues of hard, constant labor, he'll eventually make some kind of career for himself as a writer.

Ray Bradbury in *On Being a Writer,* edited by Bill Strickland, 1989

It is sometimes fashionable to dismiss the short story and to attribute its apparent decline to the greater versatility of the novel and to the rise of nonfiction. But the trouble does not lie with the form but with the practitioners. A really good short story writer will always find an audience. J.D. Salinger, John Cheever and John Updike have been remarkably successful, and the reason is that they are all masters of the form. They all have a good ear and eye for detail.

Frank McShane, *The Life of John O'Hara,* 1980

After the Second World War, society changed and the market for short stories waned. *Collier's* died, as did *The Saturday Evening Post.* In a mere instant, as history is reckoned, the audience for quality short fiction all but vanished; the demand, instead, was for nonfiction and journalism.

Jon Franklin, *Writing For Story,* 1994

If you want to write fiction, the best thing you can do is take two aspirins, lie down in a dark room, and wait for the feeling to pass.

If it persists, you probably ought to write a novel. Interestingly, most embryonic fiction writers accept the notion they ought to write a novel sooner or later. It's not terribly difficult to see that the world of short fiction is a world of limited opportunity. Both commercially and artistically, the short-story writer is quite strictly circumscribed.

This has not always been the case. Half a century ago, the magazine story was important in a way it has never been since. During the twenties, a prominent writer typically earned several thousand dollars for the sale of a short story to a top slick [non-pulp] magazine. These stories were apt to be talked about at parties and social gatherings, and the reputation a writer might establish in this fashion helped gain attention for any novel he might ultimately publish.

The change since those days has been remarkable. In virtually all areas, the short fiction market has shrunk in size and significance. Fewer magazines publish fiction, and every year they publish less of it. The handful of top markets pay less in today's dollars than they did in the much harder currency of fifty or sixty years ago. Pulp magazines have virtually disappeared as a market.

Lawrence Block, *Writing the Novel*, 1979

I suspect that things were much easier back when I was starting out. Editors were actually writing to young short story writers asking if they had manuscripts! It's occurred to me that if I were an unpublished young writer right now, I might very well have to stay unpublished.

Anne Tyler in *The Best American Short Stories*, edited by Anne Tyler, 1983

Foreshadowing devices in short stories have the effect of enhancing the inevitability of the action, usually without destroying the suspense or tension--in fact, correctly used, foreshadowing can enhance those effects. What foreshadowing does is prepare in advance for events that will follow later in the story, often in ways that will not be fully understood by the reader until the story is completed. For while devices of foreshadowing may sometimes be very apparent, at other times it is necessary to go back into a story to see what methods were used to make its final effects convincing.

Rust Hill, *Writing in General and the Short Story in Particular, Revised Edition*, 1987

The novelist can slowly unfold the changing lives of several characters, but the short story writer has difficulty enough in making credible the change in a single character. Any intelligent reader has a very reasonable skepticism about sudden spiritual or moral change; the author most prove to the reader that this character was well on the way toward the change before it actually takes place. Doing this takes up much of an author's story.

Jarvis A. Thurston, *Reading Modern Short Stories*, 1955

People wonder where writers get their ideas. Must they first experience what they write? Do they really rush wildly around looking for story ideas? Good writers look for "characters," because ideas grow as freely from characters as apples from trees. Every character grows not one but many fresh, unique, writable stories.

Writers who want to write good stories or plays must know their characters better than they know themselves. Better--because most of the time we are unaware of the motivating forces within us. Strange but true, it is easier to create a living, three-dimensional character than an unreal, one-dimensional character.

Lajos Egri, *The Art of Creative Writing*, 1990

I've had this conversation with many fiction writing students...Basically what's happening is this: The student is telling you that he has given up trying to write stories about people because he can't find anything to say about them, and wants your blessing as he launches a new student career of writing words about words.

Give him nothing. This is a crucial moment in his life. If you let him go he's likely to end up with a doctoral degree in rhetoric and will spend the rest of his life teaching undergrads how to write words about words. The best thing to do is to put him up against the wall and threaten to shoot him if he doesn't shut up with that silly stuff.

Martin Russ, *Showdown Semester*, 1980

Virtually all magazines have printed rejection slips. Some make their points succinctly with little attempts to soften the blow. The basic message is straightforward: "We've decided not to publish your story." Some rejection forms make a half-hearted effort to explain the obvious: "We're not reading fiction for the time being" or "another editor may think differently" (i.e., the problem may be ours and not yours). A few try diplomacy: "We're grateful for the chance to read your work." And others are mildly apologetic: "We're sorry that the quantity of manuscripts we consider makes it impossible to reply to each one personally." At bottom, however, the message is no more and likely no less than, simply, "No."

Michael Curtis in *On Writing Short Stories,* edited by Tom Bailey, 2000

This country used to be crazy about short stories. New stories would appear every week in the *Saturday Evening Post* or in *The New Yorker,* and every middle-class literate person would be talking about it: "Hey, did you read that story by Salinger?" or "Hey, did you read that story by Ray Bradbury?"

Kurt Vonnegut, *Palm Sunday,* 1981

Guggenheim, all those prizes and grants--you know how they go--more money is given to people who already have money. I know a professor who can't write. He wins a prize every year--usually the same one--and he goes off to some island and works on some project, meanwhile still getting paid half-salary for doing nothing at the university he's supposed to be teaching at. On one of his island trips he put together an anthology, even put me in it, but didn't have the decency to send me a copy of the book.

Charles Bukowski in *Charles Bukowski: Selected Letters 1965-1970,* edited by Seamus Cooney, 2004

I wish my students could write simply and clearly, and keep a story moving as well. They are damned if they will tell a story simply and directly, and I have discovered the reason for this. It is not the fault of their previous teachers. It is their own fault: they have no stories to tell. I am going to take them on walks, and make them look at people. I have just ordered them to buy a book, which is to be the core text for my workshop. The book? That Steichen collection of photographs, *The Family of Man*

Kurt Vonnegut in *Kurt Vonnegut: Letters,* edited by Dan Wakefield, 2012

I've followed this writing game a long time. Strange thing. Take a guy who has been editing a magazine. You see him published here and there. Then he decides to stop publishing his mag and devote himself to his "art." He then vanishes and is never heard from. He's no longer there to play you publish me and I'll publish you. And this happens as well with the magazines of more expensive format and a larger readership. What the hell does this tell you?

Charles Bukowski in *Charles Bukowski: Selected Letters 1987-1994*, edited by Seamus Cooney, 2004

I met Raymond Carver one time, long ago. We drank all night. In the morning we went out for breakfast and he couldn't eat. I ate his breakfast and mine. I remember him telling me, "I'm going to be famous now. A friend of mine has just been appointed editor of *Esquire* and he's going to publish everything I send him." I never got much out of Carver and still can't quite see what the fuss is all about. You asked, so I told you.

Charles Bukowski in *Charles Bukowski: Selected Letters 1987-1994*, edited by Seamus Cooney, 2004

8 HUMOR

Humor writers mine their personal experiences for material. They may tell a story using narrative techniques, or they may relate personal experiences to make a point and offer an opinion. Humor writers gain a lot of help in craft by learning how to structure jokes, work with timing, and deliver punch lines.

Elizabeth Lyon, *A Writers's Guide to Nonfiction,* 2003

Once you've developed skills in observing humor, you're ready to use basic comic elements. Some jokes are *really* old, tracing back to medieval times. Despite variations in individual funny bones, however, these jokes have survived for centuries because they work. Certain elements are almost *always* able to make people laugh.

[Like basic plot structures, you can use the comic elements as dependable foundations for creative adaptation…Here is a starting list: timing, mime, slapstick, repetition, switches, exaggeration, extremes, indecision, convention suspension and wordplay.]

Patricia Case in *How to Write Funny,* John B. Kachuba, editor, 2001

If people expect me to be funny, they are in for a rude shock. I figure my job ends when I leave the typewriter and get out of the swivel chair. People make a mistake when they confuse a writer with a performer.

S.J. Perelman, in *People, Books & Book People,* edited by David W. McCullough, 1981

Comedian Bob Hope's heir at NBC, Johnny Carson, not to mention Carson's legion of successors, proves that Hope's flippant, topical monologue has never left us. There's also Hope's obvious influence on comedians in the 1970s who played versions of themselves as show-business boors, like Albert Brooks and Steve Martin.

Ben Schwartz, *Bookforum,* Dec/Jan, 2015

There may be a certain risk with humor. Someone said it's not only ten times harder, it's fifty times harder to bring an audience to laughter than to bring it to tears. With humor, it's easier to bomb...You don't want to be corny. Corny is something that's not funny.

Gail Galloway Adams in *How to Write Funny,* John B. Kachuba, editor, 2001

It is not hard to write funny stuff. All you have to do is procure a pen and paper, and some ink, and then sit down and write it as it occurs to you. The writing is not hard, but the occurring--that, my friend, is the difficulty.

Stephen Leacock in *Becoming a Writer* edited by Dorthea Brande, 1934

Humor is difficult. Other kinds of stories don't have to hit the bull's-eye. The outer rings have their rewards too. A story can be fairly suspenseful, moderately romantic, somewhat terrifying, and so on. This is *not* the case with humor. A story is either funny or it is not funny. Nothing in between. The humor target contains only a bull's-eye.

Isaac Asimov, *I, Asimov,* 1996

Unlike tragedy, a sense of humor is determined by many factors: our age, our socioeconomic backgrounds, our culture. What most of us consider tragic is fairly static, though something tragic can be *made* funny by comic techniques such as repetition. In Nathanael West's *A Cool Million,* the hero keeps losing limbs and other parts of himself as he makes his way in the world until there is very little that's left of him. You lose one limb or all your limbs at once, that's tragic. But if you lose them little by little, as well as an eye, your teeth, your hair, you start defying logic, and once you've transcended logic, most people will laugh in spite of themselves, even if they find something a little horrifying at the same time.

Simply put, tragedy has serious and logical consequences. Cause and effect. Comedy usually doesn't. You throw a person off a tall building in a comedy, he bounces. You throw someone off a building in a tragedy, don't wait for the bounce.

Robin Hemley in *How to Write Funny*, John B. Kachuba, editor, 2001

Comic novels often offend as many people as they please because each reader's capacity for tolerating irreverence is different; what seems tame to one reader seems right to another, what seems corrosive to one reader seems hilarious to another.

Jane Smiley, *13 Ways of Looking at the Novel*, 2005

The best humor is *concise*. Ask yourself: Is this line needed? Can I make this line shorter? Is this aside that funny? Can I format this joke differently to make it move quicker? Here's an example of a lean joke: George W. Bush's plan to gain environmentalists' support for his energy policy: solar-powered oil pumps.

J. Kevin Wolfe in *How to Write Funny*, John B. Kachuba editor, 2001

The world likes humor, but treats it patronizingly. It feels if a thing is funny it can be presumed to something other than great. Writers know this, and those who take their literary selves with great seriousness are of considerable pains never to associate their names with anything funny or flippant or nonsensical or "light." They suspect it would hurt their reputation, and they are right.

E. B. White, *The Second Tree From The Corner*, 1954

A friend of mine once told me about a guy who murdered his first wife and put her in a freezer. He had her in a storage locker and his second wife stopped paying the bill for it, so the contents were auctioned off, and one lucky buyer purchased a freezer with a dead woman inside.

Gruesome certainly, but I could easily imagine a darkly comic story about such a situation.

Robin Hemley in *How to Write Funny* edited by John B. Kachuba, 2001

What is the secret of writing funny? If I knew, I would write my own ticket. But I venture this thought: The art begins with a sense of sadness. This is the clown's gift.

James J. Kilpatrick, *The Writer's Art*, 1994

Be careful with exaggeration, one of the main tools of humor writing. Exaggeration, generally speaking, should be outside the realm of possibility, but somehow within the realm of visual imagination.

Patrick McManus, *The Deer on a Bicycle*, 2000

I like to read stores where people suffer a lot. If there's no suffering, I kind of tune out...I do have a weakness for funny characters who can't shut up to save their lives...

Gary Shteyngart, *The New York Times Book Review*, February 2, 2014

One of the most famous lines in the history of comedy is from "The Jack Benny Show." Throughout his career, Benny developed the persona of the ultimate skinflint. On one show, a robber pulled a gun on Benny and threatened, "Your money or your life." Finally Benny spoke: "I'm thinking it over."

For the cheapskate Benny persona, this was a rough decision that required some real thought. And it is a perfect example of comedy derived from character. This was not a joke superimposed onto a situation; it grew organically out of the Benny character.

David Evans in *How To Write Funny,* John B. Bachuba, editor, 2001

Pretense is a common trait of many humorous characters. An audience will laugh at any character that lacks self-knowledge--one who is a fraud and tries to publicly present himself as a authority figure deserving of respect. When exposed by other characters as a fraud, the audience will laugh. When these pretentious characters try to cover up and continue their pretensions, the reader will laugh again because these characters are not a threat to them.

Richard Michaels Stefanik, writersstore.com, 2000

Any good story will have some humor somewhere, whether it's in the situation, the dialogue, the action. But if I want laugh-out-loud funny, I'm going to grab anything by Carl Hiaasen, and I know I'm going to get a good story with memorably quirky characters along with the laughs.

Nora Roberts, *The New York Times Book Review,* February 11, 2015

Fiction without irony is like painting without perspective. Irony exposes the incongruities of everyday life--the half-truths, deceptions and self-deceptions that help us all get through the day. Things are never what they seem, and the essence of ironic humor is the lack of fit between life as it is and life as we imagine it should be. We think the world should make sense: It doesn't. We think life should be dignified: It never is. We think life should have a serious purpose...But of course the purpose always turns out to be very silly in the end. Irony is the writer's richest and most inexhaustible humor resource.

The genre of the campus novel, from Kingsley Amis to Richard Russo, is a perfect example. Higher education is meant to be serious business; universities are meant to be serious places. So it's funny when, in Russo's *Straight Man,* the chair of the English department hides in the ceiling space over the faculty offices to eavesdrop on a meeting between colleagues...

Another reason why irony is such a powerful source of humor is that, as Voltaire observed long ago, life is absurd, but we try to make sense of it. This doomed effort creates some of the best comedy....

David Bouchier in *How to Write Funny,* John B. Kachuba, editor, 2001

Wordplay itself is not usually funny, only clever, unless it is attached to some other psychological force in the narrative...Most of the humor I'm interested in has to do with awkwardness: the makeshift theater that springs up between people at really awkward times...Bad jokes may be an expression of that awkwardness, without being inherently funny themselves. Of course, in including humor in a narrative a writer isn't doing anything especially artificial. Humor is just part of the texture of human conversation and life. In real life people are always funny.

Lorrie Moore, *The Paris Review,* Spring/Summer 2001

Satire is the opposite of truth telling. Satire is a big lie mobilized to get a comic effect. Sometimes the lie is mere exaggeration, sometimes it is a complete invention. Either way, satire is an attack weapon. It inflates the faults and foibles of powerful people or conventional ideas, with the intention of making them look ridiculous. "Humor belongs to the losers," said Garrison Keillor, and that's what satire is about. It's a kind of revenge, often very sweet and always triggered with anger.

Jonathan Swift was the father of modern satire. In scathing books like *A Tale of a Tub, The Battle of the Books,* and *Gulliver's Travels,* Swift mocked the pretensions and prejudices of his own time. His technique was quite simple and works as well today as it did in the 1700s. He picked his target, imagined a fantastic metaphor and exaggerated everything. For example, in *Gulliver,* he created a deadly satire on prejudice with the story of the "Big Endians" and the "Little Endians," two groups locked in eternal battle over which end to open a boiled egg.

Kurt Vonnegut and Joseph Heller crafted marvelous satires on the Second World War, using Swift's tools of exaggeration, fantasy and aggressive ridicule. But contemporary satire is harder. Politics and popular culture have moved almost beyond the reach of ridicule. It's difficult to come up with something so bizarre that it won't actually happen before your piece appears in print. So satire can be risky for a fiction writer, who always risks being upstaged by reality.

David Bouchier in *How to Write Funny,* John B. Kachuba, editor, 2001

Writing funny pieces is a legitimate form of activity, but the durable humor in literature, I suspect, is not the contrived humor of a comedian commenting on the news but the sly and almost imperceptible ingredient that sometimes gets into writing. I think of Jane Austen, a deeply humorous woman. I think of Thoreau, a man of some humor along with his bile.

E.B. White in *Writers at Work, Eighth Series,* edited by George Plimpton, 1988

Humor can either be a genre in its own right, or an important ingredient in many other genres. Shakespeare wrote comedies, tragedies, and romances. Even in the most tragic of his tales, he knew the importance of inserting a humorous scene every so often to bring the audience some comic relief from all the death, deceit, and unrequited love in the rest of the play. While joke writing is a subsection of the genre, and a potentially lucrative one, it would be a mistake to confuse the ability to tell a joke with the ability to write humor.

Gordon Kirkland in *Novel & Short Story Writer's Market,* edited by Anne Bowling and Vanessa Lyman, 2002

Most writers aren't relentlessly funny from beginning to end, and they don't have to be. A pinch of humor that works is better than a potful that doesn't. For most of us humor is merely seasoning; it's not the whole dish.

Patricia O'Conner, *Words Fail Me,* 1999

Sociologists, linguists and biologists say that our ability to laugh and desire to do so isn't all fun and games, but actually serves two essential life functions: to bond with members of our "tribe," and to lessen tension and anxiety. Both of these are also excellent reasons to incorporate humor in your nonfiction. As a communication tool, effective use of humor can humanize you, cementing your bond with readers. It can also help your work stand out in a crowded market. And as advertising studies have shown, humor enhances how much we like what we're reading and how well we remember it afterward.

Anne Jasheway, writersdigest.com, August 9, 2011

Humor is good when it stems from the truth. In fact, truth alone is often humorous. But the humor of artifice--whose worst device is exaggeration--always makes me a little ill because it is just another con game...I suppose that the worst is Bob Hope with his flip little cute exaggerations and his name droppings. I don't keep up much with the world and he drops these names I never heard of, all supposing to *mean* something.

Charles Bukowski in *Charles Bukowski: Selected Letters 1965-1970,* edited by Seamus Cooney, 2004

Humor is the hardest to write, easiest to sell, and best rewarded. There are only a few who are able to do it. If you are able, do it by all means.

Jack London in *Jack London,* edited by Dale L. Walker, 1979

Humor, like beauty, is in the eye of the beholder. What's uproariously funny to one person may leave another cold. What's funny today may seem insensitive tomorrow. This is certainly true with Leo Rosten's 1937 book *The Education of Hyman Kaplan,* which describes the very funny struggles of a group of adult immigrants learning English. Many readers may find

Rosten's book patronizing at best and offensive at worst. Issues of political correctness--the death knell for humor--arise, too

Nancy Pearl, *Book Lust*, 2003

Any well-written nonfiction story can and should engage the emotions. In even the most serious of topics, there is usually room for a touch of humor, and the contrast helps heighten the story's impact. Pathos, too, can emerge in the unlikeliest settings, and can be all the more effective for being unexpected. This doesn't mean that material has to be thigh-slapping hilarious, or tear-jerking sorrowful. Most often, humor and pathos are subtle, growing naturally out of the events being described.

James B. Stewart, *Follow the Story*, 1998

Humor is the secret weapon of the nonfiction writer. It's secret because so few writers realize that humor is often their best tool--and sometimes their only tool--for making an important point....

Few Americans understand this. We dismiss our humorists as triflers because they never settled down to "real" work. The Pulitzer Prizes go to authors like Ernest Hemingway and William Faulkner, who are (God knows) serious and are therefore certified as men of literature. The prizes seldom go to people like George Ade, H. L. Mencken, Ring Lardner, S. J. Perelman, Art Buckwald, Jules Feiffer, Woody Allen and Garrison Keillor, who seem to be just fooling around.

They're not fooling around. They are as serious in purpose as Hemingway or Faulkner--a national asset in forcing the country to see itself clearly. Humor, to them, is urgent work.

William Zinsser, *On Writing Well*, 1975

9 CRIME FICTION

The Golden Age of detective fiction occurred between the two world wars, when several crucial developments changed the genre forever. The stories became more literate and the detectives more believable--no longer were they persons of super human intellect who could look at someone's shoes and determine where they had just been by the type of dirt collected there. Also, much more emphasis was put on period and character as opposed to merely constructing a clever puzzle.

Jay Pearsal, *Mystery & Crime*, 1995

I never read romantic novels, ever; I didn't enjoy them. And as I never liked fantasy and I never liked science fiction. I suppose that leaves for one's comfort reading the detective story. The form is often quite nostalgic; if you're reading some of the earlier ones it's a different world, it's a more ordered world, it's a safer world--despite the fact they're dealing with murder.

You're back in this English village with the well-known characters; there's a sense of nostalgia and security about them and in the end a terrible crime is solved and peace and order is restored. And in real life it isn't, and in modern detective stories, especially mine, it isn't restored, but in most classical English detective stories it is.

You know it's going to turn out right, that virtue is going to be rewarded and evil is going to be punished. So these detective stories do have that ability to provide for the reader some kind of solace. I don't think we choose our genre, I think that a genre chooses us.

P. D. James, "On Writing: Authors Reveal the Secrets of Their Craft," theguardian.com, March 25, 2011

The resilience of detective fiction, and particularly the fact that so many distinguished and powerful people are apparently under its spell, has puzzled both its admirers and its detractors and spawned a number of notable critical studies which attempt to explain this puzzling phenomenon. In "The Guilty Vicarage," W. H. Auden wrote that his reading of detective stories was an addiction, the symptoms being the intensity of his craving, the specificity of the story, which, for him, had to be set in rural England, and last, its immediacy. He forgot the story as soon as he had finished the book and had no wish to read it again. Should he begin a detective story and then discover it was one he had already read, he was unable to continue. In all this the distinguished poet differed from me and, I suspect, from many other lovers of the genre. I enjoy rereading my favorite mysteries although I know full well how the book will end, and although I can understand the attraction of a rural setting, I am frequently happy to venture with my favorite detectives onto unfamiliar territory.

P. D. James, *Talking About Detective Fiction*, 2009

Most readers come to a mystery novel because the genre promises an actual story, a characteristic that many find lacking in so-called mainstream fiction.

Jeremiah Healy in *Writing Mysteries by Sue Grafton*, 1992

The reading of detective stories is simply a kind of vice that, for silliness and minor harmfulness, ranks somewhere between crossword puzzles and smoking.

Edmund Wilson (1895-1972), The literary critic who wrote, in 1945, the famous *New Yorker* article, "Who Cares Who Killed Roger Ackroyd?" Mr. Wilson was not an Agatha Christie fan or a lover of genre crime fiction. He was, in that regard, a literary snob.

It may well be that when the historians of literature come to discourse upon the fiction produced by the English-speaking peoples in the first half of the twentieth century, they will pass somewhat lightly over the compositions of the "serious" novelists and turn their attention to the immense and varied achievement of the detective writers.

W. Somerset Maugham (1874-1965) English playwright, novelist and short story writer

In a narrative constructed around a mystery, the central mystery, if anything, takes on an outsize importance, one that threatens to blot out everything else. On some level, the only thing that matters in a mystery story is the last chapter. You may think that's unfair, but it's just the way the genre works....

One theory about the ideal structure of a mystery story...holds that in a mystery there are essentially two kinds of plot: an apparent plot and a revealed plot. The apparent plot is everything that happens up to the final chapter of the story... is immediately apparent, until the very end. The revealed plot is what really turns out to be the case after all the mysteries have been revealed.

In a really good mystery...the difference between these two kinds of plots isn't just mechanical, it is interpretive. It isn't just about who-appears-to-have dunit and who-really-dunit. It's about what it all--the world, good and evil, women and men, family, justice, society, the truth at the heart of humanity-- really means: what it seems to mean when we're wandering in the darkness, and what it means when we come into the light.

Another theory holds that what the structure of a mystery is really about is story and discourse, signifier and signified. The mystery, in its opening chapters, posits the existence of a coherent, meaningful story: the body in the woods, the blood spatter, the knife in the grass, the partial footprint. But the story is hidden, its meaning obscured. The narrative that proceeds from this point is not, itself, the story--it is, rather, discourse, the system of talk and empty signification and endless deferment that surrounds the story, like planets orbiting a star that can be glimpsed only glancingly, never directly. The story, usually, is revealed in the final chapter, but the story that preceded the story--the story of the detectives finding clues, signifiers throbbing with a meaning that lay just outside their grasp--that wasn't the story.

Andrew De Young, "'True Detective': Just Another Murder Mystery, After All," The Stake, March 13, 2014

The crime novel is where the social novel went. If you want to write about the underbelly of America, if you want to write about the America nobody wants to look at, you turn to the crime novel. I don't bristle at the "you're a mystery writer" or "you're a crime writer" thing. I don't have an issue with that. But I do think that personally, when I sit down to write I'm writing an urban novel, writing about urban realities.

Dennis Lehane, powells.com, 2003

Most critics date the emergence of the classical *detective story* with the publication of Edgar Allan Poe's *The Murders in the Rue Morgue*, 1841. British versions by such writers as Arthur Conan Doyle tend to place emphasis on style, a few specific locales, and logic. American versions, which flourished from the twenties onward, carry with them a pulpier prose, a larger scope, and a heavy charge of sensationalism.

Lance Olsen, *Rebel Yell*, 1998

You know you're reading a great mystery novel when you're up at three in the morning, unable to put it down. When you finally fall asleep, the characters go romping around in your dreams. When you get to the final page, you smack yourself in the head because the solution seems obvious in retrospect yet came as a complete surprise.

Page-turning suspense. Rich characterization. A credible surprise ending. Sounds pretty simple, but writing a mystery novel is not for the faint of heart...Be prepared to keep three or four intertwined pots spinning. Get ready to master the art of misdirection so readers will ogle those red herrings you've sprinkled while ignoring the real clues in plain sight. Don't be surprised when you find yourself riding herd on a load of characters who won't go where you want them to.

On top of that, you'll need dogged determination and intestinal fortitude to stick with it, through the first draft and endless revisions, until your words are polished to lapidary perfection. It wouldn't hurt, either, to have the hide of a rhinoceros to withstand the inevitable rejections. Talent being equal, what separates many a published mystery writer from an unpublished one is sheer stamina. Only gluttons for punishment need apply.

Halle Ephron, *Writing and Selling Your Mystery Novel*, 2005

The protagonist, who is home alone with a bad cold, hears a rustling sound from the lower floor and, instead of calling 911 or acting logically to the danger, sets off to investigate the darkened basement with a butcher knife. At this point, your reader starts groaning out loud. Don't send your character into danger without a thought to the consequences; instead, make certain that she takes appropriate action. Perhaps she attempts to dial for help, but discovers that the criminal has cut the phone wires. Or, she can attempt to escape, but then suddenly he's looming at the door, blocking her way. The lesson here is that when the going gets tough, a protagonist fights back to the best of her ability.

Jessica Page Morrell, *Between the Lines*, 2006

Good writers know how to create suspense; better writers know how to prolong it. Creating effective suspense is not that easy, and the best writers know they shouldn't let it go once it exists...

Nearly all suspenseful elements can be prolonged. You can prolong danger in endless ways, even when you think you can't: a character can survive a dangerous operation only to develop a dangerous infection, or a character can get through one dangerous obstacle only to be faced with another.

Noah Lukeman, *The Plot Thickens*, 2002

Investigation is the meat and potatoes of mystery fiction. The sleuth talks to people, does research, snoops around, and makes observations. Facts emerge. Maybe an eyewitness gives an account of what he saw. A wife has unexplained bruises on her face. The brother of a victim avoids eye contact with his questioner. A will leaves a millionaire's estate to an obscure charity. A bloody knife is found in a laundry bin. A love letter is discovered tucked into last week's newspaper.

Some facts will turn out to be clues that lead to the killer's true identity. Some will turn out to be red herrings--evidence that leads in a false direction. On top of that, a lot of the information your sleuth notes will turn out to be nothing more than the irrelevant minutiae of everyday life inserted into scenes to give a sense of realism and camouflage the clues.

Hallie Ephron, *Writing and Selling Your Mystery Novel*, 2005

Old-fashioned suspense is more engaging than immediate violence. A great thriller is more about creating a sense of unease, a queasiness that comes with knowing something is not quite right. It's why I love unreliable narrators--there's something so wonderfully unnerving about realizing midway through a book that you've put yourself in the hands of someone who is not to be trusted.

Gillian Flynn, *The New York Times Book Review*, May 11, 2014

The Postman Always Rings Twice had nothing to do with the mail service. The title was a private joke of crime novelist James Cain. His postman would ring his doorbell twice whenever the many-times rejected book's manuscript came back from a publisher.

Erin Barrett and Jack Mingo, *It Takes a Certain Type To Be A Writer*, 2003

The nature of the mystery novel is such that your protagonist will be tested. He'll be insulted, lied to, bullied, humiliated, cheated, threatened, and injured. He'll see other people duped, scapegoated, and hurt. Characters, like real people, show their mettle in the do-or-die situations.

Hallie Ephron, *Writing and Selling Your Mystery Novel,* 2005

Often I start working out a story in terms of its villain. Sometimes he's more interesting than anyone else. I'm curious about what makes a murderer who he is. Was he born missing some human quality? Did his early environment shape him? Or was it a combination of both?

Sandra Scoppettone in *Writing Mysteries,* edited by Sue Grafton, 2002

Though [writer Roger Rosenblatt] studied at Harvard, and even taught there, his most important education came from popular fiction. Above all, detective fiction, starting with Sherlock Holmes.

"I wanted to be Holmes, himself," he writes early in [his book, *The Boy Detective*]. "The detective I concocted for myself was not exactly like him. What I imagined was a composite made up of Holmes's power of observation, Hercule Poirot's powers of deduction, Sam Spade's straight talk, Miss Marple's stick-to-itiveness, and Philip Marlowe's courage and sense of honor--he who traveled the 'mean streets,' like mine, and was 'neither tarnished nor afraid.' The fact that, as far as I could tell, I lacked every single one of these qualities, and saw no prospect of every achieving them, presented no discouragement."

From Pete Hamill's review of Rosenblatt's book *The Boy Detective* in *The New York Times Book Review,* November 17, 2013

The term mystery, as in mystery novel, is an umbrella that shelters a variety of subgenres: the traditional whodunit, the private eye, the classic puzzle, the police procedural, action/adventure, thriller, espionage, the novels of psychological and romantic suspense.

Sue Grafton, *Writing Mysteries,* 1992

A "cozy" is a mystery novel with a light tone and an element of fun; the setting is usually a small community and the protagonist is an amateur sleuth who's a member of the community. Sex and violence occur, for the most part, offstage. Agatha Christie's Miss Jane Marple remains the quintessential cozy protagonist.

Hallie Ephron, *Writing and Selling Your Mystery Novel,* 2005

The *most important* apparent *disadvantage* you'll face with an amateur sleuth has to do with the suspension of belief--why is this amateur detective attempting to solve this murder? Why not let the cops do it? Why does this amateur keep tripping over dead bodies? And why doesn't she mind her own business?

Nancy Pickard in *Writing Mysteries,* edited by Sue Grafton, 1992

Who wants to be a mystery writer? Who wants to be a crime novelist when you can be a plain old novelist with a capital "N"? You are known by the company you keep. I mean, do you want to be mentioned in the same breath as Agatha Christie and a bunch of people like that?

James Ellroy, barcelonareview.com, April 16, 2001

Literary murders are as old as the book of Genesis. But no one before Edgar Allan Poe, as far as we know, ever wrote a story in which the central plot question was "who did it?" and the hero was a detective [C. Auguste Dupin] who correctly deduced the answer to that question.

William G. Tapply, *The Elements of Mystery Fiction,* 1995

The tradition of the mystery or crime novel is an old and honored one, but it's quality has been debased. And possibly nothing has done more harm to the nature of mystery fiction than the notion that it should concern itself more with "whodunit" than why the deed was done. Chief among those responsible for this decline in Agatha Christie.

Thomas H. Cook, themysteryguild.com, 2003

Most of my fiction writing has been in the murder mystery novel genre, specifically whodunits, in which there usually are four to six suspects. One of the most difficult aspects of writing whodunits is to give all of these suspects roughly equal motives for having committed the murder. The idea is to keep the reader guessing as long as possible.

I try to adhere to the doctrine of fair play in the plot. That is, I put in clues so that the reader could conceivably identify the murderer. Having said that, I bury the clues by making them hard to spot. Many of these clues are embedded in seemingly innocuous details. [In real life, people often commit murder with virtually no motive that makes any sense. Moreover, people with the most obvious motives often turn out to be innocent. In the murder mystery genre the plots have to make sense. In true crime they just have to be true.]

Robert Goldsborough in *The 101 Habits of Highly Successful Novelists*, Andrew McAleer, editor, 2008

The whodunit and the thriller are in their most typical manifestations deeply conventional and ideologically conservative literary forms, in which good triumphs over evil, law over anarchy, truth over lies.

David Lodge, *The Practice of Writing*, 1996

At their core, spy novels are about secrets. Secrets create power. Power determines how we live. That's a formula for fiction that matters--matters to us in this world where making sense of what's really going on turns out to be a lifelong endeavor, one that fiction lets us do from the safety of own sheltered lives...

Spy novels remind us of our past and reflect our future. Alan Furst's WW II era novels bring to life heroic struggles of the "greatest generation," while novels written long before 9/11 by Tom Harris and Tom Clancy foreshadowed dramatic hijacked aircraft terrorist attacks targeting American civilians...

In spy novels we're guaranteed a fictional journey in which something happens. A secret will be stolen or protected, a spy will be caught or escape, the conspiracy will triumph or be crushed. A spy novel can be set anywhere with as much action as you want--sabers in the courtyard or switchblades in the alley, snipers, runaway carriages, strangers on a train, parachuting commandos, car chases, kung fu, high-tech weaponry and low-minded thugs...

Right versus wrong, good versus evil, the essential nature of power and politics, all that and more unfold is a safe, fictional package for us to enjoy.

James Grady, *Parade*, March 1, 2015

The most frequently repeated rule of detective fiction is the most nonsensical. It says, "you must play fair with the reader," meaning that in the course of the narrative the reader must see and hear everything that the detective sees and hears. I don't know why mystery writers have insisted on it, since every good writer of detective stories has violated this rule over and over again.

Rex Stout in *The Writer's Book*, edited by Helen Hull, 1959

There is nothing easier than to write a detective story. For a start there is at least one corpse, more in American detective stories. Then there is an inspector or a superintendent who conducts the inquiry and who has the right to probe the past and present life of each of the characters. And finally there are the suspects, in varying numbers and different degrees of camouflage as the author decides will best lead to the final denouement.

Georges Simenon, *The Man Who Wasn't Margret* by Patrick Marnham, 1994

"Down these mean streets a man must go who is not himself mean," Raymond Chandler wrote in his article, "The Simple Art of Murder" which could be called the manifesto of the American hard-boiled detective novel. This man, the detective, "is neither tarnished nor afraid. He is the hero, he is everything. He must be a complete man and a common man and yet an unusual man. He must be, to use a rather weathered phrase, a man of honor, by instinct, by inevitability, without thought of and certainly without saying it."

It's a worthy aesthetic, and Chandler was certainly the master of it, even back in 1944, when he wrote "The Simple Art of Murder." The essay was a repudiation of the English school of murder mystery--best represented by Agatha Christie--or, more specifically, the countless American knockoffs thereof, genteel, stilted puzzles set in "Miami hotels and Cape Code summer colonies," rather than manor houses. Chandler held up Dashiell Hammett as the exemplar of what he referred to as the new "realist" school of crime fiction, yet Chandler was Hammett's equal, if not his superior in the style that would also become known as noir.

Laura Miller, salon.com, September 7, 2014

We must cut off the modern detective story from the novel proper, put it in quite another category, one with its own traditions, conventions and demands, and thus develop a completely independent critical approach to it. I feel, in fact, that however we react to novels of the American hard-boiled school, nothing but harm can be done by an attempt to see them as "realistic" or closer to the novel proper than other varieties of crime fiction.

Robert Barnard, *A Talent to Deceive,* 1990

In traditional hard-boiled crime fiction, if the hero is a police officer, he'll be the departmental maverick, too honest and decent to engage in office politics yet laser-focused on nailing the perp. Often there's a murdered relative, almost always female, to juice this crusader's motivation. His marriage will have fallen apart because he's too stoic and too devoted to the job to sustain a real relationship. But he'll be devoted to his kid and is a one-woman romantic at heart, even if hardly anybody ever gets near his heart. He'll brood a lot and go home alone. He'll have a temper but a righteous one. He might drink too much or be too ready with his fists, but that just makes him a bit of an antihero, that familiar figure from cable TV dramas…

It's all getting awfully predictable, which may explain why this reader can't bear to finish yet another novel about such a hero. I've found, instead that the crime novels I open with the keenest anticipation these days are almost always by women. These are books that trespass the established boundaries of the genre by lingering over characters who used to serve as mere furniture in the old-style hard-boiled fiction. They may dare not to offer a solution to every mystery or to have their sleuths arrive at those solutions by non-rational means. Their prose ranges from the matter-of-fact to the intoxicating, and the battlefields they depict are not the sleazy nightclubs, back alleys, diners and shabby offices of the archetypal detective novel, but a far more intimate and treacherous terrain: family, marriage, friendship.

Laura Miller, salon.com, September 7, 2014

The crime fiction thriller is an extension of the fairy tale. It is melodrama so embellished as to create the illusion that the story being told, however unlikely, could be true.

Eric Ambler in *The Mystery Lovers' Book of Quotations,* edited by Jane Horning, 1988

Perhaps you have made a decision to write a legal thriller because you have been a participant in a dramatic courtroom battle--as a defense attorney whose skill exonerated an innocent client, as the beneficiary of family heirlooms in a hard-fought will contest, or as a juror who second-guessed the tactics of the litigators throughout a protracted trial. Maybe your fascination with this category of crime novels is that you have practiced law on the civil side but have fantasized about delivering the stirring summation in a high-profile murder trial. Or maybe you simply enjoy the prospect of entering this world because you like lawyers.

Once you have selected this sub-genre as your setting, I think there are critical issues to face before you start pounding out the pages. Whether you are writing a courtroom drama or using a legal eagle as an amateur sleuth, remember that you have chosen to portray a profession--like medicine--that requires an advanced degree and is governed by a lot of rules and procedures. Even if your characters are going to break those rules, you have to know what they are in order to heighten the tension of any ethical dilemma or criminal verdict...

I prefer to read books written by experienced lawyers or by authors who have studied the practice seriously. They know the language and attitude of the courtroom, they move their characters about it with ease, they sit them at the proper counsel table, they craft their arguments to the judge with appropriate rhetoric, and they know when to make objections. Many other readers who have no reason to be familiar with legal procedure won't care about getting those details right, so you first need to figure out who your target audience might be.

Linda Fairstein in *Writing Mysteries,* Sue Grafton, editor, 2002

Like its first cousin, the mystery novel, the police procedural features a well-structured, fast-paced chronicle of crimes and punishments. Unlike the mystery, the police procedural stresses the step-by-step procedures followed by professional detectives in solving their cases: processing the crime scene to collect physical evidence; canvassing the neighborhood for witnesses or suspects; postmortem examination of the body to determine the cause and manner of death; identifying the victim; tracing the background of the victim; investigating associates of the victim; examining the method of operation of the perpetrator; and continuing with the follow-up investigation.

O'Neil DeNoux in *The Writer's Handbook,* edited by Sylvia K. Burack, 1994

Suspense novels are deservedly popular, but very hard to define. They are not murder mysteries. They are not just straight novels, because something nasty and frightening is bound to happen. That is the promise to the reader. They are not spy stories, and they are certainly not police procedurals. In a suspense novel, the element of character matters very much indeed. The hero/heroine is pitted, not against organized crime or international terrorism, but against a personal enemy, a personal problem; the conflict is on an individual, adversarial level.

Joan Aiken in *The Writer's Handbook,* edited by Sylvia K. Burack, 2004

Historical mystery fiction are for those who enjoy going to a different time as well as place. To create believability, an author of well-written historical mysteries has to do without the conveniences of modern methods and forensics, while incorporating myriad details that authors of modern-set mysteries can take for granted. These authors not only incorporate such details, but do so smoothly so that there are no disjointed pauses for explanation, no interruption of the reader's pleasure in the story.

Margaret Frazer, *The 3rd Degree,* March 2001

Although it's widely acknowledged that the human capacity for self-delusion is boundless, it can often be difficult to get through psychological crime novels of the "How well do you know your husband/wife/best friend?" variety without becoming so irritated by the protagonist's willful obtuseness that you end up wanted to give him, or more usually her, a good shake.

Laura Wilson, *The Guardian,* September 19, 2004

As Raymond Chandler himself would later admit, the typical real life private detective was not as he imagined his protagonist Philip Marlowe, an intellectual whose idea of a good time was a quiet night at home with a bottle of rye and a book of chess problems. The real PI was an ex-cop with the brains of a turtle who spent his time finding out where people had moved to.

John Baxter, *A Pound of Paper,* 2003

The detectives in Scandinavian crime fiction share many attributes with their American and British counterparts. Many are unkempt, unhealthy and sometimes fatalistic characters, but are nevertheless humane and brilliant sleuths. They doggedly pursue the criminal element, usually (but not always) winning the day at the expense of maintaining a normal family or social life. Some are alcoholics whose human interactions are limited to station and squad car. Some even develop relationships with the victims, or even worse, the criminal.

Key to the appeal of Scandinavian crime literature is the stoic nature of its detectives and their peculiarly close relationship with death. One conjures up a brooding Bergmanesque figure contemplating the long dark winter. Another narrative component just as vital is the often bleak Scandinavian landscape which serves to mirror the thoughts of the characters. Ancient stone and dark shores inhabit these stories such that the landscape becomes an important narrative agent, even a character itself. Readers will also find fascinating the supernatural strain pervading this literature: Ancient beliefs in ghosts, changelings, and other natural spirits thrive in contemporary Nordic noir.

Jeremy Megraw, nypl.org, January 14, 2013

Some mystery novels don't reach the discovery of the body until many pages into the story...Mystery writers have freedom to spend quite a few pages establishing the character of the detective or setting up the society in which the murder will take place. But the audience is quite aware that a murder *will* take place, but will become impatient if the writer takes too long getting to it.

Orson Scott Card, *How to Write Science Fiction & Fantasy*, 1990

An editor rejected my first mystery novel with these words: "I think it would take something really unusual to convince me to take on a new mystery series--an American/Jewish plumber who solves cases by listening at people's drain pipes, or something like that."

William G. Tapply, *Elements of Mystery Fiction*, 1995

The backdrop of a mystery, the world in which the action takes place--the scenery so to speak--has the potential to be as important as character or plot. Indeed, if painted vividly enough it can become a character itself; or it can determine plot. It can set a mood, create an atmosphere. It can add richness and color.

Julie Smith in *Writing Mysteries,* edited by Sue Grafton, 2002

Many suspense novels and thrillers are based on the drama of the hunter and the hunted. Often a chase requires a one step forward, two steps backward approach. For example, after chasing down many false leads, a police detective finally discovers the suspect's hideout and hurries to secure a search warrant. The scene could end on his assistant rushing into the room with the warrant, and the detective grabbing his keys and heading for the car. Naturally the reader will be curious about where the villain lives and will keep reading. Or the scene might end with the detective arriving at the hideout to discover that the villain has vanished along with all traces of its illegal operation. The question is not only where he has gone, but who tipped him off.

Jessica Page Morrell, *Between the Lines,* 2006

I write from 10 AM to 6 PM, Monday to Friday. I try to write eight pages a day. When I had a 9-to-5 job, I used to write at night and on weekends, but not anymore.

Ed McBain, bookreporter.com, January 21, 2000

A mystery writer who waits patiently for a mood to encompass him, for an idea to strike, may find starvation, or other employment, striking first. The professional in this field cannot write one book every three or four years. Three or four a year would be more like it.

Richard Lockridge in *Writer's Book,* edited by Helen Hull, 1950

It is never very sensible to act as an evangelist for the detective story: if someone says, "I've never been able to acquire a taste for crime fiction-- who do you recommend I try?" The sensible answer probably is: "Don't bother. If you have tried and you haven't responded, then probably the response isn't in you." It *is* a pity to have become so sophisticated in one's reading as to have lost the elementary response to fiction as a *story*.

Robert Barnard, *A Talent to Deceive,* 1990

CRIME NOVELISTS

I do not think Raymond Chandler should be judged by conventional literary standards. This is not fiction in the sense that Tolstoy or Balzac or Hemingway wrote fiction. As crime fiction, it belongs to a genre whose kinship is with other kinds of pop art, including the cartoon, the old radio serial, and what is known as science fiction…Of its kind, *Farewell, My Lovely* is a masterpiece. It belongs to a class of writing for which we have no name.

Clifton Fadiman in *Fifty Years,* edited by Clifton Fadiman, 1965

I write a scene and I read it over and think it stinks. Three days later--having done nothing in between but stew--I reread it and think it is great. So there you are. You can't bank on me. I may be all washed up.

Raymond Chandler in *Selected Letters of Raymond Chandler,* edited by Frank MacShane, 1981

In the late 1930s Raymond Chandler extolled the virtues of Dashiell Hammet (who, he felt, took murder out of the library and put it back on the streets where it belonged) and defined the hard-boiled detective genre in an essay for the *Atlantic Monthly* entitled, "The Simple Art of Murder." He might have been writing a justification of his own work as well: uncluttered prose, lots of metaphors, a wisecracking detective (Philip Marlowe), and the mean streets of a tough and uncaring city.

Nancy Pearl, *Book Lust,* 2003

Dashiell Hammett produced work so stark, yet so complex, that any attempt to dismiss him as a mystery writer would be a glaring error. In *Red Harvest,* 1929, he deals with mob control and mob wars in a town called Personville, nicknamed Poisonville. The bad guys are bad, and the good guys are bad in a good way, and the whole book is a morality play. Forces of light and dark run through the actions of tough guys. The value of traditional male ideals is enhanced because even some awfully cynical people can still hold them.

Jack Cady, *The American Writer,* 1999

The fact that some genre writers write better than some of their literary counterparts doesn't automatically consecrate their books. Although a simile by Raymond Chandler and by the legion of his imitators is the difference between a live wire and a wet noodle, Chandler's novels are not quite literature. The assessment is Chandler's own, tendered precisely because he was literary. "To accept a mediocre form and make something like literature out of it is in itself rather an accomplishment." So it is. And there are a number of such accomplishments by the likes of Patricia Highsmith, Charles McCarry, Ruth Rendell, P.D. James, Donald Westlake, Lawrence Block, and dozens of others.

Arthur Krystal, *The New Yorker*, October 24, 2012

During her lifetime, Agatha Christie (1890-1976) sold more than two billion books, topped only by Shakespeare and the Bible. Hercule Poirot, her principal detective, appeared in 33 novels.

Reader's Digest, December 2014

Agatha Christie nearly pulled off a real-life hoax worthy of her mystery novels. Upset that her husband was leaving her for another woman, she set up an incriminating scene that almost got him arrested for her "murder." Luckily for him, an employee at a distant seaside hotel saw news photos of Christie and recognized her as the woman who had slipped into the hotel under an assumed name. Although Christie claimed amnesia, the police were not amused after having wasted a week of searching rivers and bogs.

Erin Barrett and Jack Mingo, *It Takes a Certain Type To Be A Writer*, 2003

Erle Stanley Gardner is credited by the *Guinness Book of World Records* as being the fastest author of this century. It was his habit to tape 3-by-5 inch index cards around his study. Each index card explained where and when certain key incidents would occur in each detective novel. He then dictated to a crew of secretaries some ten thousand words a day, on up to seven different [mystery] novels at a time.

The Writer's Home Companion (1987) edited by James Charlton and Lisbeth Mark

Raymond Chandler is reported to have said he couldn't find an ending to one of his excellent stories unless he took time to get drunk. Up to a point I accept his report. For alcohol can stimulate imagination. It can find inventions. But I'll lay my bottom dollar, as one not unacquainted with booze, that Chandler had to sober up to write that ending.

B. Guthrie Jr., *Field Guide to Writing Fiction*, 1991

Mystery writer P.D. James, who brought realistic modern characters to the classical British detective story, has died. She was 94. James' books, many featuring sleuth Adam Dalgliesh, sold millions in many countries and most were just as popular when adapted for television. James died Thursday November 27, 2014 at her home in Oxford in southern England.

Because of the quality and careful structure of her writing--and her rather elegant, intellectual detective Dalgliesh--she was at first seen as a natural successor to writers like Dorothy L. Sayers, creator of Lord Peter Wimsey in the between-the-wars "Golden Age" of the mystery novel. But James' books were strong on character, avoided stereotype and touched on distinctly modern problems including drugs, child abuse and nuclear contamination...

Although there was nothing remotely "genteel" about P.D. James' writing, she was criticized by some younger writers of gritty urban crime novels. They accused her of snobbery because she liked to write abut middle-class murderers, preferably intelligent and well-educated, who agonized over right and wrong and spent time planning and justifying their crimes. Dalgliesh of Scotland Yard, hero of more than a dozen of James' novels, is a decidedly gentlemanly detective, who writes poetry, loves jazz and drives a Jaguar.

Phyllis Dorothy James was born in Oxford on August 3, 1920. Her father was a tax collector and there was not enough money for her to go to college, a fact she always regretted...She did not start producing her mysteries until she was nearly 40, and then wrote only early in the morning before going to the civil service job with which she supported her family. Her husband, Connor Banty White, had returned from the war mentally broken and remained so until his death in 1964...

James' first novel, *Cover Her Face*, was published in 1962 under her maiden name and was an immediate critical success, but she continued to work in the Home Office until 1979...

James was often spoken of as an heir to Agatha Christie and Arthur Conan Doyle, icons of the classic British mystery, but her admirers thought she transcended both.

Jill Lawless, "Mystery Novelist P.D. James Dead at 94," thestar.com, November 27, 2014

Mickey Spillane, addressing a Mystery Writer's of America convention, warned his fans not to look closely for symbolic depth in his novels. Of his famous protagonist, Spillane said, "Mike Hammer drinks beer, not cognac, because I can't spell cognac."

James Charlton and Lisbeth Mark, *The Writer's Home Companion*, 1987

I lived to kill the scum and the lice that wanted to kill themselves. I lived to kill so that others could live. I lived to kill because my soul was a hardened thing that reveled in the thought of taking the blood of the bastards who made murder their business. I lived because I could laugh it off and others couldn't. I was the evil that opposed other evil, leaving the good and the meek in the middle to live and inherit the earth.

Mike Hammer in Mickey Spillane's *One Lonely Night*, 1961

James Ellroy [*The Black Dahlia, The Big Nowhere, LA Confidential, American Tabloid*, and others] is a cult. For many, he's a you're-in-or-you're out cult, because he's intense and absolute and violent in every respect--emotionally, linguistically, and physically. He's a brash writer who spins marvelously complicated, suspenseful plots. He is fluent in local period dialect that captures everything dirty, transient, prejudiced, profane, and provincial about the way cops and robbers, movie stars, and politicians talk. His thick, relentless dialogue (fully peppered with all the nasty racist and sexist things you might imagine that hard-boiled cops would say) combines with a compressed, impressionistic aesthetic that puts the language somewhere between *A Clockwork Orange* and *Ulysses*.

Minna Procter, *Bookforum*, Oct./Nov./Dec., 2014

SHERLOCK HOLMES

Sherlock Holmes is the quintessential man of the British Empire--self-confident and self-reliant, athletic and active, intelligent and moral, a Tory in values but free of snobbery and political cant. And he likes to solve puzzles. And he is discreet, important, and famous. He ought to get tedious and even ridiculous, but he doesn't.

Jane Smiley, *13 Ways of Looking at the Novel*, 2005

Sherlock Holmes remains one of the few household names in English fiction, arguably the most famous character in literature after Hamlet, and one with whom the public has an extraordinarily intimate acquaintance. Everyone knows his catchphrase, "Elementary, my dear Watson!", although few are aware it is nowhere to be found in the stories. His eccentricities--pinning correspondence to the mantelshelf with a jackknife and keeping tobacco in the heel of a Turkish slipper, for example--are common knowledge. He is a valuable asset to the British tourist industry, known to 87 percent of visitors to Britain, and is one of London's major attractions--indeed, Japanese and Russians often cite him as their main reason for visiting the city. Misguided souls still write to him at his Baker Street "consulting rooms," in the hope that his genius may solve their problems, even though--had he ever existed--he would be long since dead.

Russell Miller, *The Adventure of Arthur Conan Doyle*, 2008

No one wants to read about perfect characters. Since no reader is perfect, there is nothing more disagreeable than spending free time immersed in a story about an individual who leaps tall buildings of emotion, psyche, body, and spirit in a single bound. Would anyone want a person as a friend, tediously perfect in every way? Probably not. Thus, a character possessing perfection in one area should possess imperfection in another area.

Sir Arthur Conan Doyle understood this, which is one of the reasons that his Sherlock Holmes has stood the test of time for more than one hundred years and counting. Holmes has the perfect intellect. The man is a virtual machine of cogitation. But he's an emotional black hole incapable of a sustained relationship with anyone except Dr. Watson, and on top of that, he abuses drugs. He has a series of rather quirky habits, and he's unbearably supercilious. As a character "package," he emerges unforgettably from the pages of Conon Doyle's stories. Consequently, it's difficult to believe that any reader of works written in English might *not* know who Sherlock Holmes is.

Elizabeth George, *Write Away*, 2004

Reading ten Leslie Charteris novels in succession cruelly highlights his weaknesses. Likewise Agatha Christie and even Arthur Conan Doyle. "Sherlock Holmes after all is mostly an attitude and a few dozen lines of unforgettable dialogue," wrote Raymond Chandler. And once you'd grasped the attitude and heard the lines, why read on?

John Baxter, *A Pound of Paper*, 2003

Dr. Watson in the Sherlock Holmes stories…is the inviting voice of the entire series. He is intelligent, observant and faithful, the way we want doctors to be. He is also guileless and naive, where Holmes is neither, and that is the ultimate limitation in each mystery. But his lack of cunning is why we trust him--and why Holmes does, too.

Atul Gawande, *The New York Times Book Review*, October 26, 2014

A. Conan Doyle grew to detest his detective Sherlock Holmes and killed him off with satisfaction. The rest of the world didn't agree: London stockbrokers wore armbands, the public deluged newspapers with letters of mourning and outrage, and a woman even picketed Doyle's house with a sign that called him a murderer.

Erin Barrett and Jack Mingo, *It Takes a Certain Type to be a Writer*, 2003

Arthur Conan Doyle was naturally gratified by his success but increasingly concerned that Sherlock Homes was damaging his aspirations to be considered a serious writer. As early as November 1891, only four years after Holmes's first appearance in print, he had written to his mother revealing that he was thinking of "slaying" Holmes in the final story of the first series. "He takes my mind from better things," he explained. Mary Doyle was horrified that he should think of eliminating the source of such a handsome income and urgently advised him to reconsider.

Russell Miller, *The Adventures of Arthur Conan Doyle*, 2008

Sherlock Holmes died in 1893 but then came back to life ten years later. After writing twenty-four Holmes stories in six years, Arthur Conan Doyle had grown weary of the popular hero and wanted to focus on writing historical novels. So he figured he could put an end to the whole thing by having Holmes plunge to his death from Switzerland's Reichenbach Falls, holding his arch-enemy, Professor Moriarity, in a mutual death grip.

Although public outcry was enormous, Doyle remained adamant about not bringing Holmes back. Ten years later, though, *McClure's* magazine in the United States offered Doyle $5,000 per story if he'd bring his detective back to life. That was the equivalent of nearly $100,000 in today's money, and Doyle couldn't resist. His first story had Holmes coming out of hiding after ten years, and Doyle wrote Holmes stories for a quarter of a century before retiring himself and his detective for good in 1927.

Erin Barrett and Jack Mingo, *It Takes a Certain Type To Be a Writer*, 2003

You mentioned your name, as if I should recognize it, but I assure you that, beyond the obvious facts that you are a bachelor, a solicitor, a Freemason, and an asthmatic, I know nothing whatever about you.

Sherlock Holmes in Arthur Conan Doyle's "The Adventure of the Norwood Builder"

The birth of the modern crime lab can be traced directly to fiction. Sir Arthur Conan Doyle was a physician and keen observer of his patients' abnormalities. He was a splendid writer, as well, and when he created Sherlock Holmes, he also imprinted on popular culture the idea that when the elements of science are coupled with applied logic, crimes can be solved. Doyle also knew that the way to brand the concept in the public's hearts and minds was to package the science in the form of a uniquely fascinating man. After all, it had worked before, in Charles Dicken's *Bleak House,* published in 1853. In that novel, Inspector Bucket personified all that amazed the public about Scotland Yard.

By the time Doyle was writing, in the 1880s, London had had a police force for fifty years and the detectives of Scotland Yard since 1842. Starting in the 1860s, those detectives had added crime scene analysis to their toolbox of skills, and the forensic sciences took a great leap forward. But when Doyle captured it all in the form of Holmes, he did more than just sell books. One avid fan was Edmund Locard, who was influenced by the writing and went on to build the world's first forensic laboratory in Lyons, France in 1910. [The so-called Locard Principle: the criminal leaves part of himself at the crime scene and takes part of it with him.]

The idea of crime labs spread throughout the world. In 1932, the Federal Bureau of Investigation opened its lab under Director J. Edgar Hoover. [Philadelphia, Los Angeles and Detroit formed crime labs in the 1920s.]

Michael Baden, M.D. and Marion Roach, *Dead Reckoning,* 2001

Sir A. Conan Doyle's detective Sherlock Holmes was the epitome of rationalism and logic. However, Doyle himself was not. He believed deeply in ghosts, fairies, and other spiritualistic claptrap, and was duped over and over again by charlatans and hoaxers.

Erin Barrett and Jack Mingo, *It Takes A Certain Type To Be A Writer*, 2003

10 SCIENCE FICTION

Science fiction is the fiction of ideas. Ideas excite me, and as soon as I get excited, the adrenaline gets going and the next thing I know I'm borrowing energy from the ideas themselves. Science fiction is any idea that occurs in the head and doesn't exist yet, but soon will, and will change everything for everybody and nothing will ever be the same again. As soon as you have an idea that changes some small part of the world you are writing science fiction. It is always the art of the possible, never the impossible.

Ray Bradbury, *The Paris Review*, Spring 2010

Many of the writers who have inspired me most are outside the science fiction genre. Humorists like Robert Benchley and James Thurber, screenwriters like Ben Hecht and William Goldman, and journalist/columnists like H. L. Mencken, Mike Royko and Molly Ivins. They inspire me because they were good with words and they were also in command of their genres...

I believe the best way to grow a genre--in this case science fiction--is to bring new elements into it. This is why I always recommend to aspiring science fiction and fantasy writers that they read outside the genre as much as they read inside it...

My favorite thing about science fiction and fantasy right now is that it has so many genuinely good writers in it. I am biased, but I can say that the best writers in our genre can hold their own against any writers in any genre...

John Scalzi, "Science Fiction Author John Scalzi Explains How Not To Be Boring," by Brian A. Klems, writersdigest.com, July 20, 2011

Science fiction is that form of literature which deals with the effects of technological change in an imaged future, an alternative present or re-conceived history...

Science fiction, at the center, holds that the encroachment of technological or social change will make the future different and that it will *feel* different to those within it. In a technologically altered culture, people will regard themselves and their lives in ways that we cannot apprehend. That is the base of the science fiction vision, but the more important part comes as corollary: the effects of a changed technology upon us will be more profound than change brought about by psychological or social pressure... It will be *these* changes--those imposed extrinsically by force-- which really matter; that is what the science fiction writer is saying, and in their inevitability and power they trivialize the close psychological interactions in which most of us transact our lives.

Barry N. Malzberg, *Breakfast in the Ruins*, 2007

One of the hallmarks of science fiction is its intense originality. Science Fiction has few limits on topics or scope, and has wandered far into speculation about the future, future societies, and technological change. Along the way, science fiction writers have explored fiction's classic themes of life and death, human failure, and challenges intrinsic to any worthwhile story. To catch an editor's eye, you must have something different in your story, something you handle especially well--a vivid character, an intriguing background, a compelling theme.

Paula E. Downing in *The Writer's Handbook*, edited by Sylvia K. Burack, 1994

Science fiction is often accused (by those who don't like it) of being unnecessarily esoteric. You can't understand the stuff, we are told, unless you've already read a fat pile of it. Science Fiction writers use devices not readily comprehensible to an outside reader. Take faster-than-light travel, hyperspace, fourth and fifth dimensions...The truth is that anything worth knowing demands effort, and the science fiction understandable only to science fiction readers is almost invariably the very best kind written.

Gordon Eklund in *Epoch*, edited by Roger Elwood and Rober Silverberg, 1975

Science Fiction is the only branch of literature whose poorer examples are almost invariably used by critics outside the form to attack all of it. A lousy western is a lousy western, a seriously intentioned novel that falls apart is a disaster...but a science fiction novel that fails illuminates the inadequacy of the genre, the hollowness of the fantastic vision, the banality of the sci-fi writer...this phenomenon is as old as the American genre itself...and as fresh as the latest rotten book.

Barry N. Malzberg, "The Engines of the Night" 1980, reprinted in *Breakfast in the Ruins*, 2007

As a writer of science fiction and fantasy, and on behalf of all the variations and sub-genres such as urban fantasy, alternate history and steampunk which collectively make up "speculative fiction," I'd argue that genre fiction is different from literary fiction.

Whether it's dealing with ray guns and rocket ships, swords, sorcery or fur and fangbangers, speculative fiction's unifying, identifying characteristic is that it doesn't attempt to mimic real life in the way that literary fiction does. It stands apart from the world we know. It takes us away to an entirely secondary realm, be that Middle Earth or Westeros, or to an alternate present where vampires and werewolves really do exist and you ring 666 to report a supernatural crime...

Speculative fiction can be considerably harder to write than literary fiction...When readers are paying close attention to every hint and clue, the writer needs to have internal logic, consistency of character and scene-setting absolutely nailed down. Readers have to be convinced that this unfamiliar world is solidly real if they're ever going to suspend disbelief and accept the unreal, whether that's magic and dragons or faster-than-light travel.

Juliet McKenna, *The Guardian*, April 18, 2014

The term "science fiction" hadn't been invented in 1870 when the American magazine *Atlantic Monthly* published the first part of Edward Everett Hale's delightfully eccentric novella *The Brick Moon*. Readers lacked a ready-made pigeonhole for it, confronted by a fantasy about a group of visionaries who decide to make a 200-foot-wide sphere of house-bricks, paint it white, and launch it into orbit.

Jules Verne's *From The Earth to the Moon* had appeared five years earlier, so Hale's work was not unprecedented, but while Verne chose to send his voyagers aloft using a giant cannon, Hale opts for the equally unfeasible but somehow more pleasing solution of a giant flywheel.

Andrew Crumey, *"The Brick Moon,"* theguardian.com, May 14, 2011

Inspired by Edgar Allan Poe and other contemporary novelists, Jules Verne became the world's first full-time science fiction writer. He wrote nearly a hundred novels, some simply tales of travel and adventure but most based upon scientific speculation. He sent his characters around the world in a submarine in *Twenty Leagues Under the Sea* 1870 and around the moon in a huge artillery shell in *From Earth to the Moon*, 1865.

L. Sprague de Camp, *L. Sprague de Camp*, 1972

When it became known that the earth was only one of a family of planets circling the sun, the question arose: was there life on other planets? Many later speculated about this. In his *Micromegas* (1752), the French writer Voltaire brought to earth an eight-mile-high visitor from Sirus and a slightly smaller native of Saturn. Because of their size, these beings found it hard to decide whether there was intelligent life on earth.

L. Sprague de Camp, *3000 Years of Fantasy and Science Fiction*, 1972

Bishop Francis Godwin wrote the first story in English of flight into space. His *The Man in the Moon*, 1638 had birds pull a raft through space to the moon. He anticipated Newton's theory of gravity and had the pull of the moon much lighter than that of the earth.

Lester del Ray, *The World of Science Fiction*, 1979

To the American literary community--to the American arts establishment--the science fiction writers of the forties were invisible. There is no more graceful way to put this. There were, for the first half of the decade, almost no books at all: no anthologies, no reprints, no second-serial rights. Novels and stories were written for genre magazines of limited circulation, were published and went out of print, presumably forever....

It must be understood that in certain respects science fiction was no different for its writers, offered nothing less, than did the other branches of popular literature. It was pulp and appeared in the torrent of pulp magazines which by the hundreds got on in various degrees of health until wartime paper shortages and, finally, the curse of television put almost all of them in the ground by the beginning of the fifties. Western and romance writers, adventure and sports pulp writers, also worked for a half cent to two cents a word and knew that when the magazines went off sale their work would never be seen by a nonrelative or non-lover again.

Barry N. Malzberg, reprinted in *Breakfast in the Ruins*, 2007

No science fiction novel in the fifties sold more than one hundred thousand copies. Science fiction itself was regarded with lack of interest or contempt outside of the genre walls. Its very audience was an unorganized constituency, much like audiences for contemporary men's magazines. They might like it, buy it, need it, but they were not in the main evangelical and those who were, simply increased the popular perception of science fiction as a strange field, incestuous and defensive. The genre made no impression upon the academic/literary nexus which controls critical perception and audiences in this country.

Barry N. Malzberg, *The Man Who Loved the Midnight Lady*, 1980

From its earliest days, when Hugo Gernsback first inserted stories in the monthly *Electrical Experimenter*, the primary outlet and market for science fiction was magazines. The *Experimenter* was the size of *Life*. So was *Amazing Stories*, the all-fiction magazine Gersback launched in 1926. In the thirties, the pulp magazines shrank to standard quarto, but doubled in thickness as publishers used the cheapest paper around.

John Baxter, *A Pound of Paper*, 2003

Short story writing is the best place to start in the science fiction field. Many writers who start with short stories go on to acquire novel contracts. I'd say there are almost no science fiction novelists who were not published first in magazines.

Kim Mohan in *Novel & Short Story Writer's Market*, edited by Robin Gee, 1994

Some writers whose careers have been largely based on science fiction writing have never been categorized that way. Kurt Vonnegut and John Hershey were never within the science fiction ghetto. One surprising result of the ghettoizing of speculative fiction, however, is that writers have enormous freedom within its walls. It's as if, having once been confined within our cage, the keepers of the zoo of literature don't much care what we do as long as we stay behind bars.

Orson Scott Card, *How to Write Science Fiction and Fantasy*, 1990

I don't think *science fiction* is a good name for it, but it's the name that we've got. It is different from other kinds of writing, I suppose, so it deserves a name of its own. But where I get prickly and combative is if I'm just called a sci-fi writer. I'm not. I'm a novelist and poet. Don't shove me into your damn pigeonhole, where I don't fit, because I'm all over. My tentacles are coming out of the pigeonhole in all directions.

Ursula K. Le Guin, *Paris Review*, Fall 2013

Years ago Sir Arthur C. Clarke commented that he preferred reading science fiction because it's the only realistic fiction--by which he meant that it's the only one that incorporates the concept that the world is changing and being changed by human activities.

James Gunn, LJworld.com, 2006

Arthur C. Clarke was a scientist, and his work sits squarely in the tradition of "hard SF"--a largely detestable term, but we're stuck with it--which is to say, science fiction with one eye on strict scientific plausibility. Much hard science fiction is stylistically dry, with little concern for character or what one might consider the finer literary virtues. There was rather more to Clarke than mere nuts and bolts descriptions, though. On a good day, he could rise to the genuinely poetic.

Alstair Reynolds, "*The City and the Stars* by Arthur C. Clarke," theguardian.com, May 14, 2011

There is a co-dependency between science and science fiction. Many scientists and engineers acknowledge that science fiction helped to spark their imagination of what was possible in science...

Sometimes science fiction authors just make things up, but untutored imaginings tend not to make the best science fiction. As JBS Haldane put it: "the universe is not only queerer than we suppose, but queerer than we can suppose." We need scientific input to sustain a rich science fictional imagination...

Some science fiction writers are (or were until retirement) full-time scientists and academic researchers in their own right. Astrophysicist Fred Hoyle, who coined the term "Big Bang", claimed to write his science fiction in order to publish ideas that would not fit into scientific journals. Back in the 1960s, Fred Pohl edited *The Expert Dreamers* and Groff Conklin edited *Great Science Fiction by Scientists*, with stories by George Gamow, JBS Haldane, Fred Hoyle, Julian Huxley, Norbet Weiner, and others. Some authors who were originally researchers have been successful enough to quit the day job in favor of fiction...

Not all science fiction writers have science PhDs. Many of the Golden Age writers had little formal education. James White, for example wanted to be a medical doctor, but couldn't afford the training; that didn't stop him writing the marvelous alien doctors in space series called *Sector General.* Many science fiction writers have arts and humanities backgrounds, yet manage to write good hard science-based science fiction.

Susan Stepney, *The Guardian,* January 21, 2015

Daniel Defoe's immortal *Robinson Crusoe* is a metaphor for a man stranded on an alien planet. Crusoe is an exile, and exile has proved a perennial theme within the genre of science fiction.

Brian Aldiss, "The Stars of SF Pick the Best Science Fiction," theguardian.com, May 14, 2011

Stephen H. Doyle, in *Habitable Planets for Man,* attempted to estimate the abundance of planets in which human beings could live without life-support systems such as domes or spacesuits. He estimated that there were something like 600 million human-habitable planets in our galaxy alone. Other galaxies should have comparable numbers.

Stanley Schmidt, *Aliens and Alien Societies,* 1995

Dystopia has appeared in science fiction from the genre's inception, but the past decade has observed an unprecedented rise in its authorship. Once a literary niche within a niche, mankind is now destroyed with clockwork regularity by nuclear weapons, computers gone rogue, nanotechnology, and man-made viruses...We have plagues and we have zombies and we have zombie plagues.

Michael Solana, wired.com, August 24, 2014

"It's so easy to make money with science fiction stories that say civilization is garbage, our institutions will never be helpful, and your neighbors are all useless sheep who could never be counted on in a crisis," says David Brin, a science fiction writer who thinks we've gotten too fond of speculative technological bummers. Movies like "Blade Runner," "The Matrix," "Children of Men," and more recently "The Hunger Games" and "Divergent," all express some version of this dark world-view.

Neal Stephenson, the author of *Cryponomicon,* usually writes exactly those kinds of dystopian stories. In his fiction, he tends to explore the dark side of technology. But a couple of years ago he got a public wake up call.

On stage at a writer's conference, Stephenson was complaining that there were no big scientific projects to inspire people these days. But Michael Crow, the president of Arizona State University, shot back, "You're the one slacking off." By "you", Crow meant science fiction writers.

Adam Wernick, pri.org, July 29, 2014

I have deliberately cultivated a simple and even colloquial style. In the past, virtually all writing was ornate. Read a Victorian novel, for instance. Read even Dickens, the best of all the Victorians. It is only comparatively recently that writing has, in the hands of some writers, become simple and clear. But how does one go about writing clearly? I don't know. I presume you have to start with an orderly mind and a knack for marshaling your thoughts so that you know exactly what you want to say. Beyond that, I am helpless.

Isaac Asimov (1920-1992), *I. Asimov: A Memoir,* 1994

Peter S. Prescott says in his *Newsweek* piece on science fiction (December 22, 1975): "Few science fiction writers aim higher than what a teen-age intelligence can grasp, and the smart ones--like Kurt Vonnegut, carefully satirize targets--racism, pollution, teachers--that teen-agers are conditioned to dislike."

That unsupported allegation about me will now become a part of my dossier at *Newsweek*. I ask you to put this letter in the same folder, so that more honest reporters than Mr. Prescott may learn the following about me:

I have never written with teen-agers in mind, nor are teen-agers the chief readers of my books. I am the first science fiction writer to win a Guggenheim, the first to become a member of the National Institute of Arts and Letters, the first to have a novel become a finalist for a National Book Award. I have been on the faculties of the University of Iowa and Harvard, and was most recently a Distinguished Professor of Literature at CCNY.

Mr. Prescott is entitled to loathe everything I have ever done, which he clearly does. But he should not be a liar. *Newsweek* should not be a liar.

Kurt Vonnegut, *Kurt Vonnegut: Letters*, edited by Dan Wakefield, 2012

It seemed to me that midcentury mainstream American science fiction had often been triumphalist and militaristic, a sort of folk propaganda for American exceptionalism. I was tired of America-is-the-future, the world as a white monoculture, the protagonist as a good guy from the middle class or above. I wanted more elbow- room. I wanted to make room for antiheroes.

William Gibson, *Paris Review*, Summer, 2011

I can write nonfiction science without thinking because it requires no thought. I already know it. Science fiction, however, is far more delicate a job and requires the deeper and most prolonged thought.

Isaac Asimov, *I Asimov*, 1996

As a result of our media's obsession with the alleged connection between artistic genius and madness, Phil Dick was introduced to mainstream America as a caricature: a disheveled prophet, a hack churning out boilerplate genre fiction, a speed-freak. None of these impressions of Phil, taken without awareness of the sensationalism that generated them, advances our understanding of his life and work. Today the myth of Philip K. Dick threatens to drown out what evidence remains of his turbulent life.

David Gill in Anne R. Dick's *The Search for Philip K. Dick*, 1995

A writer of conventional fiction, unless he is extremely inventive, starts with innumerable givens. His plot must wind its way through them like a road through the contours of a mountain pass. But a science fiction writer, if he really uses his medium, need take very little for granted. He is not creating a road but an entire world--mountains, pass and all.

Tom O'Reilly in *Critical Encounters,* edited by Dick Riley, 1996

Different people read for different reasons, but to reproduce the mundane circumstances of their everyday lives is generally not one of them. There are literary writers who understand this and those who don't--hence the preponderance of divorce novels, teen angst novels, and dealing-with-aging parent novels that do little more than take us to where we've already been and tell us what we already know.

Those who write science fiction and other forms of speculative fiction generally understand that while what we know and understand has its charms, the reason most of us read is to experience something fundamentally new.

Susan Defreitas, litreactor.com, September 24, 2014

In each and every science fiction story, the entire background must be supplied to the reader. The writer cannot say, "You know what I mean," when he mentions a laser handgun, even though he could simply use the word pistol in a detective story and the reader would instantly know what he meant. This is one reason why science fiction short stories are so difficult to do well. More often, the writer will start out to produce a short story and end up with a novelette--about twenty thousand words instead of five to seven thousand.

Ben Bova, *Notes to a Science Fiction Writer,* 1975

Science fiction readers are frequently also mystery fans, and books that combine a science fiction setting with a mystery plot range from more or less straightforward detective stores with a future setting to uncompromising science fiction stories that have solving a mystery as a key plot element.

Peter Hack in *Science Fiction Writer's Market Place and Sourcebook,* edited by David G. Tompkins, 1994

Aliens--nonhuman beings, usually intelligent and sentient, usually from places other than Earth--are of the most familiar elements of science fiction. Even people who don't read science fiction have become well acquainted with quite a few of them through television shows and movies. "E.T." was the title character of one of the highest-grossing movies ever made; the *Star Wars* movies popularized wookies, Yoda and Jabba the Hut; *Star Trek* offered a steady parade of nonhuman life-forms, some of them regular members of the cast.

Movies have been dealing with aliens for much longer. Invasions of giant spiders and such have long been a staple of low-budget horror films, while occasionally a film would try something a bit more sophisticated like H. G. Wells' *War of the Worlds.* The same novel inspired Orson Wells' 1938 radio broadcast that literally terrified thousands of listeners.

Printed science fiction has also featured a great many aliens, often with more care and finesse than they've usually received in the visual and broadcast media...

Some writers have made a specialty of creating fascinating, believable aliens, along with their cultures and the worlds that produced them...Intelligent nonhumans have been an important element in literature much longer than what we now know as science fiction. Gods, demons and talking animals appear in the most ancient mythologies. The folklores of many lands have produced elves, dragons and trolls that have persisted in some form into the written fantasy of today.

Stanley Schmidt, *Aliens and Alien Societies,* 1995

The shortest science fiction story on record, which is always attributed to that most prolific author, Anonymous, is in its entirety: "The last man on Earth sat in a room. There was a knock on the door." These two lines have the hallmarks of a good science fiction story: It's accessible, there's at least one mind-bending idea, it has an interesting character, and you want to find out what happens next.

Nancy Pearl, *Book Lust,* 2003

You can't write science fiction well if you haven't read it, though not all who try to write it know this. But nor can you write science fiction if you haven't read anything else. Genre is a rich dialect, in which you can say certain things in a particularly satisfying way, but if it gives up connection with the general literary language it becomes a jargon, meaningful only to an inner circle of readers. Useful models may be found outside the genre. I learned a lot from reading the ever-subversive Virginia Woolf.

Ursula K. LeGuin, "Virginia Woolf," theguardian.com, May 14, 2011

I think science fiction, along with jazz, is America's great contribution to world culture. It's as great as jazz, as profligate, and wonderful. What disappoints me about it is that most of its practitioners have not been as good as they should have been, and the fact that science fiction emerged as a genre of commercial literature, forced to make adjustments and compromises to accommodate a mass audience, which was not its aesthetic interest. I don't segregate myself from those who do so. The readership has contributed to this debasement, I suppose, but any readership does. Norman Spinrod said the worst thing about science fiction is fandom. I don't disagree with that at all. Fandom has destroyed some authors. The need to be a hero.

Barry N. Malzberg, *The Man Who Loved the Midnight Lady*, 1980

Writers of science fiction are, first and foremost, voracious readers, and they're often very savvy about the genre they work in. Whereas most literary writers have only the barest conception of where their work fits in the current publishing milieu. This is because many of them have been studying classic literature.

The literary divisions are a little clearer within genre fiction--to an almost laughable degree (hence paranormal young adult romance, alternative historical fantasy, "furry" fiction, and virtually everything ending in the suffix-*punk*). But despite the fact that the differences between various types of literary fiction are more subtle, it behooves anyone serious about publishing to get savvy about them…

The more knowledgeable you are about the imaginative space you're working in, the less likely you are to reinvent the wheel, and the more likely you are to get a handle on who your readers are and what they like.

Susan Defreitas, litreactor.com, September 24, 2014

A science fiction story is one in which the story couldn't happen without its scientific content. The story can't contradict what we currently accept as scientific fact, such as the possibility of going faster than light, but it can speculate on what may turn out to be fact--such as a way to travel though some kind of space where the speed of light is not a factor.

A fantasy story is one in which the conditions are flatly contrary to scientific fact. Magic works. Supernatural beings intervene in human affairs. People have destinies, often foretold long before their birth. [In science fiction there are rocket ships; in fantasy, magic carpets.]

Crawford Kilian, *Writing Science Fiction and Fantasy*, 1998

11 THE FANTASY NOVEL

What does fantasy ask of us? It asks us to pay something extra. It compels us to an adjustment that is different to an adjustment required by a work of art. The other novelists say "Here is something that might occur in our lives," the fantasist says "Here's something that could not occur. I must ask you to first accept my book as a whole, and secondly to accept certain things in my book." Many readers can grant the first request, but refuse the second. "One knows a book isn't real," they say, "still one does expect it to be natural."

E. M. Forster, *Aspects of the Novel*, 1927

The fantasy genre is a much more accessible form of literature than science fiction. You don't have to possess any pre-existing knowledge to get into fantasy. In science fiction, however, you do because it has all of that science in there.

Terry Brooks, scifi.com, 2003

If the story is set in a universe that follows the same rules as ours, it's science fiction. If it's set in a universe that doesn't follow our rules, it's fantasy. [It's the rocket ship versus the magic carpet.]

Orson Scott Card, *How to Write Science Fiction and Fantasy*, 1990

What does it mean to say that science fiction tries to make its speculations plausible while fantasy does not? Basically, fantasy writers don't expect you to believe that the things they're describing could actually happen, but only to *pretend* that they could for the duration of a story. Fantasy readers understand that and willingly play along. Science fiction writers, on the other hand, try to create worlds and futures (and aliens) that really *could* exist and do the things they describe. Their readers expect that of them, and write critical letters to editors and authors when they find holes in the logic (or the assumptions) that would make a science fiction story impossible...

Often the same basic story material can be treated as *either* science fiction or fantasy, depending on how the writer approaches it. For example, the old fable of "The Goose That Laid the Golden Eggs" is fantasy because real geese don't lay golden eggs and the story makes no attempt to convince you they could. It merely asks you to consider what might happen *if* one did. Isaac Asimov's short story "Pate de Foie Gras" takes this basic idea and turns it into science fiction by postulating a biochemical mechanism so that readers can judge for themselves whether it might actually work...

Fantasy is fun; but for some readers there is something extra special about a story that not only stretches the imagination, but just might be a real possibility.

Stanley Schmidt, *Aliens and Alien Societies,* 1995

From the earliest myths and legends, through different cultures, fantasy has been with us. Think of the Arabian Nights stories, the Arthurian Romances, Spenser's *The Fairie Queen,* Shakespeare's *A Midsummer Night's Dream,* Lord Byron's *Manfred,* Mary Shelly's *Frankenstein,* Bram Stoker's *Dracula,* and the works of Edgar Allen Poe, Lovecraft, Lord Dunsany, and George MacDonald.

Whether these stories are set in our world or a secondary world where magical creatures and/or people exist, they all share a common theme: the exploration of the human condition. Even the much maligned medieval/quest fantasies offer their readers the chance to vicariously explore a wondrous world, battle evil and restore justice. Even a lowly Hobbit can change the course of the world by destroying the Ring.

That is the appeal of the Tolkienesque fantasy. In our modern world where politicians prove corrupt, large corporations rip off customers and terrorists kill ordinary people going about their daily lives, the traditional quest fantasy provides an antidote to cynicism. Fantasy, deriving from the word fantastic, exercises our sense of wonder.

Rowena Cory Daniells, *The Australian Literature Review,* June 17, 2010

I still see fantasy as escapist literature. Whether the storytelling itself or by the ideas behind the story, readers want to be transported beyond their mundane existence by the genre.

Betsy Mitchell, *Writer's Digest*, 1999

So many writers think fantasy is easy. All you have to do is rip off some elves, goblins, and a few other things from Tolkien and spend about 10 minutes making up imaginary words and another 10 minutes working up a rough idea of the country and a little local history and bingo, you're in business. You're a fantasist. It's not like that. What made Tolkien unique is that he spent 50 years building his world, and he built it from the inside out.

Peter S. Beagle in *The Writer's Handbook*, edited by Alfrieda Abbe, 2004

To name a few sub-fantasy genres: There's *Epic Fantasy* involving thick books and very long series; *High Fantasy*, usually very traditional and Tolkienesque; *Dark Fantasy* that mixes in horror or grim themes; *Grimdark Fantasy* employing a dystopian element in the world or plot; *Steampunk*, a mix of fantasy and old Victorian clockwork and steam elements; *Arcanepunk*, a blend of science fiction and fantasy; *Historical Fantasy* incorporating magic into historical fiction often mixed with the sword and sorcery sub-genre; and *Urban Fantasy* which blends the ideas of magic and myth with modern day worlds.

Joanna Penn, thecreativepenn.com, June 27, 2013

A *fable* is a brief tale, in prose or verse, to illustrate a moral. Often involving unusual or supernatural incidents, *fables* sometimes contain animals, as in *Aesop's Fables*, Rudyard Kipling's *The Jungle Book*, and George Orwell's *Animal Farm*.

Rod L. Evans, *The Artful Nuance*, 1997

Fantasy celebrates the non-rational. Wrapped in a cloak of magic, it dares a rational reader to object to a frog suddenly being turned into a prince. Where an explanation would be required in science fiction, fantasy says: "Because it did." Though fantasy may offer some cause and effect--the prince probably did something wrong in the first place to cause him to be turned into a warty amphibian--no scientific rationale is required.

Philip Martin in *The Writer's Guide to Fantasy and Literature,* edited by Philip Martin, 2002

Fantasy, I'm convinced, is the genre that's constantly waiting for you to let down your guard, and pull the rug from under your feet without any warning.

On the face of it, I should have no problem with fantasy. I am, after all, a fan of science fiction, someone who grew up reading comic books filled with fantastic, amazing tales of people who can do things far outside the reach of mortal men, whether it's flying faster than speeding bullets or shambling through the world as an undead monster seemingly unable to remain six feet under. Surely superheroes and science fiction are fantasies? If I can accept them easily enough, why do I have such a problem with the fantasy genre?

The trouble, I suspect, is in the world-building aspect of each genre. Superheroes, for the most part, exist in worlds that are intentionally meant to mirror our own, with the differences becoming part of the story and out in the open. The same applies to much of science fiction; although the far future may be filled with inventions and ideas that don't exist in our world. They too have to be specifically mentioned in order for them to exist and matter. There's a sense that forewarned is forearmed.

In fantasy, I can assume that all bets are off. Fantasy stories tend to take place in worlds that are *like* ours, but not ours, where countries have different names, and magic--something that *purposefully* defies categorization, and thus threatens *deus ex machina* twists and resolutions--is witnessed and wielded without a shrug. As much as I appreciate imagination, there's something about fantasy that feels *too* far removed from the world in which I live....

Graeme McMillan, "Fantasy Genre," entertainment.time.com, April 5, 2013

At the heart of most traditional fantasy milieu is a culture derived from that of the European Middle Ages, in large part the medieval societies of what are now Great Britain, France and Germany. The culture is a synthesis of both the Roman culture that dominated Western Europe for some five centuries and of the Germanic culture that eventually overran and absorbed it. Three major institutions formed the basis of medieval society and dictated how most people lived. These were feudalism, manorialism and Christianity.

Michael J. Varbola in *The Writer's Complete Fantasy Reference,* edited by the editors of Writer's Digest Books, 1998

Among the fantasy genre's greatest hits are: *The Wind in the Willows* (1908), *The Wizard of Oz* (1900), and *Alice's Adventures in Wonderland* (1865). These books are embraced by adults and children alike.

Philip Martin in *The Writers Handbook,* edited by Alfrieda Abbe, 2004

The "portal fantasy" is a mainstay in the fantasy genre. In this type of novel, someone from our world discovers a pathway to another world where he or she is our relatable explorer. We discover this new world through this narrator's eyes. It's a tried and true fantasy plot.

Charlie Jane Anders, i09.com, January 26, 2012

I learned years ago from Lester del Ray that the secret to writing good fantasy is to make certain it relates to what we know about our own world. Readers must be able to identify with the material in such a way that they recognize and believe the core truths of the storytelling. It doesn't matter if you are writing epic fantasy, contemporary fantasy, dark urban fantasy, comic fantasy, or something else altogether, there has to be truth in the material. Otherwise readers are going to have a tough time suspending disbelief long enough to stay interested.

Terry Brooks, *Sometimes The Magic Works,* 2003

More than other genres, supernatural fiction is defined by atmosphere and characterization. By atmosphere I mean the author's ability to evoke a mood or place viscerally by the use of original and elegant, almost seductive language. The most successful supernatural novels are set in our world. Their narrative tension, their very ability to frighten and transport us, derives from a conflict between the macabre and the mundane, between everyday reality and the threatening other--whether revenant [a ghost that returns], werewolf, or demonic godling--that seeks to destroy it.

Elizabeth Hand in *The Writer's Guide to Fantasy and Literature,* edited by Philip Martin, 2002

Sword-and-sorcery fiction is to fantasy what the western is to the historical novel, or perhaps more precisely, what the hardboiled private-eye story is to mystery fiction. It is a subgenre based on a prefabricated image, without which it cannot be identified at all: the cowboy in the middle of the dusty street, ready to draw; the private-eye in the trench coat; the brawny scantily-clad swordsman, glaring defiantly at menaces supernatural and otherwise, with an even less-clad shapely wench cowering somewhere in the background.

Darrell Schweitzer in *How To Write Tales of Horror, Fantasy & Science Fiction,* edited by J.N. Williamson, 1991

Ray Bradbury's rocket ships were not souped-up fighter jets. Instead, they were the latter-day descendent of Joseph Conrad's sailing ships: You traveled on them not so much to encounter adventures as to think about what the encounter might mean. His Mars was not an arid red desert, it was filled with towns where old ladies puttered around on the same kinds of charming but pointless errands little old lades do in Marcel Proust's *Cambray.*

One way to sum up Ray Bradbury is to notice that he is just about the only American science fiction writer to claim, proudly, the label "fantasy" for his books. *Fahrenheit 451* was his only real science fiction novel, he said. You might even locate him in a middle ground between the best American fantasy literature and the hyper-masculine world of *Astounding Science Fiction.*

John Plotz, slate.com, June 6, 2012

The first novel I published was the fifth I'd written and when it sold I was working on novel thirteen. What finally made the difference? Harry Potter. I slid into publication on Harry Potter's big, beautiful coattails. When I first started writing you couldn't sell a fantasy novel for teens to save your life. An editor once told me, "First you have to sell three or four realistic novels, about real kids, preferably humorous. If they do well then maybe, *maybe* someone will look at your fantasy." Then Harry Potter hit, and every editor in the country started pulling fantasy out of their slush piles.

Hilari Bell in *How I Got Published,* edited by Ray White and Duane Lindsay, 2007

12 THE HORROR NOVEL

A man bursts spontaneously into flames. Disembodied voices speak. Something lurks behind the closet door. A victim of religious mania kills his wife and children. These episodes can be found in *Wieland*, or *The Transformation*, published in 1798. It is the first American horror novel, written by Charles B. Brockden Brown, a Philadelphian of Quaker stock who is recognized as the father of American literature. He was, in other words, the first American crazy enough to try to support himself solely by writing fiction.

Douglas E. Winter, *Faces of Fear*, 1985

A source of modern fantasy was the Gothic novel, invented in Germany and introduced to England by Horace Walpol's *The Castle of Otranto* (1764). This novel of medieval murder and spookery has all the elements that became standard props of the Gothic horror story: a wicked tyrant, an imperiled virgin, an impoverished young hero of noble blood, a monk, a castle with trapdoors and secret passages, a ruined monastery, and *two* ghosts. Who could ask for more?

L. Sprague de Camp, *3000 Years of Fantasy and Science Fiction*, 1972

The horror genre has a great literary history. Hawthorne, Henry James, Edgar Allan Poe, many others found a depth and seriousness in it which made horror more valid, more interesting and worthy, than the general run of mystery fiction. Horror was about the invention of clever puzzles. It dealt with profound emotions and real mysteries, not who had left the

137

footprints under the gorse-bush and how the key to the library had wound up in the colonel's golf bag. Horror could touch people, change them, make them think. While horror fiction was certainly entertaining, there was much more to the genre than mere weightless entertainment.

Peter Straub in *How to Write Tales of Horror, Fantasy & Science Fiction*, edited by J.N. Williamson, 1991

The Great Depression only enhanced America's interest in things supernatural and horrifying. A number of horror-themed radio shows sprung up including "The Shadow" (1930) and "The Spider" (1933). Both spawned successful spinoffs in the form of novellas and comic books. Yet the 1930s also marked the last decade of the pulp magazine. Publisher Henry Steeger visited the French Grand Guignol Theater for inspiration and returned to revive the *Dime Mystery Novels* series. He added *Terror Tales and Horror Stories* over the next two years. All these pulps survived until 1941. The very real horrors of World War II overshadowed fictional ones. It wasn't until the 1950s that the horror genre hit its stride.

Kristin Masters, blog.bookstellingyouwhy.com, October 24, 2013

New technology brought new possibilities for horror film makers of the 1980s. Soon the emphasis shifted to gore for gore's sake, and the film genre fell out of favor with mainstream audiences. But the horror novel was enjoying an excellent reputation for quality writing, despite the growth in formulaic shocker stories. In 1981, Thomas Harris published the first novel in his Hannibal Lecter series. This novel remains one of the most commercially successful portraits of a serial killer, and it heralded the start of the serial-killer craze of the ensuing decades...In recent years, the archetypes of vampires, werewolves, and zombies have come to dominate the horror genre.

Kristin Masters, blog.bookstellingyouwhy.com, October 24, 2013

Bloody acts of violence need not be graphically described. My position is simple. I detest the Vomit Bag School of Horror--books and stories featuring gore for gore's sake, designed strictly for the purpose of grossing out the reader.

William E. Nolan, *How To Write Horror Fiction*, 1990

Horror fiction upsets apple carts, burns old buildings, and stampedes the horses; it questions and yearns for answers, and takes nothing for granted. It's not safe, and it probably rots your teeth, too. Horror fiction can be a guide through a nightmare world, entered freely and by the reader's own will. And since horror can be many, many things and go in many, many directions, that guided nightmare ride can shock, educate, illuminate, threaten, shriek, and whisper before it lets the reader loose.

Robert McCammon, *Twilight Zone* Magazine, October 1966

I have very strong opinions of what the horror genre should be and this has earned me few friends in the franchised horror product schoolyard. All writers of horror, thriller, drama, and adventure stories, because of the material they consider in their work, are serial killers with a physical OFF switch. They have to put themselves into the heads of their maniac creations. It's so easy to put a knife in someone's eye, that's not the point of horror. The point of horror is to make people feel revolted and oppressed and angered in some fundamental way. One has to get under the skin of the reader. You do this by breaking moral boundaries. You do this by breaking narrative structure. You do this by mixing up genres. The horror writer has to expect to be hated, loathed, derided--for only when he can achieve this status of ogre can his art mean anything to a populace sucked dry by the corporate franchising of the horror ethos.

Mike Philbin in *The Writer's Guide to Fantasy and Literature*, edited by Philip Martin, 2002

It seems to me that horror, as I'm trying to write it, actually encompasses everything I want to write. But on the other hand, if a theme comes along and takes the book in a different direction that turns out not to be horror, then that's fine. Horror fiction, particularly supernatural horror fiction, came out of the mainstream. There's hardly a major writer of short fiction who hasn't written a ghost story at some stage, and often that may be what they are mostly remembered for...What has happened is that books have been packaged by publishers into genres and it is this which has caused the split between mainstream and horror fiction. Obviously there is some fiction which is pure horror, and there's nothing wrong with a story that sets out to do nothing but frighten the reader any more than there's nothing wrong with a comedy which sets out to be nothing but funny or a romance that sets out to do nothing but make you take out your box of tissue. At the same time, I think that horror fiction is often much more than that, and that's certainly the kind I've always tried to write.

Ramsey Campbell in *How to Write Tales of Horror, Fantasy & Science Fiction,* edited by J. N. Williamson, 1991

For a while now, so-called "literary" and "genre" fiction have been moving from outright opposition to a cautious rapprochement. Literary writers such as Jonathan Lethem, Donna Tartt and Michael Chabon increasingly deploy tropes and images from genre, while genre writers have upped their stakes considerably in terms of complexity, moral resonance and style. Sophie Hannah, Josh Bazell and Denise Mina have reinvented crime fiction; Charles Yu, Iain M. Banks and M. John Harrison have given a literary uplift to science fiction; while China Mieville, Jeff VanderMeer and Kelly Link have done the same for fantasy. But horror--the third aspect of "speculative fiction"--has had markedly less success in this regard.

Stuart Kelly, *The Guardian,* November 7, 2012

Fear is fun. Being frightened is delicious. We tend to giggle when we're really scared--partly to expel the tension, partly because we're having such a good time. I'm not talking *real* fear. No one enjoys encountering a knife at the throat, or facing a loaded gun, or fighting the horrors of cancer. But a book or movie or a TV show can't physically hurt us. Instead, they provide an escape hatch, a way for us to deal with the fact that death is as natural as birth and that no one gets out of life alive. Manufactured horror on a page, in a theater, or on a television screen, allows us to transcend our own mortality--at least for the duration of the story. It's a way to surmount the horrors of the real world. And, as I say, it's a lot of fun. That's why we allow ourselves to be frightened over and over. By tapping into our primal fears, bringing the things of darkness into the light, we achieve an act of personal triumph. We feel brave; we've faced the monster and *survived.* We emerge with a grin and a giggle, we've put Old Mr. Death in his place.

William E. Nolan, *How to Write Horror Fiction,* 1990

In pure horror stories--dark fantasy--anything goes, usually straight for the throat. Monsters attack the house, crawl down the chimney, slither or slouch in Zombie ranks closer and closer with each step to the front porch. These fantastic creatures are evil to the core: from slurping, sucking alien monsters to cursed cars that kill their owners. Early in these stories evil begins to appear, usually after a brief opening of calm and tranquility, in small measures.

Philip Martin in *The Writer's Guide to Fantasy and Literature*, edited by Philip Martin, 2002

Louis L'Amour, the western writer, and I might both stand at the edge of a small pond in Colorado, and we both might have an idea at exactly the same time. We might both feel the urge to sit down and try to work it out in words. His story might be about water rights in a dry season, my story would more likely be about some dreadful, hulking thing rising out of the still waters to carry off sheep...and horses...and finally people. Louis L'Amour's "obsession" centers on the history of the American west; I write fearsomes. We're both a little bit nuts.

Stephen King, *Secret Windows: Essays and Fiction on the Craft of Writing*, 2000

I write horror novels because I want to scare sleeping minds awake and expose readers to things they don't already know, so they'll see things they've never seen from viewpoints they've never experienced, and question assumptions they've never questioned...

Of course some people get grumpy when you wake them, angry when your stories don't validate their beliefs, and uncomfortable if they see something of themselves in the monsters you create. But as Marquis de Sade wrote in response to his critics, "Evil recognizes evil, and the recognition is always painful."

Dean Anderson in *On Writing Horror*, Mort Castle, editor, 2007

Writing horror isn't so easy. With any type of fiction, it's difficult to think of something that hasn't already been done. With horror fiction, it's especially true. Creepy basements, loud noises from the attic, hidden rooms, Indian burial grounds, old hotels, multiple personality disorder, etc.--it's all been done before, and it's all out there. These clichés shouldn't restrain you, however. They've simply defined the space you're working in. You know what's out there, now create your own story.

Cris Freese, writersdigest.com, October 25, 2013

Horror is a genre with certain identifiable characteristics. When people who enjoy horror read your story, they are not reading it in a vacuum. They are reading it as part of a genre, constantly comparing your story to other horror stories they've read. If I had never read Edgar Allan Poe's "The Tell-Tale Heart" and then a story very much like it, readers who know Poe's story may not be quite as thrilled with my big surprise ending as I had hoped. To them it's no surprise. They've read it before, only a better version.

To be a creative, innovative horror writer, you must read a lot of everything--and a lot of that everything must be horror. You may be thinking: *How can I be creative and original with all these other authors' ideas floating around in my head?* This is critical: The sheer amount of material floating around in your head will actually prevent you copying from any *one* author in particular.

Instead, you will find a tiny piece of character from this book, a tiny piece of plot from that book, a certain stylistic technique from that other--to combine into something totally new. It is the writer who reads only Stephen King who will turn out stories that sound like Stephen King--on a very bad day.

Jeanne Cavelos in *On Writing Horror,* Mort Castle, editor, 2007

In a horror novel or short story, there is one primary rule: Make your characters as realistic as possible.

Reality is your bridge into the fantastic. If readers empathize with your characters and truly believe in them as projections of real life, then they will follow them into whatever fantastic situations you provide. You will achieve what Coleridge termed "the willing suspension of disbelief." Your reader will *want* to believe your story, no matter how improbable it may be in objective reality.

William E. Nolan, *How to Write Horror Fiction,* 1990

Let us start with an observable fact: Many commercially successful novels and motion pictures pay only slight attention to historical accuracy. This is just as true in horror fiction as it is in other types of historical storytelling. Let us also observe that these inaccuracies are found in many outstanding works of literature and drama, and that faithfulness to history does not, by itself, create compelling stories.

Richard Gillian in *On Writing Horror,* Mort Castle, editor, 2007

Exposing your children to horror-nuanced children's literature at an early age is a positive thing. And here's why: 1. It gets children interested--exhilarated--about reading. I remember that as a kid, I was fascinated by *any* book that dealt with monsters or ghosts or anything weird. It was thrilling to open up and experience some of these books. There was a sense that I was pushing the boundaries, exploring new territory, doing something that bordered on naughty. It was a little scary and a lot of fun. 2. By exploring the dark side of humanity and the nature of fear, kids learn more about themselves and hopefully become more empowered because of it. 3. There are life lessons to be learned. Don't take that shortcut through the cemetery. Staying out late and not telling your parents where you are can be dangerous. Walking into a forest late at night looking for a wayward pet is a bad idea. Don't take candy from strangers. 4. These children's horror stories create a broader knowledge of literature and history.

Paul Allen, barnesandnoble.com, April 29, 2013

In the literature of horror, a handicap has frequently been that of verisimilitude, the creative weakness or flatness of character. H.P. Lovecraft spoke of the "weird" rather than the Gothic, which seems to me, for all my admiration of Lovecraft's masterly work, unnecessarily restricting. To Lovecraft, too, "phenomena" rather than "persons" are the logical heroes of stories, one consequence of which is two-dimensional, stereotypical characters about whom it is difficult to care. Situations and plots may be formulaic, language merely serviceable, and not a vehicle for the impassioned inwardness of which "weirdness" is one attempt at definition, but only one. The standards for horror fiction should be no less than those for "serious, literary" fiction in which originality of concept, depth of characters, and attentiveness to language are vitally important.

Joyce Carol Oates in *On Writing Horror*, Mort Castle, editor, 2007

For the modern reader, *Frankenstein* fails in its intention to depict and evoke horror. In part this is a failure of style, and in part is a failure of technique--the author dwells too little on grisly details. We have to take the horror too much secondhand. Though the events of the novel are horrifying--three murders, a wrongful conviction, another death--the author, for whatever reason of sensibility or youth, chooses not to make a spectacle of them.

While *Frankenstein* worked in its day, it has since become a model of what not to do if you really want to frighten the reader.

Jane Smiley, *13 Ways of Looking at The Novel*, 2005

Suppose you have a strong desire to use a ghost, vampire or werewolf as your central horror novel menace. Is it still possible to utilize such conventional monsters? Will editors buy yet another vampire novel when so many have already been written?

The answer is yes: Editors are always receptive to novels and stories containing supernatural monsters, but they must be freshly presented; your stories must offer new insights and a fresh approach.

William F. Nolan, *How to Write Horror Fiction*, 1990

Horror is an extremely popular genre in teen fiction. It's easy to see why. A good horror story will take a relatively normal individual, Our Hero, and pit them against a malevolent, often mysterious enemy, The Monster. Our Hero must struggle to understand this monster, its strengths and weaknesses. Then he must face it. Often, Our Hero conquers the unknown beast, sometimes not, and until some understanding of The Monster is found, Our Hero, faced with the unknown is often powerless against it. Teens deal with parents, teachers, peers, and a world full of rules they have yet to fully understand.

Teen fiction, at its best, examines these confusing emotional issues; therefore, the coming-of-age theme is essential. Characters face the unknown and take steps to gain power over it. They are forced to make life-defining decisions by examining who they are and taking actions that set the stage for the adults they will become.

This is what makes horror so compelling for a teen audience (besides the cool monsters, of course). Horror looks at issues of death, alienation, insecurity, physical changes, loss of faith, and the inherent fear of the unknown. On some level, horror fiction shows teens that even the greatest obstacles can be faced and survived. The most well known example of this comes from the television series *Buffy the Vampire Slayer*, in which the idea presented is that high school is, quite literally, *hell*.

Thomas Pendleton in *On Writing Horror*, Mort Castle, editor, 2007

In a story or novel, when should your monster be introduced? Should you have him, her, or it attack your protagonist in the beginning, perhaps on the opening page?

There is no set rule as to how soon you should bring your monster center-stage front, but in nearly all of the best horror fiction, an *aura* of menace and potential danger is established right away; the monster is not introduced until much later, allowing you to provide tension and suspense for your readers as they nervously await meeting your menace at full force. The *actions* of the monster can and should be dramatized early; a murder, or a scene during which the *effect* of the monster is shown without a full revelation of the creature itself.

William F. Nolan, *How to Write Horror Fiction*, 1990

I like to get ten pages a day, which amounts to 2,000 words. That's 180,000 words over a three-month span, a goodish length for a book--something in which the reader can get happily lost, if the tale is done well and stays fresh. On some days those ten pages come easily; I'm up and out and doing errands by eleven-thirty in the morning. More frequently, as I grow older, I find myself eating lunch at my desk and finishing the day's work around one-thirty in the afternoon. Sometimes, when the words come hard, I'm still fiddling around at teatime. Either way is fine with me, but only under dire circumstances do I allow myself to shut down before I get my 2,000 words.

Stephen King, *On Writing*, 2000

Researchers from the University of Wales found that fiction readers had the strangest dreams. Fantasy fans had more nightmares and more dreams in which they were aware they were dreaming. Romance novel readers' dreams were the most emotionally intense. And children who read scary books were three times more likely to have nightmares.

Erin Barrett and Jack Mingo, *It Takes a Certain Type To Be a Writer*, 2003

The weaving of the real and unreal is part of a fast-growing strain of fiction some call slipstream. The label slipstream encompasses writing that slips in and out of conventional genres, borrowing from science fiction, fantasy and horror. The approach, sometimes also called "fantastika," "interstitial" and "the new weird," often combines the unexpected with the ordinary.

Anna Russell, *The Wall Street Journal*, February 4, 2014

13 THE ROMANCE NOVEL

In 2008 in the United States romance fiction is said to have been worth $1.37 billion in actual book sales, quite apart from subsidiary rights income. Over 7,000 novels were published in the genre. The Romance Writers of America Association provides the...flag-waving statistics that 74 million people read at least one romance novel in 2008. Most readers--perhaps as many as 90 percent--are female.

Michael Schmidt, *The Novel: A Biography,* 2014

Though love and romance have long been a part of the literary world, the romance novel as we know it today originated in the early twentieth century in England. The publishing firm of Mills & Boon, established in 1908, brought out the work of such authors as Agatha Christie and Jack London-- and also published romantic fiction. The firm soon realized that its hardcover romances, sold mostly to libraries, were more in demand than many of its regular titles. As the years passed, romantic fiction outstripped other book sales by even greater margins, and eventually the firm dropped other types of books in order to concentrate on publishing romantic novels.

In the late 1950s, the success of Mills & Boon romances was noted by a Canadian publishing company, Harlequin Books, which began publishing Mills & Boon books North America as Harlequin Romances. The two firms merged in the early 1970s, with Mills & Boon becoming a branch office of Harlequin. Harlequin began setting up independent publishing offices around the world and started to publish romances in translation. In 1981, the firms became a division of the Torstar Corporation, a Canadian communications company.

For a number of years, Mills & Boon continued to be the sole acquiring editorial office, buying books from British authors. Though it began publishing American author Janet Dailey in the 1970s, Mills & Boon didn't truly open up to other American authors until the early 1980s.

Leigh Michaels, *On Writing Romance,* 2007

Women read and write romance novels. That writing does not appear in serious literary publications, though, because serious publications do not publish in the genre. These publications might claim they exclude romance novels not because they are often by women or appeal to women, but because they're frivolous, poorly written crap. And some romances are crap. *Fifty Shades of Grey* is a terrible book, and I couldn't even manage three pages of the last Nora Roberts novel I tried. But there are plenty of mediocre books of all sorts, up to and including literary fiction. Is the self-conscious virtuosity of Jonathan Lethem's *As She Crawled Across the Table*, with its thunking ironies and predictable magical realist absurdities, really any less formulaic than romance fiction? Certainly the book's exploration of love and creation seems clumsy compared to Judith Ivory's Regency romance, *Black Silk*...

I'm sure there are many people--and indeed many women--who prefer Lethem to Ivory. The point isn't that all people everywhere should like what I like. The point is that certain authors and certain perspectives are excluded before a literary conversation can even begin.

The typical excuse for that exclusion is genre, not gender. But those two words have a common root, and are intertwined in many ways. Romance is seen as unserious and frivolous because women are seen as unserious and frivolous, and romance is written largely by women for women, about concerns traditionally seen as feminine....

Noah Berlatsky, salon.com, February 25, 2014

The romantic heroine emerged in the late eighteenth century as the archetypal female figure in modern European culture. Romantic writers like Rousseau and Coleridge made the female heroine's sexual powers both dangerous and unpredictable, mirroring the spontaneity of nature. But they also made her essentially passive, someone acted upon rather that her own agent. As an erotic being whose sensuality was very much of this world, and whose intellect was of minor importance, she stood in sharp contrast to the medieval and early modern woman spiritual figure, who sublimated her sexuality in the search for a closer union with God and was capable of learned comment on theology.

Jill Ker Conway, *When Memory Speaks*, 1998

In the romance novel the domineering male becomes the catalyst that makes the empowerment fantasy work. The heroine isn't as big as he is; she isn't as strong, as old, as worldly; many times she isn't well-educated. Yet despite all these limitations she confronts him--not with physical strength but with intelligence and courage. And what happens? She always wins! Guts and brains every time. What a comforting fantasy this is for a frizzled, overburdened, anxiety-ridden reader.

Susan Elizabeth Phillips in *Dangerous Men and Adventurous Women,* edited by Jayne Ann Krentz, 1992

I think there are several dynamics that attract us to bad boy heroes who are mad, bad, and dangerous to know--at least in novels and movies. They're hot, hunky, and irreverent. I think a lot of us have the fantasy of meeting a bad boy with snake-charmer eyes, a wicked smile, and a smooth tongue. We are caught up in the overwhelming desire for such a man and we just can't fight it.

Rachael Gibson, likebooks.com, 2005

What a romance novel does is describe the *progress of the love story,* from meeting to that moment when the heroine and the hero decide to commit to each other. At that point they *expect* to live happily thereafter. Whether they do or not is another story--the straight novel, if you like, after the romance.

Donna Baker, *Writing a Romance Novel,* 1997

Traditionally, the romance novel hero is the Byronic type--dark and brooding, writhing inside with all the residual anguish of his shadowed past. He's world-weary, cynical, quick-tempered and prone to fits of guilt and depression. He is strong, virile, powerful, and lost. Adept at many things that carry with them the respect and admiration of the world (particularly the world of other males), he is not fully competent in the arena where women excel--the arena of his emotions, which are violently out of control.

Linda Barlow in *Dangerous Men and Adventurous Women* edited by Jayne Ann Krentz, 1992

There is a place in romance, in my own fantasies, for the laconic cowboy, for the over-civilized power broker, for the gentle prince and the burned-out spy. They all have their appeal, their merits, their stories to tell. But the vampire myth strikes deep in my soul. Deep in my heart I want more than just a man. I want a fallen angel, someone who would rather reign in hell than serve in heaven, a creature of light and darkness, good and evil, love and hate. A creature of life and death. The threat that kind of hero offers is essential to his appeal.

Anne Stuart Krentz in *Dangerous Men And Adventurous Women,* edited by Jayne Ann Krentz, 1992

In romance novels, the general theme is the taming of a man.

Nicholas Sparks in *Writer's Digest,* October 2003

Relationship is what drives the romance story. Whatever plot there is, whatever outside influences there are, it is all about who these people are and what they're going to bring to each other.

Nora Roberts, *Writer's Digest,* June 2001

In a romance novel, falling in love creates problems for both hero and heroine, but ultimately love's power provides the solution. During the romantic journey, characters must experience both internal and external conflict as they struggle to achieve their goals.

Vanessa Grant in *The Writer's Handbook,* edited by Alfrieda Abbe, 2002

Two rules: All romance novels must have a happy ending that revolves between the hero and the heroine in the form of a lifelong commitment, and the love story revolves around one hero and one heroine--no adultery.

Charis McEachern, *Writer's Digest,* March 1999

Strong, appealing characters, sensuous writing, and an understanding on how to create sexual tension are the key elements of good romance novels. Writing strong love scenes that are neither too sappy nor too graphic is one of the challenges of the genre.

Judith Rosen in *The Writer's Handbook,* edited by Alfrieda Abbe, 2002

The theme of the man who is "saved by the love of a good woman" is common in both life and romance. In reality, savior complexes are dangerous because they encourage women to stay with abusive mates, but that is another story, one that belongs in "woman's fiction" rather than "romance." What matters in a romance context is that healing the wounded hero is a fantasy of incredible potency.

Mary Jo Putney in *Dangerous Men and Adventurous Women*, edited by Jayne Ann Krentz, 1992

The romance novel is based on the idea of an innate emotional justice in the universe, that the way the world works is that good people are rewarded and bad people are punished. The mystery genre is based on the same assumption, only there is a moral justice, a sense of fair play in human and legal interaction: because the good guys take risks and struggle, the murderers get punished and good triumphs in a safe world. So in romance, the lovers who take risks and struggle for each other and their relationships are rewarded with emotional justice, unconditional love in a emotionally safe world.

Jennifer Crusie, *Romance Writer's Report*, March 2000

We romance writers get to make people happy. We assure our readers that no matter how bad things get, our heroines will always win in the end. We confirm what romance readers believe in their heart of hearts: Love will conquer all.

Julie Beard, *Complete Idiot's Guide to Getting Your Romance Published*, 2000

Category romances are marketed monthly under imprints readers have learned to associate with romance. Each book bearing the same imprint carries a distinctive cover design its readers recognize. To reduce costs, all books in the line have a fixed page length. Once printed, they are marketed in a block. Single-title romance novels are not part of a category line, their page length is not fixed, and each is sold on an individual basis.

Vanessa Grant, *Writing Romance*, 2001

A Regency period heroine may find herself in dire straits and approach crisis in many ways, but never at the expense of dignity and self-respect. Otherwise, she becomes too tawdry to qualify as a heroine for the romance genre.

Alice Orr, *No More Rejections*, 2004

The Regency period of British history has fascinated me for a long time. I've read Jane Austen's books many times, as well as a lot of other fiction and nonfiction about the period. When I first decided to write a novel set in London in the early 1800s, I reread several of my general sources on what life was like in the period, mostly books on the social history of England. Then I read biographies and autobiographies, starting with several about Jane Austen and then branching out into books on Lord Wellington and the Prince Regent (later George IV). I asked my friends for recommendations.

Then I hit the library, looking for specific things, like a street map of London in 1817 and books on period slang. *The 1811 Dictionary of the Vulgar Tongue* turned out be invaluable for dialogue. Along the way, I kept running across other fascinating things that I hadn't known to look for.

Patricia C. Wrede in *Children's Writer's and Illustrator's Market*, edited by Chuck Sambuchino, 2013

Publishers (like television executives) have this "thing." They find something that sells, and they do it and do it and do it until they have killed it. If you're around long enough you'll see Regency romance novels come in, be beaten to death, go out, then come back seven to ten years later. I was dropped by Avon in the mid-eighties because traditional Regencies weren't selling and they weren't going to do them anymore. Ten months later, they called and asked me for three more. Now traditional Regencies are dying again. I have my own theory on that--the publishers tried putting graphic sex in them, that was a mistake. Traditional Regencies were perfect little gems, never with a large following, but always there, always to be counted on by older readers and for young women just getting into reading romance. Traditional Regencies introduced several generations of readers to romance.

Kasey Michaels, likesbooks.com, 2005

The attitudes between men and women have to be politically correct even when you're writing Regency and Georgian period historical romance novels. You're going to alienate readers if you have terribly domineering men and very submissive women. That might be an historically accurate way to look at men and women, but you really can't get away with that in modern novels. You have to somehow skirt around that and make the heroes sensitive to women and respect them even while obviously they were more domineering than modern men would be. You have to do the corresponding thing with women. They have to be a little less submissive.

Mary Balogh, likebooks.com, 1998

I think historical romances are difficult to produce as films because of the expense of the sets and costuming. But I know there is a tremendous demand in Hollywood for modern day romantic comedies. Certainly a good contemporary, with a lot of witty sparring, could very easily translate into film.

Patricia Cabot, likesbooks.com, 2001

I don't wholly agree with the label "romance." It is for me chiefly a marketing label, not a creative one. When Kathleen Woodiwiss and Margaret Mitchell were penning their first books, they weren't writing "romance." They were writing from their hearts like any other writer. Publishing labeled the books "romance." Publishing, in trying to imitate the success of these books, had superimposed rules and defined a genre. The best "romance writers" write from their hearts and break "rules" all over the place.

Judith Ivory, booktalk.com, 2005

The detractors of romance novels--usually people who haven't read any--often say the stories are simplistic and childish, and they contain no big words and very little plot--just a bunch of sex scenes separated by filler and fluff. A common view of romance is that there's only one story; all the authors do is change the characters' names and hair color and crank out another book.

Critics of romance also accuse the stories--and their authors by extension--of presenting a world in which women are helpless. Romance, they say, encourages young readers to fantasize about Prince Charming riding to their rescue, to think their only important goal is to find a man to take care of them. The books are accused of limiting women by idealizing romantic relationships, making women unable to relate to real men because they're holding out for a wonderful Harlequin hero.

In fact, rather than trailing behind the times, romance novels have actually been on the cutting edge of society. Long before divorce was common, for instance, romance novels explored the circumstances in which it might be better to dissolve a marriage than to continue it...

Even early romances often featured working-women and emphasized the importance of economic independence for women. While some heroines are indeed young, inexperienced, and in need of assistance, the usual romance heroine is perfectly competent. Finding her ideal man isn't a necessity; it's a bonus.

Modern romance novels tell a young woman that she can be successful, useful, and valuable on her own; that there are men who will respect her and treat her well; and that such men are worth waiting for.

Leigh Michaels, *On Writing Romance,* 2007

Years ago we followed the loving couple to the bedroom door, only to have it closed in our face. Now, not only do we go all the way with them in the bedroom, we often find that they don't wait to get there. Sex can take place almost anywhere--in a parked car, in the middle of a field, on the side of a mountain [not a good idea]--just like in real life. Nor does the heroine always have a wedding ring on her finger.

Donna Baker, *Writing a Romantic Novel,* 1997

One of the most critically important moments in the first section of your Romance novel is the first meeting of the hero and heroine. This moment may be the first time the two of them lay eyes on each other. Or it may be their first meeting after a long separation, if they've had a previous relationship. Or they may see each other regularly, but this is the first meeting that is significant to the plot and conflict--the first encounter connected with the event that is going to change their lives.

This first meeting sets the stage for the interaction of the rest of the book. If the readers don't see it happening, they will feel cheated and left out, and won't likely be involved enough with the characters to want to continue reading.

Yet many beginning writers tell about the first meeting, rather than show it as it happens. Or they include just a couple of lines of dialogue between hero and heroine, then jump to a scene hours later where the heroine is telling her best friend in five pages of dialogue how gorgeous the hero is. Or they have the hero think about how he reacted to the heroine.

Leigh Michaels, *On Writing Romance*, 2007

To be real, your romance novel characters have to be imperfect. They must have problems or no one will be interested in reading about them. But while heroes and heroines have almost certainly created some of their own problems, they can't have done so out of stupidity or shortsightedness, or readers will have trouble empathizing. There is usually a good motive-- sometimes a noble one--for the actions that lead them into trouble. If for example, the heroine's credit cards are maxed, it's probably not because she has a closet full of clothes and shoes. She might, on the other hand, have been buying clothes and shoes for the occupants of a homeless shelter. If the hero's about to declare bankruptcy, it's not because he's been buying yachts and diamonds--but he might have been pouring money into a faltering business so his employees could continue to draw a paycheck. [Becoming poor to help the poor is stupid. Going broke and sticking creditors to keep people employed is not only stupid it's unethical. In this example I don't like the hero or the heroine.]

Leigh Michaels, *On Writing Romance*, 2007

It's that fantasy about taming the bad boy, and you can't get any worse than a vampire. They have been alive for 600 years. They've experienced everything. Then all of a sudden they meet this great heroine, who basically is a breath of fresh air. Falling in love, trying to find that spark again in their lives--that is a great romantic fantasy.

Erika Tsang, *Time*, February 27, 2006

Because there have been thousands of romance novels published, it is inevitable that some of them have featured similar plots. Usually the fact that the characters in each book are different makes even the similar plots distinctive, too. But there are plot points that have been so overused that they've worn out and require an entirely new approach to make them unpredictable and exciting again.

The only way to be aware of all these problem areas is to read a lot. Some of the standards that appear in far too many romance novels include the heroine running smack into the hero (usually feeling as if she's hit a solid wall when she collides with his impressive chest); the hero walking in on the heroine in her bath; the heroine walking in on the hero while he's clad only in a towel; the heroine falling, so the hero has to catch her; the heroine breaking the heel off her shoe; the hero and heroine feeling an electrical jolt on first touch; the heroine seeing fireworks with the first kiss.

Leigh Michaels, *On Writing Romance,* 2007

When I was writing romance, I realized that I needed more than just relationships to pull the characters through three hundred pages. I didn't like writing the detailed sex scenes, but I loved the action parts. So I decided to move into crime fiction. Truth is, I made a sort of hybrid--I took the things I loved about the romance and squashed those things into a mystery/adventure format. It's always risky to try something new like that, but it will work if you give the reader something compelling and appropriate for the emerging market.

Janet Evanovich, *How I Write,* 2006

[There was a time when editors like Maxwell Perkins of Scribner's and Sons played a hands-on role in getting a book ready for publication. Those days are long gone. In the 1960s, editor Don Preston had the almost impossible job of getting a glitzy, gossipy novel by an amateurish writer named Jacqueline Susann into publishable form. The manuscript, entitled *Valley of the Dolls*, became a national bestseller thanks in large part to Don Preston's editorial skills. This is Preston's evaluation of Susann's manuscript]:
    "She is a painfully dull, inept, clumsy, undisciplined, rambling and thoroughly amateurish writer whose every sentence, paragraph and scene cries for the hand of a pro. She wastes endless pages on utter trivia, writes wide-eyed romantic scenes that would not make the back pages of *True Confessions*, hauls out every terrible show biz cliché, lets every good scene fall apart in endless talk and allows her book to ramble aimlessly. I really don't think there is a page of this manuscript that can stand in present form. And after it is done, we will be left with a faster, slicker, more readable mediocrity."

Don Preston as cited in Barbara Seaman's *Lovely Me: The Life of Jacqueline Susann,* 1987

Feminism is not keen on romance fiction, but sometimes its modern offspring, chick-lit, passes muster. This is a rapidly aging but still contemporary kind of romance that is more complex than the conventional romance. [Chick-lit] entails family and other woman friends with whom the protagonist shares experiences. [This stuff can be brutal to read.] The term was first used in publishing in 1995 and it has stuck, though claims that chick-lit is postfeminist are exaggerated. The sex in chick-lit books is more frank, sometimes comical, and generally more nuanced that in the traditional romance, where it can be peremptory and usually out of sight.

Michael Schmidt, *The Novel: A Biography,* 2014

Most people who hate romance novels will admit--if pressed and if they're honest--they haven't actually read one since the 1970s when the so-called bodice ripper novels represented the genre.

Linda Lael Miller in *Novel and Short Story Writer's Market,* edited by Anne Bowling and Vanessa Lyman, 2002

Many romance readers won't try a novel written in first-person, single person point of view. As romances go, it can be a challenge to reveal enough about the main character's love interest to make the romance seem convincing. In other words, to understand what that other person sees in the main character. What do you do to reveal these emotions to the reader?

Holly Cook, likesbooks.com, 2013

Every romance novel I've seen that's been turned into a movie has been terrible. I'm not sure why Hollywood can't get it right, but they can't, and I don't want to watch one of my babies get destroyed.

Susan Elizabeth Phillips in *The Making of a Bestseller,* by Brian Hill and Dee Power, 2005

Every novel I write is harder than the last book. You would think that it would get easier in time, but it doesn't because the challenges are bigger, and your ego pushes you to do better. You want your writing to be cleaner, and I don't want to repeat myself--and that gets hard after so many books-- but you don't want the same plot line, and the same characters, you want to keep it fresh. That's one of the hardest things, but it's just absolutely necessary.

Nora Roberts in *Novel And Short Story Writer's Market*, edited by Robin Gee, 1994

14 CHILDREN'S BOOKS

A child only reads 600 books in the course of his childhood, and *all of those 600 have already been written.* There are hundreds of contemporary books for children--many of them first class. There are also the classics. So what need is there for you to write another children's book? You should enter this literary field because you have a strong urge to tell the kind of story *that you think children will enjoy.* And preferably because there is some particular story that is clamoring to be let out of your mind.

Joan Aiken in *Fiction Writer's Market,* edited by Laurie Henry, 1987

Writing for young people is a great responsibility, because their minds are impressionable and what they read can effect not only their current lives but their future ones as well. Writing for them should be approached with a serious regard for the possible influence of your words. Do not plan to write for children because you think it easy, or the writing does not need to be as good as that in books for adults. Requirements for good juvenile writing are far more strict than they are for adult fiction.

Lee Wyndham, *Writing for Children & Teenagers,* 1988

Even famous authors of books intended for adult readers have found that their fame does not transfer easily into the children's market. Renown in one area of writing does not necessarily smooth a path into an entirely *different* genre. And that is precisely what writing for children is: a different and separate writing area, *not* an easier one. It has its own difficulties and calls on special and specific skills from its practitioners.

Allan Frewin Jones and Lesly Pollinger, *Writing for Children and Getting Published,* 1996

Children's books are *not* watered down adult books. They demand certain abilities of their authors, not the least of which is that of being able to tap into the minds and souls of young people and to project the voice of those people to the reader. You, as an experienced adult, have to see things objectively and yet have the ability to recall feelings and attitudes and viewpoints of your early years to the point that you can write about children convincingly.

Barbara Seuling, *How to Write a Children's Book and Get It Published*, 1991

To write for children involves a close affinity with one's own childhood. If you have this, it follows that you will have that same affinity for childhood in general.

Irene Hunt in *Pauses*, edited by Lee Bennett Hopkins, 1995

It's striking how long children's book can last. One explanation may be the way in which they're read. They become part of our emotional autobiographies, acquiring associations and memories, more like music than prose. Another explanation may lie in the fact that children's books are designed with re-reading in mind. For all children's writers are conscious that his or her books may be re-read by children themselves.

S. F. Said, *The Guardian*, February 16, 2015

Not every successful book for children is a rounded story, with a beginning a middle and an end. Many are more linear, a series of adventures, which don't really deserve the name of plot. This works perfectly well as long as the events are sufficiently amusing or exciting or both.

Treld Pelky Bicknell and Felicity Trotman, *How to Write and Illustrate Children's Books and Get Them Published*, 2000

Children read to find out what happens next: Anxiety feeds suspense. The Harry Potter and Lemony Snicket books have proven this.

Francine Prose, *The New York Times Book Review*, October 26, 2014

While some young readers can think abstractly, most children understand fiction quite literally. This means you have to be careful about what you suggest to them. Perhaps you have a story idea about a little girl who is lonely. Suddenly, a magical man arrives and takes her away on a fantastic adventure. That may be a solid story idea, but your young reader might also take that story line literally, and the repercussions of that in today's world could be very dangerous.

Tracy E. Dils, *You Can Write Children's Books*, 1998

The goal in writing popular books for both adults and children is identical: Fiction is *entertainment*. Your children's book should not be designed to teach a lesson, send a message, or expound upon a moral theme. A theme, such as *honesty is the best policy* or *perseverance pays*, may be implicit in the storyline, but the point should be made subtly by the outcome of the plot.

Sam McCarver in *The Writer's Handbook*, edited by Alfrieda Abbe, 2004

Children and adolescents have their own distinctive ideas concerning humor, politics, and prose, and their tastes in these matters may strike older readers as sophomoric, gauche, ill-informed, or just dead wrong. Conversely, the young have a way of noticing that good manners can be oppressive, that the past is often irrelevant, and that emperors are sometimes naked. In short, the young are not lesser beings; they're just different.

Thomas M. Disch, *The Dreams Our Stuff Is Made Of*, 1998

I have always child-tested my books. I go into classrooms to read my manuscripts to boys and girls before they go to the publisher. I accept children's criticisms and enjoy their comments.

Mary Garelick in *Pauses*, edited by Lee Bennett Hopkins, 1995

My child would enjoy the phone book if I sat her on my lap and read it to her. Test your children's manuscript on discerning adults and ask, "Does it engage you?"

Stephen Roxburgh, *Byline*, January 2000

Before you begin to write your children's book, make sure that you are clear in your own mind whether you are writing *about* children, or *for* them. Do you have a reader in prospect? If there is any doubt or ambiguity about this, your work will suffer. If you try to write for children, but hope that adults will be reading the book, too, an element of insincerity is almost certain to slip into your style.

Joan Aiken, *The Way to Write for Children*, 1999

As adults, we often forget that children can comprehend more than they can articulate, and we end up communicating to them below their level, leaving them bored. Or, the opposite can happen: children are growing up faster than we did and act very sophisticated although their vocabulary skills are underdeveloped. Striking the balance between writing below or above their level is tricky.

Alijandra Mogilner, *Children's Writer's Word Book*, 1999

Novels for children and young adults are soothing and reaffirm the young reader's sense of worthiness. The child, who may have few friends, gathers around himself or herself an array of characters who are entertaining and forgiving and enlightening.

Jane Smiley, *13 Ways of Looking at The Novel*, 2005

Children of both sexes in the 10 to 12 year age group predominantly read fiction, with the most popular genre amongst both boys and girls being adventure stories. Girls choose more romances, horror/ghost stories and poetry books. Boys choose more science fiction, comedy, sports and war/spy books.

Lyn Pritchard, penguin.com, 1999

Most children enjoy the sound of language for its own sake. They wallow in repetitions and luscious word-sounds and the crunch and slither of onomatopoeia [words that sound like what they mean], they fall in love with impressive words and use them in all the wrong places.

Ursula K. LeGuin, *Steering the Craft*, 1998

As America's postwar baby boomers grew up, dipped a toe in child psychology studies at college and started families of their own, children's book publishers took note of a new, pop cultural sensitivity to a wide array of developmentally-based childhood trials and tribulations. Picture books about potty training, tantrum throwing, the death of a pet and other emotionally charged topics proliferated, and were often shelved together at the library under the catchall heading of "bibliotherapy."

Leonard S. Marcus, *The New York Times Book Review,* July 13, 2014

If an editor says your children's story is "slight," this may mean you have no significant theme. Don't blurt out your theme. Let it emerge from the story. If you must come out and say it, do it in dialogue, not narration. Avoid preaching. Children's stories should be explorations of life--not Sunday school lessons. Keep your theme positive. If writing about a special problem, offer constructive ways for your reader to deal with it.

Aaron Shepard, *The Business of Writing For Children,* 2000

Tall tales are a highly specialized form of children's book humor. You need to be awfully good, for the classic tales you compete with are superb. Take Jim Bridger who discovered that it took eight hours for an echo to return from a distant mountain. He turned it into an alarm clock by shouting "wake up!" before he went to bed.

Sid Fleischman in *The ABC's of Writing For Children,* edited by Elizabeth Koehler-Pentacoff, 2003

Harry Potter, like many heroes of fantasy, is endearing because he is rather ordinary. Surrounded by magic, he is the quintessential young, insecure schoolboy, seeking friendship from peers and respect from adults, learning to trust others, trying to stand up for what he thinks is right. While engaging in ongoing struggles with evil creatures of darkness, he is also fond of sports, wizard trading cards, and jelly beans. In the best of fantasy, the world is infused with magic--but victory comes in the end, after all is said and done, from very human values of faith, courage and perseverance.

Philip Martin in *The Writer's Guide to Fantasy and Literature,* edited by Philip Martin, 2002

For writers, the Harry Potter effect has been twofold. On the one hand, it has been encouraging. The increased sales of children's books have been good for them, and there's more of a sense of value for children's books. But the downside to this has been that a lot of people have thought, *I could write Harry Potter. They must be looking for another Harry Potter.* It is so untrue. I will go on record as saying we won't see another Harry Potter for fifty years.

David Levithan in *Agents, Editors, and You* edited by Michelle Howry, 2002

I hate to see [in a children's book] a whiny character who's in the middle of a fight with one of his parents, slamming doors, rolling eyes and displaying all sorts of stereotypical behavior. I hate seeing character "stats" ("Hi, I'm Brian. I'm 10 years and 35 days old with brown hair and green eyes.") I also tend to have a hard time bonding with characters who talk to the reader ("Let me tell you about the summer when I...")

Kelly Sonnack in *2013 Children's and Illustrator's Market*, edited by Chuck Sambuchino, 2012

Perhaps the most polarizing book written for children is *The Rainbow Fish*, by Marcus Pfister. To its fans, it's a sparkling illustrated story about a beautiful but arrogant fish who learns humility by giving away its shiny scales to less fortunate fish. To detractors, it's a socialist screed that encourages "an attitude of greed and entitlement," as one customer wrote in a review on Amazon.com.

John Williams "Books to Love and Hate," *The New York Times Book Review*, October 5, 2014

When writing for nine-to twelve-year-olds, the endings don't have to be happy. But they do have to be satisfying in some fundamental way. In younger books, stories deal primarily with situations and feelings the child might encounter. In middle-grade stories the endings grow out of the characters, their internal changes, and their ability to understand and cope with the world around them. As a consequence, the endings of these books are more complex.

For instance, sometimes life doesn't turn out the way the hero wants it to. Yet she does get some of what she needs--an understanding of how the world works, perhaps, or a newly found ability to cope with a confusing and challenging event. She might have to accept adverse circumstances or even mourn a deep loss. But in all of these situations, the hero learns something. She changes, grows and begins to get a firmer grasp on the complexity of the world around her.

Nancy Lamb, *Crafting Stories for Children,* 2001

Middle-grade fiction (ages 9-13) is perhaps the most satisfying category for a writer. Children are still children, but their curiosity is unbounded and the writer who can enthrall them will be cherished. Statistics have shown that this age is also known for having the most readers as a group. To satisfy these voracious and varied readers, think about writing thrillers, literary novels, fantasy and science fiction, gripping historical fiction, humor, and books about contemporary problems.

Olga Litowinsky, *Writing and Publishing Books For Children,* 1992

Books for young adults often explore the gulf in understanding between parents and children. You can only do this if you enter the world of the young person and address the conflict from their point of view. Try to remember the battles you had as a teenager with those adults who wielded authority over you, be they parents, teachers, the police or whomever. How did *you* feel when these people tried to impose their will on you?

Allan Frewin Jones and Lesly Pollinger, *Writing For Children and Getting Published,* 1996

This is not a hard and fast rule, but generally younger children's books are written with a single point of view. This means the story is told through the eyes and thoughts of the main character. Don't tell the reader the thoughts or feelings of any character except through their speech and actions. [No internal monologues.]

Bethany Robers, bethanyroberts.com, 2001

Too much backstory kills a children's book by slowing the pace to a crawl. This is especially deadly in a young adult novel, where pacing is generally faster than in adult books.

Ricki Schultz in *Children's Writer's and Illustrator's Market*, edited by Chuck Sambuchino, 2013

These days, you don't have to be a parent to be familiar with popular teen book titles like *Harry Potter, The Hunger Games* or *Twilight*. These titles have sold millions of copies of books and spawned merchandise empires, been adopted into blockbuster films, and have permeated our pop-culture lives.

Young adult literature is a booming business and has been one of the fastest growing book categories for publishers in recent years with more than 715 million books sold in 2013...Even though this genre is aimed at audiences 12 to 18, more non-teenagers are picking up these titles. In fact, a 2014 report showed that 77 percent of young adult literature buyers were actually adults, with the largest segment of buyers--43 percent, ages 18 to 29...And given the difficult economic climate the publishing industry has faced over the last few years, more young adult buyers has been a blessing...

Tracy Wholf, "Why Adults are Buzzing About Young Adult Literature," PBS News Hour, October 4, 2014

One of the problems with thrillers or crime stories where children or young people are the lead characters is that ingenious methods need to be thought up to explain why adults do not take over the whole investigation. A major part of your skill as a children's author of such plot-driven books will be to come up with plausible reasons why your protagonists do not tell any adults what is going on, and concocting events that are viable and reasonable in a world fraught with "stranger dangers."

Allan Frewin Jones and Lesley Pollinger, *Writing for Children*, 1996

Most young adult novels are over 30,000 words long or 120-250 pages. Although younger adult novels can deal with intense and serious subjects, they are often mysteries and thrillers--stories engrossing enough to appeal to younger kids as well as older ones. The older young adult novels deal with more complex subjects.

What distinguishes a young adult novel from an adult novel is often nothing more than subject matter. These books are complicated, sophisticated and challenging. They are not limited in what issues can be discussed, nor are they in any way "kids' books." By this age level, there is a high tolerance for ambivalence in both character and plot, as well as a general acceptance of complex and painful subjects.

Nancy Lamb, *Crafting Stories for Children,* 2001

Babies recognize faces and other babies and all the little things they have around them--the dish that they eat out of and their highchair. It would be silly to do a board [picture] book with atmosphere and landscapes for a tiny child who has no experience of that.

Helen Oxenbury in *Ways of Telling,* edited by Leonard S. Marcus, 2002

The most successful children's book authors are author-illustrators who illustrate their own books. Almost invariably, though, these people are primarily artists, their art is stronger than their writing, and all of them have enormous talent and experience as professional illustrators. These are some of the best artists in the nation. They are the people you'll be competing with if you choose to illustrate your own books.

Staton Rabin in *The Writer's Handbook,* edited by Alfrieda Abbe, 2005

Rhyming! So many writers think children's picture books need to rhyme. There are some editors who won't even look at books in rhyme, and a lot more who are extremely wary of them, so it limits a literary agent on where the manuscript can go and the likelihood of it selling. These books are also particularly hard to execute perfectly.

Kelly Sonnack in *2013 Children's and Illustrator's Market,* edited by Chuck Sambuchino, 2012

With little children, the way stories are resolved is critical. The endings of the more serious stories offer comfort and closure to fragile psyches. Little children need to feel safe, to feel protected from the vagaries of a capricious world. Time enough for them to learn about unpredictability and its messy aftermath.

It's no accident that fairy tales end with "And they all lived happily ever after." Endings such as this give children a sense of security, a feeling they can cope with the circumstances they confront in their daily lives.

Nancy Lamb, *Crafting Stories For Children*, 2001

Most chapter books (ages 7-10) are 1,500 to 10,000 words long or forty to eighty pages. These books, divided into eight to ten short chapters, are written for kids who can read and who can handle reasonably complicated plots and simple subplots. Written with a lot of dialogue, the vocabulary in chapter books is challenging, and words can often be understood in the context of the sentence. Most chapters are self-contained with a beginning, middle and end. But some chapters move the plot forward by means of cliffhanger endings.

Nancy Lamb, *Writer's Guide to Crafting Stories For Children*, 2001

Around the end of the second grade, many children spurn heavily illustrated picture books and look for what they call "chapter books." Finally, children can read on their own, and publishers provide easy-to-read books that invite them to read with a simple vocabulary, short sentences, and a lot of white space. If the book in broken into chapters, children feel that they're reading a "grown-up" book.

Olga Litowinsky, *Writing and Publishing Books For Children, 1992*

If you want to write or illustrate books for kids, the number one piece of advice you're going to hear is "Join the SCBWI." I'll bet money on it.

SCBWI stands for the Society of Children's Book Writers and Illustrators, and is a world-wide organization that links together those who want to create content for kids. There are many regional chapters in the United States, and plenty internationally as well. The group holds meetings, has annual conferences (both regional and national) and provides both a support system as well as a wealth of online resources.

Chuck Sambuchino in *Children's Writer's and Illustrator's Market*, edited by Chuck Sambuchino, 2013

Children's magazines are a great place for unpublished Children's writers and illustrators to break into the market. Writers, illustrators and photographers alike my find it easier to get book assignments if they have tearsheets from magazines. Having magazine work under your belt shows you're professional and have experience working with editors and art directors and meeting deadlines.

But magazines aren't merely a breaking-in-point. Writing, illustration and photo assignments for magazines let you see your work in print quickly, and the magazine market can offer steady work and regular paychecks. Book authors and illustrators may have to wait a year or two before receiving royalties from a project. The magazine market is also a good place to use research material that didn't make it into a book project you're working on. You may even work on a magazine idea that blossoms into a book project.

Chuck Sambuchino in *Children Writer's And Illustrator's Market,* edited by Chuck Sambuchino, 2013

When I was young I longed to write a great novel that would win me fame. My first book, *Mother Goose in Prose* (1914) was written to amuse children. For, aside from my evident inability to do anything "great," I have learned to regard fame as the will-o-the-wisp which, when caught, is not worth the possession. But to please a child is a sweet and lovely thing that warms one's heart and brings it own reward.

L. Frank Baum in *L. Frank Baum* by Katharine M. Rogers, 2002

For aspiring children's picture book illustrators, a blog is the best free tool you have to break into children's book publishing today. With proper blogging, you can demonstrate that you have the skills, knowledge, and a desire to illustrate picture books. Blogs are unique in that they allow art directors, editors, and agents the opportunity to see your work. The art you post lets visitors see what and how you illustrate--but it is the writing that gives insight on your thought process, your personality, and ultimately a peek into the kinds of projects you would like to work on in the future.

Teresa Kietlinski in *Children's Writer's And Illustrator's Market,* edited by Chuck Sambuchino, 2013

15 GENERAL NONFICTION

Writing nonfiction is like carving a rock. It sits there. It's hard. It's big. And you whittle away at something concrete. Writing fiction is like pulling things out of the air. Nothing is there but invention. It's disconcerting, thrilling.

Marie Arana in *Off the Page,* Carole Burns, editor, 2008

I prefer nonfiction to fiction. I reviewed so many novels in the 1970s that I sort of burned out on fiction. I enjoy books on travel and have an extensive women travelers collection in my personal library...My personal library contains over 28,000 volumes, so I have plenty of books at home to keep me company.

Larry McMurtry, *The New York Times Book Review,* July 13, 2014

Most of the fiction writers I know get absorbed by the idea of what *might* have happened; I feel more absorbed and gripped by the idea of what *did* happen.

Alec Wilkinson in *Writer's Market, 1994,* edited by Mark Garvey

For every short story that's published, perhaps a hundred nonfiction pieces are published as well--in newspapers, newsletters, magazines, books, online publications, and a variety of other media. For every new novel that is released, book publishers release fifteen to twenty nonfiction titles--from memoirs to textbooks to auto repair manuals. And for every successful poet or scriptwriter in the country, there are probably forty or fifty successful writers of nonfiction. [I didn't know there were that many successful poets.]

Scott Edelstein, *100 Things Every Writer Should Know*, 1999

The most popular nonfiction authors of our day might be characterized by a certain overconfident swagger, the modern prerequisite for mattering in a mixed up, insecure world. More often than not, these "authors" aren't authors at all, in the strict sense of carefully pondering their ideas and diction and lovingly crafting an argument sturdy yet supple enough to carry their work over to a mass readership. In place of the William Whytes, Vance Packards, and Betty Friedans of earlier, more confident chapters of our national bestsellerdom, we have promoted a generation of alternately jumpy and anxious shouters. Generally these public figures fall into one of two categories: television personalities who have hired hands to cobble together their sound bites; and middling non-writers suffering from extended delusions of grandeur. When it comes to hardcover nonfiction, a realm in which books *are* physical objects, plunked down on coffee tables as signifiers or comfort totems, Americans don't seem to be looking for authors or writers or artists so much as lifestyle brands in human form: placeholder thinkers whose outrage, sense of irony, or general dystopian worldview matches their own, whether it is Glenn Beck, Barack Obama, or Chelsa Handler.

It's a glum corollary of such market forces that these very popular nonfiction books aren't *books* in the traditional sense of the word so much as aspirational impulse buys. They imbue their owners with a feeling of achievement and well being upon purchase, a feeling that crucially does not require the purchaser to *actually sit and read the book in question*. Substantive, thoughtful books might pervade other lists (e-book, trade paperback, etc.), but when it comes to the top position on the hardcover nonfiction roster, accessory books by high-profile bloviators typically dominate from Al Franken's *Rush Limbaugh Is a Big Fat Idiot* to Ann Coulter's *Godless* to Edward Klein's *The Amateur* to Dinesh D'Souza's *America*.

Heather Havrilesky, "Mansplanation Nation," *Bookforum*, Dec/Jan, 2015

Clutter is the disease of American writing. We are a society strangling in unnecessary words, circular constructions, pompous frills and meaningless jargon....

The secret of good writing is to strip every sentence to its cleanest components. Every word that serves no function, every long word that could be a short word, every adverb that carries the same meaning that's already in the verb, every passive construction that leaves the reader unsure of who is doing what--these are the thousand and one adulterants that weaken the strength of a sentence. And they usually occur in proportion to education and rank. [In other words, college professors are the worst.]

William Zinsser, *On Writing Well*, originally published in 1975

There's an ethical dilemma in almost all journalism. In taking someone else's story and making it your own, in describing them on your terms, in ways they may not agree with.

Ted Conover in *The New Journalism* (2005) by Robert S. Boynton

The short story writer, playwright, and novelist deal with private life. They deal with ordinary people and elevate these people into our consciousness. The nonfiction writer has traditionally dealt with people in public life, names that are known to us. [This is not always the case. For example, four of my nonfiction books are about ordinary, nonpublic people.]

Gay Talese in *Telling True Stories*, edited by Wendy Call, 2007

Any person who can speak English grammatically can learn to write nonfiction. Nonfiction writing is not difficult, though it is a technical skill. What you need for nonfiction writing is what you need for life in general: an orderly method of thinking. Writing is literally only the skill of putting down on paper a clear thought, in clear terms. Everything else, such as drama and "jazziness," is merely the trimmings. I once said that the three most important elements of fiction are plot, plot, and plot. The equivalent in nonfiction is: clarity, clarity, and clarity.

Ayn Rand, *The Art of Nonfiction*, 2001

There are two ways, I think, to approach nonfiction writing. You can set out on your journey armed with a thesis and collect supporting facts along the way--a perfectly legitimate approach. From this prosecutorial style, we get our best polemics, satires, and exposes. Partisan, one-sided and tending to justify a preconceived viewpoint, this is the art of the legal brief and indictment. This literature more often sounds like a trumpet blast, a call to arms, than an invitation to sober analysis and reflection.

But there's another type of nonfiction writing in which the writer surrenders all preconceived belief and submits to the material. That's not to say that the latter writers are mental eunuchs without firm opinions or airheads mindlessly soaking up facts. They, too, begin their journey carrying the bulky baggage of prejudice, although they may not know it or admit to it. The difference is that they zealously search for facts that contradict their working hypotheses. They like to stub their toes on hard, uncomfortable facts strewn in their paths. They want information that will explode, like a prankster's cigar, in their faces.

Ron Chernow in *The Writing Life,* 1995

I'll bet you think that if you write a nonfiction book that is interesting, fact filled, and with touches of great writing, a publisher is sure to buy it. Wrong. You have forgotten the first basic rule. Find out who wants it.

Oscar Collier, *How to Write and Sell Your First Novel,* 1990

Learning how to write is hard enough, but deciding what to write about-- isolating a marketable subject that is appealing to you--is the most difficult task a writer must confront. Find a subject that intrigues and motives you and that will simultaneously intrigue and motivate readers. The task is double-edged. Salable subjects are around us everywhere; on the other hand, they are astoundingly elusive.

Lee Gutkind, *The Art of Creative Nonfiction,* 1997

We seem to be living in an age of know-it-alls: talk show hosts and guests, expert witnesses, pundits, gurus on every conceivable subject. The information age is exhausting. It is also dull, like a dinner party guest who never stops talking. In my view, this climate is anathema to good writing, which is rooted not in knowledge but in curiosity.

James B. Stewart, *Follow the Story,* 1998

Nonfiction writers write too much about themselves and what they think without seeking a universal focus so that readers are properly and firmly engaged. Essays that are so personal that they omit the reader are essays that will never see the light of print. The overall objective of a writer should be to make the reader tune in, not out....The uninspired writer will tell the reader about a subject, place, or personality, but the creative nonfiction writer will show that subject, place, or personality in action.

Lee Gutkind, *Keep it Real*, 2009

The act of nonfiction writing is a zone I occupy, a psychological space. After a while I lose self-consciousness and all sense of time. Before I can get to that zone, though, I have to make the leap from taking field notes to writing the first draft. Imposing order on the chaos in my notebooks is hard.

When I was younger, I filled my reporting notes with my own thoughts and feelings about things. These notes often didn't contain much information about the source of my thoughts and feelings: what I was actually *seeing*. They contained few details of clothing and place, smells, sounds, and other sensory impressions. I'm sorry about that, because I could use some of those notes now.

I learned a few things since then. I try to write down all the visible, tactile, smellable facts as well as what I hear. With that material in front of me, I have complete access to my memories of how I felt about a certain incident or scene; I don't need to know those thoughts recorded on the notebook page.

I usually take more than ten thousand pages of steno pad notes for a book. These notes include all the perishable material, the fleeting events I watched unfold in front of me. I fill another set of notebooks with library research and standard office interviews. Once I have it all, I have to organize it.

I used to make an index of all my notebooks. Creating the index forced me to review all my notes once, very carefully. I tried not to spend too much time on it; I didn't want to waste energy on something that was just a tool. The index was usually flawed, because I refused to go back and revise once I started. Now, I actually type out my notes. It doesn't seem to take much longer than making the index. Once I've done that, I review my notes several times to find the most interesting parts and to gain a sense of the whole.

Tracy Kidder in *Telling True Stories*, edited by Mark Kramer and Wendy Call, 2007

I hate writing about anyone who is familiar with the press or has a "story." I like to write about people who don't necessarily see what their story is, or what my interest might be. I like subjects who really know how to enjoy life or are immersed in whatever they are doing fully.

Adrian Nicole Leblanc in Robert S. Boynton's *The New Journalism*, 2005

The secret to the art of journalistic interviewing--and it is an art--is to let the other person think he's interviewing you. You tell him about yourself, and slowly you spin your web so that he tells you everything.

Truman Capote in *Conversations With Capote*, edited by Lawrence Grobel, 1985

When confronted with an interview subject who might not have exactly scintillating things to say, a good nonfiction writer, rather than making up better stuff, will work hard to discover other aspects of the subject that are interesting, like by talking to other people about the character in question or simply work on getting the subject to talk more and reveal himself, rather than resorting to fiction.

Lee Gutkind in *Writing Creative Nonfiction*, edited by Carolyn Forche and Philip Gerard, 2001

Some people love to talk about themselves. A few people love to talk about themselves but don't say much that is useful. They say such things as "The Lord made me do it," or "I've got to hand it to my teammates." [Being a sports journalist must be brutal.] Your job as an interviewer is to turn the subject into a storyteller. Ask questions so layered, so deep, and so odd that they elicit unusual responses. Take the person to places he wouldn't normally go. Ask questions that require descriptive answers.

Jacqui Banaszynski in *Tell True Stories*, 2007, Mark Kramer and Wendy Call, Editors

In your nonfiction writing class [the professor should] always be ready to "tie in" whatever you're talking about with its application out in the world. Undergrads are terribly conscious they they'll soon become human beings, and are delighted to know that some of the stuff they're learning may be useful after they leave this artificial hothouse called college. As a writing teacher you'll have more of an advantage in this regard than teachers of most of the other "humanities" courses.

Martin Russ, *Showdown Semester,* 1980

I write about animals because I really like animals. I'm also interested in the animalistic side of human nature, and when and why humans cross over into doing very violent things. [When animals become gratuitously violent they are acting like humans. In other words, violent human behavior is more humanistic than animalistic.] Writing about animals is a way of getting at readers' emotions. People sometimes open up their emotions to animals more easily than they do other people. You see that with the way people get so obsessed with their pets. A big thing you see in New York is a person walking their dog with a diamond-stud collar, right past a homeless person. [Unlike people, dogs do not become paranoid schizophrenics.] That interests me as well. My stories are about people, but I use animals as vehicles to get at the people.

Carole Burns, *Off the Page,* 2008

My first writing mentor, Annie Dillard, once told our college class that if you ever have the choice between visiting a far-flung place or reading about it, choose the book. [As a nonfiction writer, if I had a mentor, which I didn't, the advice would have been just the opposite.]

Virginia Pye, "Opinionator" *The New York Times,* December 29, 2013

Most people think of history as old dead stuff, and who can blame them? It's so often presented that way, like bad-tasting medicine that supposedly is good for you. History is about life and people and the writing must bring these people and their times to life. The story of our country is so strong, so compelling, so very important. I want to share the wealth.

David McCullough, *The Writing Life,* 1995

Nature writing often requires an ability to understand and interpret the findings of science. If you do not have the education or career credentials for writing about these subjects, you can rely on others who are experts, or you can write as a lay naturalist, an astute observer. However, the onus of accuracy is upon you. Although nature writing rests on science, the essay form leaves plenty of room for the writer's interaction with the environment, including one's inner emotional landscape as well as the outer landscape of the setting. One of the best ways to improve your skill in nature and outdoor writing is to read examples of it, as well as books on how to write this specialized kind of writing.

Elizabeth Lyon, *A Writer's Guide to Nonfiction*, 2003

Essays, unlike articles, intentionally include or even feature the writer's subjective viewpoint and experiences. Besides political and social commentary in newspapers, the essay form encompasses personal experiences of all kinds. Essays are further distinguished from articles by a structure suited to argue an opinion or tell a story.

Elizabeth Lyon, *A Writer's Guide to Nonfiction*, 2003

A friend of mine once wrote a "how-to" book about camping and hiking. On the book cover, as you might expect, is a photograph of the author, wearing a backpack out in the mountains somewhere. But what you wouldn't expect is that the backpack wasn't his; he had to borrow it. And what looks like a scene from Sequoia National Park actually took place in Central Park.

As you may guessed by now, this self-proclaimed "expert" on hiking and camping had never done either; but he *did* do his research. His book sold well and no one was the wiser.

Joel Saltzman, *If You Can Talk, You Can Write*, 1993

A "feature" is an article with a human-interest angle. Its purpose goes beyond news and information. A feature engages its readers in the story of people or of a single person behind a newsworthy event. This means that well-written features are meant to arouse emotions. The writer might accomplish this through humor, for instance, or by conveying the emotions of the people involved in the event...The way you write a feature can depart from strict journalistic writing and may borrow techniques from fiction.

Elizabeth Lyon, *A Writer's Guide to Nonfiction*, 2003

Take a class of writing students in a liberal arts college and assign them to write about some aspect of science, and a pitiful moan will go around the room. "No! Not science!" the moan says. The students have a common affliction: fear of science. They were told at an early age by a chemistry or a physics teacher that they don't have "a head for science."

Take an adult chemist or physicist or engineer and ask him or her to write a report, and you'll see something close to panic. "No! Don't make us write!" they say. They also have a common affliction: fear of writing. They were told at an early age by an English teacher that they don't have "a gift or words."

William Zinsser, *On Writing Well,* originally published in 1976

Science writing has a reputation for bloodlessness, but in many ways it is the most human of disciplines. Science, after all, is a quest, and as such it's one of the oldest and most enduring stories we have. It's about searching for answers, struggling with setbacks, persevering through tedium and competing with colleagues all eager to put forth their own ideas about how the world works. Perhaps most of all, it's about women and men possessed by curiosity, people who devote their lives to pursuits the rest of us find mystifying or terrifying--chasing viruses, finding undiscovered planets, dusting off dinosaurs or teasing venomous snakes.

Michelle Nijhuis, "The Science and Art of Science Writing," *The New York Times,* December 9, 2013

Today, art-book publishing is blooming in a desert. Despite ever-dwindling nourishment from sales, it is a golden age in terms of both the number of titles available and their impressive quality. No single factor explains this paradox, but if we examine the list, we do see trends. The most important may be the uncoupling of art publishing from trade book-selling. As rising exhibition attendance led to increased in-house book sales, museums and galleries came to regard trade partners as superfluous. Relying on university and specialty book distributors, they began to replace trade houses at the center of art publishing. Relatively inexpensive page-makeup software helped turn books into appealing and versatile vehicles for promotion and marketing as well as creative expression by artists and designers. Traditional forms, like artist monographs and broad art-historical surveys, became rare.

Christopher Finch, *Bookforum,* Dec/Jan, 2015

Authors write acknowledgments to acknowledge their debts, of course, to thank people who helped in some way. Ideally, your tone should be gracious but not queenly, grateful but not groveling. Humble dignity is what you should aim for. Acknowledgements also enable you to shamelessly drop names without seeming immodest. In this way, you let the reader know that while you, the author, did the real work, a great many important people stopped whatever they were doing to give you a hand.

Patricia T. O'Conner, *Words Fail Me*, 1999

16 NARRATIVE NONFICTION

Narrative is *the representation of an event or series of events.* "Event" is the key word here, though some people prefer the word "action." Without an event or an action you may have a "description," an "exposition," an "argument," a "lyric," some combination of these or something else altogether, but you won't have a narrative. "My dog has fleas" is a description of my dog, but it is not a narrative because nothing happens. "My dog was bitten by a flea" is a narrative. It tells of an event. The event is very small one--the bite of a flea--but that is enough to make it a narrative.

H. Porter Abbott, *The Cambridge Introduction to Narrative,* 2002

The object of most of your writing is to tell a story, whether it's fictional or not. The story will have a beginning, a middle, and an end, and in telling the story, you are moving the reader along, maintaining interest and attention from page to page. To facilitate this, the writer has at her disposal an array of devices--species of writing like narrative, exposition, dialogue, background. Each stage of the process... has its own particular challenges.

Ian Jackman, *The Writer's Mentor,* 2004

Story-driven nonfiction is extraordinarily successful, and there's a huge market for it. I think it's partly because when you publish a nonfiction book, especially one that's story driven as opposed to didactic or scholarly, you can target the market in a easier way.

Charlie Conrad, *Poets and Writers,* May/June 2004

Creative nonfiction requires the skills of the storyteller and the research ability of the conscientious reporter. Writers of creative nonfiction must become instant authorities on the subjects of their articles or books. They must not only understand the facts and report them using quotes from authorities, they must also see beyond them to discover their underlying meaning, and they must dramatize that meaning in an interesting, evocative, informative way--just as a good teacher does.

Theodore A. Rees Cheney, *Writing Creative Nonfiction,* 2001

I think narrative nonfiction is essentially a hybrid form, a marriage of the art of storytelling and the art of journalism--an attempt to make drama out of the observable world of real people, real places, and real events. It's a sophisticated form of nonfiction writing, possibly the highest form that harnesses the power of facts to the techniques of fiction. It constructs a central narrative, setting scenes, depicting multidimensional characters and, most important, telling the story in a compelling voice that the reader will want to hear.

Robert Vare in *Telling The Story* by Peter Rubie, 2003

The narrative is what we usually mean by the word "story." A narrative has a beginning, middle, and end. It is organized chronologically, though not necessarily strictly so. One of the most useful and simplest pieces of advice about writing I ever received was the time-honored adage "Show don't tell." The narrative shows readers what happened, often in vivid detail. Of all the forms of writing, it is the one that strives to re-create reality for the reader.

John B. Stewart, *Follow the Story,* 1998

[The term] "creative nonfiction" precisely describes what the form is all about. The word "creative" refers simply to the use of literary craft in presenting nonfiction--that is, factually accurate prose about real people and events--in a compelling, vivid manner. To put it another way, creative nonfiction writers do not make things up; they make ideas and information that already exist more interesting and often more accessible.

Lee Gutkind, *Keep It Real,* 2009

Writing a book is so hard and painful--it demands such a huge commitment of time and energy--that I won't embark on a book-length project unless the subject matter has me by the throat and won't let go....

This [book writing] is a cold and capricious business. To make a living at long-form journalism you have to possess at least a modicum of talent, but it's perhaps even more important to be stubborn and determined and, above all, lucky.

Jon Krakauer in *The New Journalism,* edited by Robert S. Boynton, 2005

Creative nonfiction differs from fiction because it is necessarily and scrupulously accurate. Creative nonfiction differs from traditional reportage because balance is unnecessary and subjectivity is not only permitted but encouraged.

Lee Gutkind, *The Art of Creative Nonfiction,* 1997

Some people criticize nonfiction writers for "appropriating" the techniques and devices of fiction writing. These techniques, except for invention of characters and detail, never belonged to fiction. They belong to storytelling.

Tracy Kidder in *Literary Journalism,* edited by Norman Sims and Mark Kramer, 1995

What I remember about my first years as a published novelist is how eager publishers were, in those early days, for new fiction. This may have been because there was no New Journalism yet--once it appeared it dealt fiction a kind of double whammy, since the New Journalists used many of the techniques of fiction while keeping the appeal of fact.

Larry McMurtry, *Walter Benjamin at the Dairy Queen,* 1999

When I write nonfiction, obviously I was not there when the events occurred. I write in a dramatic style--that is, I employ lots of dialogue. I describe feelings. I describe how the events must have taken place. I invent probable dialogue or a least possible dialogue based upon all of the research that I do.

Joseph Wambaugh in Janet Malcolm's *The Journalist and the Murderer,* 1990

Scenes (vignettes, episodes, slices of reality, and so forth) are the building blocks of creative nonfiction--the primary factor that separates and defines literary and/or creative nonfiction from traditional journalism and ordinary lifeless prose.

The uninspired writer will *tell* the reader about a subject place, or personality but the creative nonfiction writer will *show* that subject, place, or personality in action.

Lee Gutkind, *The Art of Creative Nonfiction,* 1997

Nonfiction has many of the same requirements as fiction: opening hooks baited to entice readers; personalities and settings developed appropriately; background material presented without dumping; and consistent internal logic. In fact, nonfiction's familiar traits--who, what, where, when, why, and how--translate easily into character, setting, motivation, and problem-solving action.

Carol Ottolenghi-Barga, sfwa.org, 2001

Narrative nonfiction is hard pressed to compete with concocted tales...Fiction has such built in advantages in its power to imagine inner life and present narratives free of the factual gaps inevitable in true stories. Narrative nonfiction must strive for the literary if it's to have a chance at the audience garnered by important fiction.

Amand Giridharadas, *The New York Times Book Review,* September 21, 2014

Truth to the traditional reporter encompasses objectivity, meaning that the reporter must not allow personal feelings to enter into the writing of the story. Like Jack Webb in the old and often rerun *Dragnet* TV series, they are seeking "Just the facts, ma'am." What the reporter/writer feels or thinks personally about the nature or truth of the story is irrelevant. Curiously, most everyone in the newspaper business will admit that objectivity is impossible, but that doesn't seem to diminish the intensity of their belief in the principle.

More often than not, writers turn to the creative nonfiction genre because they feel passionately about a person, place, subject, or issue and have no interest in or intention of maintaining a balanced or objective tone or viewpoint. Writers turn to creative nonfiction because they have a story to tell, often involving themselves, and they do not want to be reined in or controlled by Big Brother rules and regulations.

Lee Gutkind, *The Art of Creative Nonfiction,* 1997

The simplest ending to a nonfiction story is the climax. This is the scene that concludes a crisis, resolves a conflict, or marks a turning point in which the outcome becomes clear. An ending of this type should be considered in every narrative story. Obviously, it can be used only in a story that embraces some degree of narration, even if only a sequence of anecdotes. One approach to stories that consist of such a sequence is to break apart the principal anecdote, beginning with it, interrupting it at the point of greatest narrative suspense, then returning to it only at the end. More frequently, however, the climax is used as an ending in purely narrative stories, in which the overriding question from the outset is simply "What happened?"

James B. Steward, *Follow the Story,* 1998

When I started teaching in the English Department at the University of Pittsburgh in the early 1970s, the concept of an "artful" or "literary" nonfiction was considered, to say the least, unlikely. My colleagues snickered when I proposed teaching a "creative" nonfiction course, while the dean of the College of Arts and Sciences proclaimed that nonfiction in general--forget the use of the word *creative*--was at its best a craft, not too different from plumbing. [Actually, it's probably just as difficult to be a good plumber as it is to be a good writer. Moreover, we have enough writers.]

As the chairman of our department put it one day in a faculty meeting while we were debating the legitimacy of the course: "After all, gentlemen...we're interested in literature here--not writing." That remark and the subsequent debate had been precipitated by a contingent of students from the school newspaper who marched on the chairman's office and politely requested more nonfiction writing courses--"the creative kind."

One English colleague, aghast at this prospect, carried a dozen of his favorite books to the meeting--poetry, fiction, and nonfiction--gave a belabored mini-review of each, and then, pointing a finger at the editor of the paper and pounding a fist, stated: "After you read all these books and understand what they mean, I will consider voting for a course called Creative Nonfiction. Otherwise, I don't want to be bothered."

Luckily, most of my colleagues didn't want to be bothered fighting the school newspaper, so the course was approved--and I became one of the first people to teach creative nonfiction on a university level. This was 1973.

Lee Gutkind in *Writing Creative Nonfiction,* Carolyn Forche and Philip Gerard, editors, 2001

I don't even like interviewing people, because I feel once I've interviewed someone, it's much harder to write critically about them unless you bring up every critical feeling you have in the course of the interview.

Norman Mailer in *Conversations With Norman Mailer,* edited by J. Michael Lennon, 1988

In the introduction to his breakthrough 1973 anthology, *The New Journalism,* Tom Wolfe writes about how Jimmy Breslin, a columnist for the *New York Herald Tribune,* captured the realistic intimacy of experiences by noticing details that could act as metaphors for something larger and more all-encompassing that he wanted to say. Wolfe describes Breslin's coverage of the trial of Anthony Provenzano, a union boss charged with extortion. At the beginning, Breslin introduces the image of the bright morning sun bursting through the windows of the courtroom and reflecting off the large diamond ring on Provenzano's chubby pinky finger. Later, during a recess, Provenzano, flicking a silver cigarette holder, paces the halls, sparring with a friend who came to support him, the sun still glinting off the pinky ring.

Wolfe writes: "The story went on in that vein with Provenzano's Jersey courtiers circling around him and fawning while the sun explodes off his pinky ring. Inside the courtroom itself, however, Provenzano starts getting his. The judge starts lecturing him and the sweat starts breaking out on Provenzano's upper lip. Then the judge sentences him to seven years, and Provenzano starts twisting his pinky finger with his right hand." The ring is a badge of Provenzano's ill-gotten labors, symbolic of his arrogance and his eventual vulnerability and resounding defeat.

Lee Gutkind (the "Godfather" of creative nonfiction), *Forever Fat: Essays By the Godfather,* 2003

Historians have always crafted narratives. War. Peace. Political battles. Feuds in the hollers. Floods on the Mississippi. Hurricanes. Strikes. Assassinations. Voyages to known and unknown places. Trials of the century. Personal quests. Leaders with uncommon touches and tragic flaws. This is the stuff of great narrative and the stuff of narrative history, stories about the past told with verve and drama but also with strong arguments and thick footnotes.

Lee Gutkind, *Keep it Real*, 2009

17 JOURNALISM

There is no question that journalists at establishment media venues, including *The New York Times,* have produced some superb reporting over the last couple of decades. I don't think anyone contends that what has become (rather recently) the standard model for a reporter--concealing one's subjective perspectives or what appear to be "opinions"--produces good journalism.

But this model has also produced a lot of atrocious journalism and some toxic habits that are weakening the profession. A journalist who is petrified of appearing to express any opinions will often steer clear of declarative sentences about what is true, opting instead for a cowardly and unhelpful "here's-what-both-sides-say-and-I won't-resolve-the-conflicts" formulation. That rewards dishonesty on the part of political and corporate officials who know they can rely on "objective" reporters to amplify their falsehoods without challenge...

Worse still, this suffocating constraint on how reporters are permitted to express themselves produces a self-neutering form of journalism that becomes as ineffectual as it is boring. A failure to call torture "torture" because government officials demand that a more pleasant euphemism be used, or lazily equating a demonstrably true assertion with a demonstrably false one, drains journalism of its passion, vibrancy, vitality and soul.

Worst of all, this model rests on false conceit. Human beings are not objectively driven machines. We all intrinsically perceive and process the world through subjective prisms. What is the value in pretending otherwise?

Glenn Greenwald, *The New York Times,* October 27, 2013

In fiction, the writer's voice matters; in reporting, the writer's authority matters. The writer of fiction must invent; the journalist must not invent.

We read fiction to fortify our psyches and in the pleasure that fortification may give us...We need journalism to learn about the external world in which our psyches have to struggle along, and the quality we most need in the reporter is some measure of trustworthiness. Good journalists care about what words mean.

John Hersey, *The Writer's Craft*, 1973

I believe that impartiality is a worthwhile aspiration in journalism, even if it is not perfectly achieved. I believe that in most cases it gets you closer to the truth because it imposes a discipline of testing all assumptions, including your own. That discipline does not come naturally. I believe journalism that starts from a publicly declared predisposition is less likely to get to the truth, and less likely to be convincing to those who are not already convinced...And yes, writers are more likely to manipulate the evidence to support a declared point of view than one that is privately held, because pride is on the line.

Glenn Greenwald, *The New York Times*, October 27, 2013

As narrative nonfiction writers we care deeply about sustaining quality journalism in an age that is rather inhospitable to it, for both technological and economic reasons. Television came along in the 1960s and 1970s and replaced print journalism as the quickest, most powerful instrument for the news. On the occasion of cataclysmic events--the crashing of the NASA shuttle, John Kennedy's assassination, the September 11 attacks--people turn to television. It is the prime carrier of news. So we, print journalists, have had to go where television cameras could not. We must answer the questions that the television's images pose. We're lucky: Television news raises more questions than it answers.

Print journalists have to be better than they used to be. With network television, cable television, the Internet, and even video games, it's tougher to compete for people's time. There are more and more sources of information out there, and they demand less and less intellectual energy. People work harder; they have less time. When I started as a journalist, fifty-two years ago, I operated in an age with a single-income middle class. Now it's a two-income middle class. The writer must get better and better, become a better storyteller.

David Halberstam, "The Narrative Idea," in *Telling True Stories*, Mark Kramer and Wendy Call, Editors, 2007

[Print and TV] reporters in journalism textbooks try to provide readers and viewers with what they need to know and try to produce stories that answer Who?, What?, When?, Where?, and Why? Journalists in real world news markets are driven, either consciously or indirectly, to produce stories that are generated by a different set of Five Ws: Who cares about information? What are they willing to pay, or others willing to pay to reach them? Where can media outlets and advertisers reach them? When is this profitable? Why is it profitable? These economic concerns help predict media content and explain why information in news reports differs from an accounting of a day's most significant events.

James T. Hamilton, *All the News That's Fit to Sell*, 2004

Being a journalist, I never felt bad talking to journalism students about the profession because it's a grand, grand job. You get to leave the office, go talk to strangers, ask them anything, come back, type up their stories. That's not going to retire your student loans as quickly as it should, and it's not going to turn you into a person who's worried about what kind of new car they should buy, but that's as it should be. I mean, it beats working.

David Carr, *The Independent*, February 13, 2015

Secondary sources are most useful when they lead to primary documents. The legislative hearing transcript would be a primary document as would be a real estate deed, political candidate's campaign finance report, lawsuit, insurance policy, and discharge certificate from the military. Documents can be just like human sources because they are prepared by humans. However, unlike humans, documents do not talk back and do not claim to have been misquoted.

Steve Weinberg in *Leaving Readers Behind*, 2001

Screenwriters know that if a movie doesn't have a good ending, people will leave the theater feeling like they wasted their money. Novelists know that you can't write a good book without a good ending. Speechwriters always try to end on a high note....

But most newspaper stories dribble pitifully to an end. This is the enduring legacy of the inverted pyramid--a form that makes good endings impossible. The inverted pyramid orders information from most important to least important, robbing stories of their drama and leaving nothing to reward readers who stay with it to the last line.

It is important to recognize that the inverted pyramid never had anything to do with writing or readers or the news. Those of us who have studied the history of the form trace its emergence to the invention of the telegraph. Reporters covering far-flung news about, say, a sinking ship or a Civil War battle now had a speedy way to transmit their stories to their newspapers, but they found that they could not always rely on it. Sometimes the line would fail; sometimes their messages would be preempted by urgent official business. So they learned to transmit their information in bursts with the most important facts first.

This proved to be the perfect form to accommodate the manufacturing process in every newspaper's back shop. Stories were written and edited on paper and then sent to typographers, who set them in lead type. This type had to fit into a designated space on a newspaper page, but often it was too long. The only practical way to cut lead type was to trim it from the bottom.

We don't send our stories by telegraph anymore, and it has been more than thirty years since U.S. newspapers used lead type. Today, most are fully digital so stories can be trimmed anywhere with the stroke of a key. Furthermore, stories for online use don't have to be trimmed to fit a preexisting hole at all....

Bruce DeSilva, "Endings," in *Telling True Stories,* Mark Kramer and Wendy Call, Editors, 2007

Thousands of editors have told thousands of reporters that quotes will add essential liveliness to a story, and at the same time help cover your posterior: If someone else provides the information, you don't have to stand by it. Yet as tempting as that can be, after-the-fact quotes are anti-literary. They can take the reader away from the moment in question in some vague and indeterminate present in which the quote is uttered. They take the journalist away from his or her voice. And they take away from the writing the deep-down appeal of once-upon-a-time storytelling. Compare: *"I knew I had to get out of there," said firefighter Ken Jones* with *Jones knew he had to get out of there.* The first is boilerplate; the second, a cobblestone in the road to art.

Ben Yogoda, *The Sound On The Page,* 2004

Securing a subject's permission and cooperation, if that subject isn't a public figure, is one of the trickiest things I have to do as a nonfiction writer. It is a matter of both law and ethics. I try to make sure that private individuals understand what I'm doing, and I try to give them some sense of what the consequences might be. It's a sort of Miranda warning: *Anything you say may be used against you in my book....*

These days, publishers often require authors to get signed releases from their subjects. Lawyers tell me these sorts of releases are of limited use in cases of invasion of privacy, a very vague area of the law, and of even less use in libel cases. The releases generally say something like this: *I can write anything I want to about you. I can steal your good name. And I'll give you a free copy of the book in which I do these things.* From what I understand, most courts don't think that's a valid contract. For those reasons I've stopped getting releases from the people who appear in my books. Nonetheless, releases can be a tool to help subjects truly consider what they are doing.

Tracy Kidder, "Security Consent," in *Telling True Stores,* Mark Kramer and Wendy Call, Editors, 2007

Every journalist who is not too stupid or too full of himself to notice what is going on knows that what he does is morally indefensible. He is a kind of confidence man, preying on people's vanity, ignorance, or loneliness, gaining their trust and betraying them without remorse. Like the credulous widow who wakes up one day to find the charming young man and all her savings gone, so the consenting subject of a piece of nonfiction writing learns--when the article or book appears—*his* hard lesson.

Journalists justify their treachery in various ways according to their temperaments. The more pompous talk about freedom of speech and "the public's right to know"; the least talented talk about Art; the seemliest murmur about earning a living.

The catastrophe suffered by the subject is no simple matter of an unflattering likeness or a misrepresentation of his views; what pains him, what rankles and sometimes drives him to extremes of vengefulness, is the deception that has been practiced on him. On reading the article or book in question, he has to face the fact that the journalist--who seemed so friendly and sympathetic, so keen to understand him fully, so remarkably attuned to his vision of things--never had the slightest intention of collaborating with him on his story but always intended to write a story of his own.

Janet Malcolm, *The Journalist and the Murderer,* 1990

I'm still a sucker for the romance of journalism, but I'm also a realist. My adult lifetime graduate course has taught me that my profession's virtues,

like those of the Greek heroes, often become its vices. Its very successes--
illuminating the civil rights revolution, helping open America's eyes to
Vietnam or Nixon's depredations or financial mismanagement--induced
excess. Reporters wanted to be famous, rich, influential. As a media writer,
I've reported on a new generation of windbags, of callow people who think
they become investigative reporters by adopting a belligerent pose without
doing the hard digging, of bloviators so infatuated with their own voice
they have forgotten how to listen, of news presidents who are slaves to
ratings, and of editors terrified they may bore readers. As in any profession,
some folks take shortcuts.

Ken Auletta, *Backstory: Inside the Business of News*, 2003

A few days spent in someone else's world (however dismal, violent, pretty
or even boring that world may be) is simply not enough to experience it as
real. It is too tightly framed by one's own domestic normality. Wherever
you are today, you know that next Monday you will be home, and from the
perspective of home today will seem too exaggerated, too highly colored,
too remote to take quite seriously. So the writer slips into a style of
mechanical facetious irony as he deals with this wrong-end-of-the-telescope
view of the world. The perfervid [phony passionate] similes that are the
trademarks of the hardened magazine writer betray him as he tries to make
language itself mask and make up for the fundamental shallowness of his
experience with its synthetic energy. Emotional disengagement, self-
conscious observation, the capacity to quickly turn a muddle of not very
deeply felt sensations into a neat and vivid piece, are part of the necessary
equipment of the writer as journalist.

Jonathan Raban, *For Love & Money*, 1988

Amity Schlaes, an editorial writer for the *Wall Street Journal*, wrote an article
in *The Spectator* in January 1994, describing the white middle class' fear of
blacks after Colin Ferguson murdered six whites on a Long Island
commuter train, and after a jury in Brooklyn acquitted a young black
despite powerful evidence that he had murdered a white. She wrote that
whites were frightened because Ferguson's "manic hostility to whites is
shared by many of the city's non madmen." When copies of the article were
circulated among Schlaes' colleagues at the *Journal*, she became an outcast.
A number of her co-workers would get out of the elevator when she got
on. People who had eaten with her in the staff cafeteria refused to sit at the
same table. A delegation went to the office of the chairman of the company

that owns the *Journal*. It did not matter that Schlaes had pointed out that minorities were the greatest victims of minority crimes, or that nobody could show that a single element of her article was untrue or inaccurate. "Her crime," wrote the then editor of *The Spectator*, Dominic Lawson, "was greater than being merely wrong. She had written the truth, regardless of the offense it might cause. And in modern America, or at least in the mainstream media, that is simply not done."

Robert H. Bork, *Slouching Towards Gomorrah*, 1997

Photographers don't like to be photographed. Surgeons require nearly twice the amount of anesthesia ordinary patients require to undergo surgery. Journalists are the least receptive to professional scrutiny by their colleagues. They react, sometimes unconsciously, sometimes with the utmost deliberation, to avenge themselves.

Renata Adler, *Gone, The Last Days of the New Yorker*, 1999

Combat journalists don't engage in fighting; rather, they're journalists who cover various armed conflicts first-hand. They may be writers, photographers, photojournalists or broadcast journalists, or a combination. They also have been called war correspondents or embedded journalists when they live and work alongside a combat unit. In their determination to report accurately on the fighting, and, often the politics associated with it, combat journalists risk their lives...

Up until the Vietnam War, there was an understanding between war correspondents and the U.S. government that certain military information wouldn't be reported. Correspondents in Vietnam, however, believed the public deserved to hear and see all that was going on. With faster technology and a television in every home, the war was brought into American living rooms on a daily basis. U.S. decisions weren't always presented in a positive light. Thus the debate began over how much access war correspondents should have to information, military tactics and the actual fighting.

During the Gulf War in 1991, journalists were only permitted to travel in a "pool" and taken to certain locations where they were allowed to film and report. Journalists resented this staged environment, however, and began to sneak into unauthorized areas to report. In 1992, the major media representatives and Pentagon officials agreed to a compromise--to "embed" journalists in combat units. The journalists, under this arrangement, could report as they saw fit...

Successful combat journalists have solid reporting skills honed by experience and a passion for doing what it takes to get the story despite the dangerous and hostile conditions they may encounter. A minimum four-year degree in journalism with an emphasis on news reporting or photojournalism, plus classes in global journalism are good preparations for this job. Another way to enter the field is through the military as a combat reporter or battle correspondent. After a basis journalism course, correspondents learn on the job and are then assigned to a location. The experience gained can lead to a reporting job after leaving the military.

Barbara Bean-Mellinger, "Definition of Combat Journalists," work.chron.com, 2014

During my first twenty years or so of magazine writing I had no working method at all. On most interviews I'd try just to go through the experience, paying as much attention as I could, and then later, write the piece from memory. That worked fairly well, but I didn't realize how insulted the subjects were that I took no notes. When I finally did start taking notes--to ease their fears--I found the process of note-taking got in the way of paying attention. I never did solve that one.

John Jerome, *The Writing Trade*, 1992

The dominant and most deep-dyed trait of the journalist is his timorousness [timidity]. Where the novelist fearlessly plunges into the water of self-exposure, the journalist stands trembling on the shore in his beach robe. Not for him the strenuous athleticism--which is the novelist's daily task--of laying out his deepest griefs and shames before the world. The journalist confines himself to the clean, gentlemanly work of exposing the griefs and shames of others.

Janet Malcolm, *The Journalist and the Murderer*, 1990

I think the principal problem with the establishment press, at least in terms of political journalism, has been excess deference to, and closeness with, the most powerful political factions, precincts over which journalism is, at its best, supposed to exercise oversight and serve as a watchdog. Instead it serves as a kind of amplifying mechanism and as a servant to them.

Glenn Greenwald [The *Guardian* journalist who published surveillance stories leaked by former CIA contractor Edward Snowden.] Quoted in The Daily Caller, December 7, 2013

It takes tremendous craft for a nonfiction writer to dominate his subject. Tom Wolfe, Truman Capote, Norman Mailer and Hunter S. Thompson could pull this off, but once they became celebrities in their own right, it became harder and harder for them to act as reporters. The instant they arrived to cover a story their presence altered it. Other less-gifted writers who tried to copy them often failed when technique overwhelmed or even changed substance.

Peg Taylor in *The Writer's Handbook,* edited by Elfrieda Abbe, 2003

An inescapable truism about journalism is that form dictates content. The form of journalism--gimme a headline, gimme a story in the next hour or two, and gimme it in 500 or 250 words--subverts the content. It's easy for someone who is allowed 20,000 words and months to report a *New Yorker* story to say this, but it's nevertheless true that most editors don't allow reporters enough time or space to get a story's facts and context right.

Ken Auletta, *Backstory: Inside the Business of News,* 2003

There are parallels between journalism and clinical psychoanalysis. Both the journalist and the psychoanalyst are connoisseurs of the small, unregarded motions of life. Both pan the surface for the gold of insight. Journalism, with its mandate to notice small things, was always congenial to me. I might have also liked being an analyst. But I never would have gotten into medical school. I never went to journalism school, either. When I started doing journalism a degree from a journalism school wasn't considered necessary. In fact, it was considered a little tacky.

Janet Malcolm, *Paris Review,* Sprint 2011

The question is not whether Internet journalism will be dominant, but whether it will maintain the quality of the best print journalism. In the end it is not the delivery system that counts. It is what it delivers. There has never been such access to knowledge in all its forms. What we have to find is a way to sustain truth seeking. If we evolve the right financial model, we will enter a golden age of journalism.

Harold Evans, *My Paper Chase*, 2009

One time a newspaper sent us to a morgue to get a story on a woman whose body was being held for identification. A man believed to be her husband was brought in. Somebody pulled the sheet back; the man took one agonizing look, and cried, "My God, it's her!" When we reported this grim incident, the editor diligently changed it to "My God, it's she!"

E. B. White, *The Second Tree From the Corner*, 1954

Newspaper people speak of journalists who cover the news as police reporters, City Hall men, and Washington correspondents. Print journalists on the sports beat are usually referred to as sports *writers*. The sports writer is not expected merely to tell us what happened. Upon small, coiled springs of fact, he builds up a great padded mattress of words. His readers escape into a dream where most of the characters are titanic heroes, devouring monsters, or gargantuan buffoons.

A. J. Liebling in *Wayward Reporter* by Raymond A. Sokolov, 1980

The debate regarding blogging versus journalism involves the question of whether or not a blogger can be a journalist...Is there a sharp distinction between the two disciplines, or has time blurred that line?

Blogging is Not Journalism
   When blogging first became a popular method of content distribution, this opinion was likely the most correct view. In the earliest days of blogging, even the best blogs incorporated a good deal of opinion and were relatively light on actual journalism. Indeed, this opinion still holds a fair amount of currency to today's more developed blogosphere...

Blogging is a Training Ground For Journalists
   Other people see blogging as a step along the road to becoming a journalist...Proponents of this opinion say bloggers can gain the tools to operate in a newsroom environment...

It's Not the Source it's the Quality

Rather than judging the medium with wide sweeping strokes, blogging should be judged on the basis of content...This view, which notes a distinction between the products of personal blogs and news sites, holds water in light of expert blogs. After all, if you're looking for information, you're likely to be better served by visiting a specialist blog rather than relying on the coverage of a writer less well-versed in that particular field...As bloggers become better and more experienced, they can become some of the best resources in their given field, especially if that field is underserved...In the end, there's little that distinguishes a good blogger and a good journalist, and the line between the two is hazy at best. A blogger may inject a little bit more analysis into a post than a journalist does in a news article, but when a blogger tracks down sources, does investigative reporting, and presents the fact clearly and fairly, that is journalism, plain and simple....

Jacob Friedman, "Blogging Versus Journalism: The Ongoing Debate," thenextweb.com, August 18, 2010

Blogs are online journals consisting of brief entries displayed in chronological order on a page. They are usually written in a conversational voice and usually peppered with links and references to other sites...Blogging is confronting journalism with the rise of current-events blogs that deconstruct news coverage, spew opinion and even scoop the big media from time to time. The best news bloggers are articulate, independent thinkers. In some ways, they are the antithesis of traditional journalists, unedited, unabashedly opinionated, sporadic and personal...

A growing number of journalists are blogging on their own time...Many are freelancers and columnists who want a showcase for their collected works and an overflow bin for commentary that couldn't fit into their allotted inches or minutes...Even journalists who have no interest in running a blog can glean story tips and ideas from them...Blogs can be a rich resource, an easy publishing tool and a repository for notebook overflow. Bloggers will not usurp online newspapers, but newsrooms could borrow a few tricks from bloggers to make their own journalism better.

Barb Palser, "Journalistic Blogging," ajrarchive.org, July/August 2002

A lot of blogs about writing are self-centered, and that's *fine*, but a truly personal blog limits your reach. If there's one thing I've learned about the

Internet it's that users come to it to see "What's in it for me?" They want valuable content that speaks to their needs.

Most writing blogs--and blogs in general--are about the writer of the blog, not about the user. I write my blog to give readers valuable content because I know that's what they want from me. They don't care about my personal life. My readers visit me for writing and publishing advice, so that's what I dish up.

Mary Kole in *Children's Writer's and Illustrator's Market*, edited by Chuck Sambuchino, 2013

I have witnessed some fraught moments at *The New York Times*. Jayson Blair was a friend of mine. [Fired from *The Times* in 2003, Blair fabricated quotes from people he'd never met.] I watched Howell Raines fly into a mountain at very close distance. I saw the newspaper almost tip over when the print business plunged and the company had to borrow money at exorbitant rates from a Mexican billionaire.

David Carr, *The Independent*, February 13, 2015

THE NEW JOURNALISM

The dominance of the realistic novel in the nineteenth century created a bridge between literature and journalism, and the era's narrative masters routinely crossed it. Walt Whitman, Mark Twain, and Stephen Crane all wrote for newspapers...

Richard Harding Davis, a newspaper journalist largely forgotten in the twentieth century but celebrated in the nineteenth, was the son of an accomplished short-story writer. Polished, mass-market narrative technique powered not only his fiction, but also the wartime dispatches that made him famous. World War I, his last great campaign, gave him the material for his most frequently quoted narrative lede: "The entrance of the German army into Brussels has lost the human quality."

Jack Hart in *Telling True Stories*, edited by Mark Kramer and Wendy Call, 2007

Fiction writing is a calling...Who wouldn't choose the role of literature's divinely chosen hand-servant over that of some schmo hustling to meet a deadline? There are many days when I am that schmo, beset by overlapping commitments, late on bills, typing the same sentence over and over with minuscule variations that somehow make it worse each time, wishing I had learned a proper trade.

Dana Stevens, *The New York Times*, January 27, 2015

News is plot, event, what happened last night or this afternoon or is in process right now. News breaks fast, somebody writes it up, the gun is barely fired before the world is clued in. Story is a wider map and involves any number of whys, relating to personal history, family background, the times, the place, and cultural background. Story makes a stab at explaining how such a wonderful or terrible thing could have happened. News enjoys a brief shelf life, turns stale fast, grows a quick crust. Story addresses complicated possibilities and reasons, therefore lasts longer, maybe forever.

Beverly Lowry, in *Writing Nonfiction*, Carolyn Forche and Philip Gerard, editors, 2001

To produce successful literary journalism or creative nonfiction, the writer must achieve two goals: journalistic credibility and artistic merit.

Mark Masse, *Writer's Digest*, March 2002

In my journalistic writing, I purposefully blend information, observation, analysis, and my own reactions to the material. I tell stories, because stories allow us to think wholeheartedly, to truly understand. The greatest Latin American novelists, such as Gabriel Garcia Marquez and Mario Vargas Llosa, began as journalists. That experience has contributed to the literary school of Latin American journalism that is better written and contains much more emotional content than U.S. journalism.

Alma Guillermoprieto in *Telling The Story, Telling The Truth*, edited by Mark Kramer and Wendy Call, 2007

With the old journalism, quoted dialogue was short, relevant but not necessarily dramatic. Eyewitness accounts gave credibility to recitation of facts, and if there was dramatic fall out, so much the better. But now we change emphasis: We narrative nonfiction writers search for dialogue that will add drama that will build excitement while staying glued to facts. Often, it's extended dialogue, long passages or a series of shorter, uninterrupted passages that tell a story in the character's own words. We use this dialogue, not to modify the facts but to present the facts. The character tells us the story (or a significant portion of it) in their words, and the result is building drama.

William Noble in *The Portable Writers' Conference,* edited by Stephen Blake Mettee, 1997

New journalism is a term that Tom Wolfe has been trying to explain, on the lecture stump, for more than five years and the reason he's never been able to properly define "new journalism" is that it never actually existed, except maybe in the minds of people with a vested interest in the "old journalism"--editors, professors and book reviewers who refused to understand that some of the country's best young writers no longer recognized "the line" between fiction and journalism.

Hunter S. Thompson in *Hunter S. Thompson: The Gonzo Letters,* edited by Douglas Brinkley, 2000

On the one hand, the New Journalists preach a doctrine of truth shaped like fiction; on the other, they frequently seem to acknowledge that the truth is being mixed, from time to time, *with* fiction.

Robert Fulford, *The Triumph of Narrative,* 2000

Whether fabricating sources or inventing scene settings, four journalists made headlines by choosing fiction over fact. It was discovered in 1998 that Stephen Glass had made up nearly half of his *New Republic* magazine stories. *The New York Times* reporter Jayson Blair was fired in 2003 for fabricating quotes from people he never met...Janet Cooke, a reporter with the *Washington Post* had to return her Pulitzer in 1981 after admitting she had created, out of whole cloth, an eight-year-old heroin addict to write about. In 2014, *USA Today* reporter Jack Kelley resigned after falsely creating stories, including a piece about a drowned woman who later turned up alive.

K. C. Baker, "Under Fire," *People,* February 23, 2015

INVESTIGATIVE JOURNALISM

Investigative reporting has taken on every aspect of American society--from government, politics, business and finance to education, social welfare, culture and sports--and has won the lion's share of each year's journalism prizes. No matter how unpopular the news media may sometimes be, there has been, ever since Watergate, an expectation that the press would hold accountable those with power and influence over the rest of us. As Jon Marshal wrote in 2011, Watergate "shaped the way investigative reporting is perceived and practiced and how political leaders and the public respond to journalists."

Woodward and Bernstein's techniques were hardly original. But they became central to the ethos of investigative reporting: Become an expert on your subject. Knock on doors and talk to sources in person. Protect the confidentiality of sources when necessary. Never rely on a single source. Find documents. Follow the money. Pile one hard-won detail on top of another until a pattern becomes discernible.

Leonard Downie Jr., *Washington Post,* June 7, 2012

The news about news is often grim. Newspapers are shrinking, folding up, or being cut loose by their parent companies. Layoffs are up and staffs are down. That investigative reporter who covered the state capitol--she's not there anymore. Newspapers like the *Los Angeles Times,* the *Washington Post,* and the *Chicago Tribune* have suffered from multiple rounds of layoffs over the years...But despite a long run of journalistic tough times, the loss of advertising dollars, and the challenge of the Internet, there's been a blossoming of investigative journalism across the globe from Honduras to Myanmar, New Zealand to Indonesia.

Woodward and Bernstein may be a fading memory in this country, but journalist with names largely unknown in the U.S...are breaking one blockbuster story after another, exposing corrupt government officials and their crony corporate pals in Azerbaijan, Angola, and Costa Rica...

"We are in a golden age of investigative journalism," says Sheila Coronel. And she should know. Now the academic dean at Columbia University's Graduate School of Journalism, Coronel was the director of the Philippine Center for Investigative Journalism, whose coverage of the real estate holdings of former President Joseph Estrada--including identical houses built for his mistresses--contributed to his removal from office in 2001.

There are, to take another example, the halcyon days for watchdog journalism in Brazil. In October 2013, at an investigative journalism conference there organized by the Global Journalism Investigative Network, there were 1,350 attendees.

Anya Schiffrin, salon.com, August 31, 2014

Investigative reporting in America did not begin with Watergate. But it became entrenched in American journalism--and has been steadily spreading around the world--largely because of Watergate.

Now, 40 years after Bob Woodward and Carl Bernstein wrote their first stories about the break-in at the Democratic National Committee headquarters in Washington's Watergate office building, the future of investigative reporting is at risk in the chaotic digital reconstruction of journalism in the United States. Resource-intensive investigative reporting has become a burden for shrunken newspapers struggling to reinvent themselves and survive. Nonprofit start-ups seeking to fill the gap are financially fragile themselves, with their sustainability uncertain.

Leonard Downie Jr., *The Washington Post,* June 7, 2012

In the ever shrinking community of serious investigative reporters in New York City, Robert I. Friedman [1950-2002] will be remembered as a dedicated pro who followed his reporting wherever it took him, no matter whom it offended or what it meant for his own career. In 1993, for example, Friedman castigated the FBI in *The Village Voice* for ignoring information it had developed on the Muslim extremists behind the first bombing of the World Trade Center, warning that without stronger action, terrorists would strike at the towers again. Though the story would cost him valuable sources with the FBI, Friedman published it and won a Society of Professional Journalists Award for Best Investigative Reporting in a Weekly.

Dan Bischoff in *What Are Journalists For,* 1999

18 MEMOIRS, JOURNALS & AUTOBIOGRAPHIES

THE MEMOIR

Most people secretly believe they have a book in them, which they would write if they could find the time. And there's some truth to this notion. A lot of people do have a book in them--that is, they have had an experience that other people might want to read about. But this is not the same as "being a writer." Or put in a more sinister way: everyone can dig a hole in a cemetery, but not everyone is a grave digger. The latter takes a good deal more stamina and persistence.

Margaret Atwood, *Negotiating With the Dead*, 2002

The truth is out there. You can't miss it, in fact--it's everywhere. But even as we embrace the twenty-four hour confession cycle of social media, the popularity, and subsequent disparagement, of the memoir reveals our mixed feelings about true stories. We might be lured into tales of harrowing childhoods or devastating divorces, but our internal machinery will monitor the narratives based on the same arbitrary rubrics that guard our own personal revelations (or lack thereof): Is the author honest about his motives? Are her experiences exotic enough to teach us something new? Does he learn a big lesson at the end, or does he tumble off a cliff into a nihilistic abyss?

Blogs and Instagram and YouTube have rendered brutal honesty and statements of "my truth" about as mundane as instructions on how to dye your hair. Nevertheless, committing your life experiences to the published page is still viewed as an audacious act, one reserved for celebrated authors, public figures, or those who've lived outside the norm and endured horrors untold. For every phalanx of writing instructors exhorting their pupils to write what they know, there's an equal and opposite gaggle of critics urging them to keep their junior-varsity trials and tribulations to themselves. If your pain doesn't equal the pain of the reader, you are merely indulging yourself.

Heather Havrilesky, *Bookforum*, February/March 2015

A memoir is not a chronological, thematically tone-deaf recitation of everything remembered. That's autobiography, which should be left, in this twenty-first century, to politicians and celebrities. Oh, be honest: It should just be left...

A memoir is not an exhibition for exhibitionism's sake. If nothing's been learned from a life, is it worth sharing? Or, if nothing's been learned *yet*, shouldn't the story wait?

A memoir is not a self-administered therapy session. Memoirists speak to others and not just to themselves....

Beth Kephart, *Handling the Truth*, 2013

This is the age of the memoir. Never have personal narrative gushed so profusely from the American soil as in the closing decade of the twentieth century. Everyone has a story to tell, and everyone is telling it. Until this decade memoir writers tended to stop short of harsh reality, cloaking with modesty their most private and shameful memories. Today no remembered episode is too sordid, no family too dysfunctional, to be trotted out for the wonderment of the masses in books and magazines and on talk shows.

William Zinsser, *Inventing the Truth*, 1998

A memoir takes a certain amount of arrogance to write....One must think one's life is important or interesting enough to palm off on an unsuspecting public. At least fiction writers have the pretense that their work has more to do with their characters than with themselves. Still, I doubt you'd find much of a difference between a memoir writer and a fiction writer in the humility department.

Or maybe memoir writers tend more toward exhibitionism, are more willing--eager, in fact--to slap their cards on the table and squawk, "Read 'em and weep." The fiction writer, cagier, plays his hand close to his vest, pretends he knows how to bluff.

If you write your life down on the page, beginning with "I was born in..." and ending with, "As I pen these immortal words, I gasp my last breath," what you've probably got is a self-indulgent autobiography, not a memoir. A memoir usually deals with a portion of one's life--say, childhood--not the life in its entirety.

Robin Hemley, *Turning Life Into Fiction,* 1994

It had occurred to a friend of mine to write a memoir, and so she called asking for help. *It should be fun,* she said. I set to work creating a list of the memoirs my friend might read, for she hadn't read even so much as a single memoir yet, and I thought reading might be helpful. I sent the list and that was that--the end of the memoir, and of the friendship.

I don't mean to be insulting when I suggest that memoir writers should read memoirs...The good memoirs aren't just good stories...They are--they must be--works of art...You have to know what art is before you set out to write it. You have to have a dictionary of working terms, a means by which you can deliver up a verdict on your own sentences and their arrangements.

Beth Kephart, *Handling the Truth,* 2013

The scientific research on the benefits of so-called expressive writing is surprisingly vast. Studies have shown that writing about oneself and personal experiences can improve mood disorders, help reduce symptoms among cancer patients, improve a person's health after a heart attack, reduce doctor visits and even boost memory.

Now researchers are studying whether the power of writing--and then rewriting--your personal story can lead to behavioral changes and improve happiness. The concept is based on the idea that we all have a personal narrative that shapes our view of the world and ourselves. But sometimes our inner voice doesn't get it completely right. Some researchers believe that by writing and then editing our own stories, we can change our perceptions of ourselves and identify obstacles that stand in the way of better health. It may sound like self-help nonsense, but research suggests the effects are real....

Tara Parker-Pope, *The New York Times,* January 19, 2015

My advice to memoir writers is to embark upon a memoir for the same reason that you would embark on any other book: to fashion a text. Don't hope in a memoir to preserve your memories. If you prize your memories as they are, by all means avoid writing a memoir. It is a certain way to lose them. You can't put together a memoir without cannibalizing your own life for parts. The work replaces your memories.

Annie Dillard in *Inventing the Truth,* edited by William Zinsser, 1998

The subject of your memoir cannot be you. Not you all alone, anyway. A memoir must be about you and *something*--and that something should usually be your relationship to something interesting and bigger than yourself. With a memoir, until you have found a genuine subject, you will have nothing at all--because *"you"* are not a subject. Neither are *"you"* a story.

Stephen Koch, *Writer's Workshop,* 2003

I advocate prologue in a memoir. I feel that it helps everyone involved--the writer, the reader--if certain early declarations are made. The thrill of literary memoir isn't bound up in plot, per se, and it shouldn't be bound up in gossip. The thrill of the genre--or at least one of its chief pleasures--is all about how well the author manages to answer all the questions or explore the themes or concerns that lie at the story's heart. Coy doesn't work--or at least I don't think it does. The questions, themes, and concerns that fuel a memoir are often best enunciated at the start. And prologues are such fine, flexible containers. You can make them do whatever you want them to do.

Beth Kephart, *Handling the Truth,* 2013

Perhaps everyone has a story to tell, but many never get around to telling them, and many others tell them poorly. Many people have led fascinating lives, but falter when they attempt to tell their stories. Often, this is because they focus on content rather than form. There's a difference between a memoir and a novel. A memoir is supposed to be true. A novel isn't. The difference between fact and fiction. It's a complex distinction, and some writers blur the distinction to good effect. Others, claiming they want to write fiction, really want to write memoirs. If you base a story on an actual event, but refuse to alter it because "that's the way it really happened," you probably want to write a memoir instead of a story.

Robin Hemley, *Turning Life into Fiction,* 2006

The uncommon memoirist presents actualities honestly and imaginatively. To be honest doesn't require unfailing accuracy, since memory and POV [point of view] intrude upon reminiscing. Honesty avoids deliberate falsehoods. Honest means the writer will not be self-serving, not always at the center, not always the star, though always in the movie. Sometimes she picks herself up off the cutting-room floor.

Because the imagination is regularly attached to make-believe, these days it is rarely attached to the writing of memoirs, which are expected to be "true," that is, factual. But truth and true are not the same as fact. Historians use facts to support their interpretations of events; they draw conclusions based on evidence that is agreed upon by other historians. A memoir's evidence emerges from memory, the unreliable narrator.

Paula Fox, "Speak, Memories", *Bookforum*, Dec/Jan, 2015

Truly the modern memoir has become so debased--or liberated--as a genre that there is little difference between the memoir and what used to be called "the autobiographical novel."

Lewis Nordan in *Novel Ideas,* Barbara Shoup and Margaret Love Denman, editors, 2001

Perhaps all memoirists lie. We alter the truth on paper so as to alter it in fact; we lie about our past and invent surrogate memories the better to make sense of our lives and live the life we know was truly ours. We write about our life, not to see it as it was, but to see it as we wish others might see it, so we may borrow their gaze and begin to see our life through their eyes, not ours.

Andre Acimen in *Writers on Writing,* edited by John Darnton, 2001

If you write about your father hitting you on the head, you're up against a lot of competition with people who are writing about exactly the same experience. I used to tell students not to use certain subjects they seemed to gravitate to almost automatically at their age, such as the death of their grandparents--grandparents tend to die when you're in high school or college. I at least want to read about something I don't already know about. [How about: "Why my father hit my dead grandfather in the head." Just kidding.]

John Ashbery in Ian Jackman's *The Writer's Mentor,* 2004

All of us live with a life history in our mind, and very few of us subject it to critical analysis. But we are storytelling creatures. So it's very important to examine your own story and make sure that the plot is one you really want. When I give talks as a historian about the dominance of the romantic plot in women's telling of their life histories, I'm amused to see women investment bankers and corporate lawyers giving a wry smile, as if to say, "It's true--that's how I *do* see my life." As a young person it's important to scrutinize the plot you've internalized and find out whether it accurately represents what you want to be, because we tend to act out those life plots unless we think about them. I'm impatient with the postmodern effort to obfuscate the validity of narrative. We are time-bound creatures. We experience life along a time continuum; things happen sequentially in our lives, and we need to understand the causation. But we never really do understand it until we sit down and try to tell the story.

Jill Ker Conway in *Inventing the Truth*, edited by William Zinsser, 1998

A good memoir requires two elements--one of art, the other of craft...Regarding craft, good memoirs involve a careful act of construction...Memoir writers must manufacture a text, imposing narrative order on a jumble of half remembered events. With that feat of manipulation they arrive at a truth that is theirs alone, not quite like that of anybody else who was present at the same events.

William Zinsser in *Inventing the Truth*, edited by William Zinsser, 1998

Memoirs are for remembrance. And the remembrances of journalists, when they take book form, are what I think of as "and then I met" books. In my time as a journalist I have met many what we call great men--at least celebrated men. But in *Growing Up* I was not interested in doing an "and I met" book. My prime interest was to celebrate people that nobody heard of, people I was terribly fond of. I thought these people deserved to be known.

Russell Baker in *Inventing the Truth*, edited by William Zinsser, 1998

Coming-of-age is a literary term to describe the passage from childhood to adulthood, from a state of innocence to a state of experience. Most writing about the teenage years is about coming-of-age, for that is the point of those years. We slip free of the protection and constraints of childhood and step into the vulnerability and freedom of adulthood, and we know it.

Susan Carol Hauser, *You Can Write a Memoir,* 2001

The memoirs of the mentally ill are full of confused action, failed promise, and grinding pain; they do not tend to make good narratives.

Dr. Alice W. Flaherty, *The Midnight Disease,* 2004

The memoir genre isn't helped by all the mandatory books that politicians turn out. These first-person tales of coming to the capital, of being made a better man by victory then defeat and a forced return home, have a standard narrative arc. These books also contain an agreed upon measure of falsification and their steady consumption may wipe out the market for serious political nonfiction.

Thomas Mallon, *In Fact,* 2001

A fellow memoirist and reviewer writes: "I'm reading a memoir now where the author has written four chapters full of dialogue for events that occurred when she was four years old. Over half the book occurs before she is ten and it's all about what people said and felt. I don't see how much of this could be possibly true."

My friend's got this right: Nothing makes a reader question memoir more indignantly than the things set aside by quotation marks...

Unless you walked around your entire life with a tape recorder in your pocket, dialogue will become one of the greatest moral and storytelling conundrums you will face when writing a memoir. You may feel that you need some of it, a smattering at least, to round-out characters, change the pace, dissect the rub between what was thought and what was actually said. You may need dialogue because in life people talk to one another and readers want to know what they said. They want to know the *sound* of the relationships.

Dialogue isn't, strictly speaking, absolutely necessary in a memoir...But when it's done right, it feels essential. It seems to bring one closer to the story's heart.

Beth Kephart, *Handling the Truth,* 2013

It is a mistake to dismiss illness memoirs out of hand. The worst of them are showy and whiny. The best of them are tussling with the great human themes in an utterly contemporary context...

Disease is everywhere. How anyone could ever write about themselves or their fictional characters as not diseased is a bit beyond me. We live in a world that is spinning out more and more medicines that correspond to more and more diseases at an alarming pace...

The illness memoir is so many things: a kindly attempt to keep company; a product of our culture's love of pathology, or of our sometimes whorish selves; a story of human suffering and the attempts to make meaning within it; and finally, a reflection on this awful and absurd and somehow very funny truth, that we are rotting, rotting, even as we write. [This is why I don't read illness memoirs.]

Lauren Slater in *Writing Creative Nonfiction,* Carolyn Forche and Philip Gerard, editors, 2001

Memoirs about cats and dogs are nearly as common as cats and dogs.

John Williams, *The New York Times Book Review,* July 13, 2014

In August of 1994 I started writing *Angela's Ashes.* I was sixty-four years old...I began by writing in the past tense about my parents meeting in New York and having me. Then, suddenly--it's on page nineteen of the book--I wrote a sentence in the present tense that says: "I'm in a playground on Classon Avenue in Brooklyn with my brother Malachy. He's two, I'm three. We're on the seesaw." I meant it just as a note to myself for the next day: how to continue. But the next day I continued where I had left off, in the present tense, in the voice of the child on the seesaw. It felt very comfortable, and I just kept going with it. The whole book is in the present tense, with a great lack of punctuation and with simple sentences and a simple vocabulary. It was kind of a mosaic: bits would come to me and I'd put them down. It wasn't a linear process, though in general the narrative follows the "Once upon a time" format right to the end.

Frank McCourt in *Inventing the Truth,* edited by William Zinsser, 1998

THE JOURNAL

Because they had to preserve the family secrets, nineteenth-century women wrote for themselves as diarists much more frequently than they wrote memoirs. The diary allowed confidences no one else was supposed to hear. The mere act of sitting down to write an autobiography broke the code of female respectability, because doing so required a woman to believe that her direct experience, rather than her relationships with others, was what gave meaning to her life.

Jill Ker Conway, *When Memory Speaks*, 1998

In writing your journal give primary attention to detail; for it is detail which organizes and preserves experiences for your future self or some other reader. General statements like "We had a wonderful time," or "It was a dismal morning" make a mockery of the whole procedure, for they evaluate experience without recreating it. I kept long journals from ages two to twenty-two, chronicling events and describing emotional states, but again and again missing the physical immediacy of the experience, the tiny hooks by which experience could have been caught and held. I failed to record how we looked, what we saw, the minor eccentricities of circumstances which gave special character to a day. I ignored these elements not only through lack of training but through misplaced priorities: I mistakenly assumed that one could discuss the heart of things without discussing the immediate details of life.

Robert Grudin in *The Writer's Life* (1997) edited by Carol Edgarian and Tom Jenks

I've kept a journal on a capricious basis since I was sixteen. For me, my journal is a supplement to my imagination. I recently heard of a novelist who cuts out magazine photos of people, pastes them on his study wall, and uses them as the basis for his character descriptions. I completely approve. Writing is hard enough, and I welcome anything that helps me along. Besides, I can't help but filter what I see through my imagination, so even my most autobiographical fiction is, in a sense, wholly imagined.

Robin Hemley, *Turning Life Into Fiction*, 2006

Writers keep journals because they like to write between projects, or they have other subjects to get off their minds besides the one they are writing about. They sometimes keep a journal because they want to write about their subjects in an unstructured way. They write journals because they like to keep writing.

Shelia Bender in *The Writer's Journal,* edited by Shelia Bender, 1997

A writer's journal must not be judged by the standards of a diary. The notebooks of a writer have a very special function: in them he builds up, piece by piece, the identity of a writer to himself. Typically, writers' notebooks are crammed with statements about the will: the will to write, the will to love, the will to renounce love, the will to go on living. The journal is where a writer is heroic to himself. In it he exists solely as a perceiving, suffering, struggling being.

Susan Sontag, *Against Interpretation,* 1969

If you have not been keeping a journal or diary, it is time to start one--or a couple of them. There is a personal journal where you write your innermost feelings about life, often in a spirited, free-writing, spontaneous fashion. Then there is a writer's journal, where you record your thoughts and ideas about your writing work. In a writer's journal you conduct an ongoing, spontaneous dialogue with yourself about writing, developing the subjects and ideas you intend to or are actually writing about. I compare a writer's journal to an artist's sketchbook. It is where the masterpiece begins.

Lee Gutkind, *The Art of Creative Nonfiction,* 1997

When I began making a living as a journalist, my father [John Cheever] often suggested that if something disturbed me, I might try writing about it. Keeping a journal helped him a great deal, he said. Putting experience down on paper made it seem less chaotic, less depressing, more sympathetic. "I write to make sense of my life," he used to say.

Susan Cheever, *Home Before Dark,* 1984

Many diarists, concerned over seeming too self-absorbed, actually avoid recording their own perceptions, reactions, and feelings. They describe other people and events but forget to include themselves as observers with unique perceptions and feelings that are validly explored in a diary.

Tristine Rainer, *Your Life Story*, 1998

No matter how messy or incomplete, journals are the missing links in creative life. For centuries, they've helped beginning and seasoned writers alike trigger new work and sustain inspiration. Anne Frank used hers for the basis of a book she wanted to write after the war. She mined it for details and later rewrote entries and composed scenes. Novelist Virginia Wolf invented herself as a writer in her journal. From age 17 until four days before her death [suicide] at 60, she used journals to move from family sketches to memoir to novels.

Alexandra Johnson, *The Hidden Writer*, 1998

My journals date from about 1917 to about 1930, with a few entries of more recent date. They occupy two-thirds of a whiskey carton. How many words that would be I have no idea, but it would be an awful lot. The journals are callow, sententious, moralistic, and full of rubbish. They are also hard to ignore. They were written sometimes in longhand, sometimes typed (single typed). They contain many clippings. Extensive is the word for them. I do not hope to publish them, but I would like to get a little mileage out of them. After so many years, they tend to hold my attention even though they do not excite my admiration. I have already dipped into them on a couple of occasions, to help out on a couple of pieces.

E. B. White, *The Second Tree From the Corner*, 1954

Here is the diary of a book [*The Grapes of Wrath*] and it will be interesting to see how it works out. I have tried to keep diaries before but they don't work out because of the necessity to be honest. In matters where there is no definite truth, I gravitate toward the opposite. Sometimes where there is definite truth, I am revolted by its smugness and do the same. In this however, I shall try simply to keep a record of working days and the amount done in each and the success (as far as I can know it) of the day. Just now the work goes well. It is nearly the first of June [1938].

John Steinbeck, *Journal of a Novel*, 1969

AUTOBIOGRAPHY

Since the 1950s literary critics have written hundreds of volumes about autobiography as a genre. The questions they ask come from literary theory. Is autobiography just another form of fiction? A bastard form of the novel or of biography? What sort of story can anyone tell about her or his life when its end is as yet unknown? Is it possible to translate the chaotic ebb and flow of experience into a narrative form with a beginning, a middle and an end? When so much of our consciousness is visual, or nonverbal, how much of it can we convey through the limited medium of words? Can anyone be both subject and object of the same sentences--the speaker and the subject spoken about? Why is this drive to engage in scrutiny of one's own life so characteristic of the West?

Jill Ker Conway, *When Memory Speaks,* 1998

The first autobiography is considered to be St. Augustine's *Confessions* (c. 400), the groundbreaking exploration of the author's philosophical and emotional development during his restless youth and his conversion to Christianity.

Sherri Szeman, *Mastering Point of View,* 2001

If you would not be forgotten as soon as you are dead and rotten, either write things worth reading, or do things worth the writing.

Benjamin Franklin, *The Autobiography of Benjamin Franklin,* 1791

When Jean-Jacques Rousseau (1712-1778) completed his *Confessions* in 1770 he introduced the secular hero into European literature and recounted his own life in a form and style which influenced male life histories well into the twentieth century. Rousseau set the pattern which required the autobiographer to record the shaping influences of his childhood and the emotions of his maturity. But even as Rousseau set down his denunciation of aristocratic privilege and contrasted his real emotional life with received values, an American contemporary, Benjamin Franklin (1706-1790), was forging another male life plot, which preempted much of the foreground of nineteenth-century male autobiography. Franklin's self-presentation defined for the first time the archetypal figure of the capitalist hero, rebellious against inherited privilege, scornful of inefficiency and of waste, driven by economic motives which never figured in Rousseau's wildest dreams. While Rousseau wanted to compel an inattentive society to recognize his literary and dramatic genius, Franklin describes himself as content to accumulate wealth, and to instruct the rest of the world about the moral and economic qualities which earned him his wealth, and through it status and public recognition.

Jill Ker Conway, *When Memory Speaks*, 1998

In the eighteenth century, autobiography was one of the highest forms of literary art. Fiction was deemed unworthy, while narration of facts was aesthetically and philosophically pleasing. This prevailing convention overwhelmed fiction to such a degree that many novelists passed their works off as non-fiction, sometimes by creating prefaces written by supposedly real characters who vouched for the authenticity of the story. Whether readers really believed in the truth of these stories is hard to say.

"The Narrative Life of Frederick Douglass: An American Slave," cliffnotes.com, no date

Some writers never write about themselves because they are private, or because they do not believe it is possible for one to say anything objectively truthful or valid about oneself.

Deena Metzger, *Writing For Your Life*, 1992

More than celebrated figures in other professions, the writers of imaginative literature have proved almost incapable of separating autobiographical fancy from fact. Mark Twain had a genius for embroidering, to say nothing of inventing the events of his life.

Richard D. Aftick, *Loves and Letters*, 1965

The edited diaries of Anais Nin were set down spontaneously as natural diaries, but when Nin chose to publish them, she want back and edited and rewrote from the perspective of a later point in time. Although overlooked,

Nin's importance is in creating a new hybrid literary form, something between diary and autobiography.

Tristine Rainer, *The New Diary*, 1978

Autobiographies are written as their authors *remember* their lives, which may or may not be the way it really was. Autobiography has a limited market with commercial publishers unless the author is already well-known or has had a most unusual and interesting life.

Doris Ricker Marston, *A Guide to Writing History*, 1976

For though fame is a help in selling books, it is of small use in writing them. And though a reader may be pleased to eavesdrop on the reminiscences of famous people, he will rarely come away from such volumes with more than a nodding acquaintance. The reason for this is that famous people are usually too sensitive of their image to write anything of themselves that may jeopardize it, such as they are bored, frightened, bewildered or hollow as the drums that acclaimed them. Famous people, when they take to autobiography, are chiefly full of tidings about their pedestals and how they got on them, and how modestly they occupy them, and how many other people on pedestals they know.

Ben Hecht, *A Child of the Century*, 1985

I have tried autobiography and found that I am not to be trusted with it. I hate the restrictiveness of facts; I just can't control my impulse to rearrange, suppress, add, heighten, invent, and improve. Accuracy means less to me that suggestiveness; my memory is as much an inventor as a recorder, and when it has operated it has operated almost as freely as if no personal history were involved.

Wallace Stegner, *On Teaching and Writing Fiction*, 2002

This is what the New Autobiography genre is: the discovery of the unique story or stories your life makes. It is the application of story structure to your life experiences to give them meaning. It's reading your life as if it were a dream, asking, "What hidden significance do these characters and these events have for me?" It's shaping these elements into what is compelling to read as a contemporary novel. The New Autobiography asks that you perceive your life as a writer would, not simplistically, but with the mystery and complexity of literature.

Tristine Rainer, *Your Life as Story*, 1998

19 BIOGRAPHY

In our society, the journalist ranks with the philanthropist as a person who has something extremely valuable to dispense (his currency is the strangely intoxicating substance called publicity), and who is consequently treated with a deference quite out of proportion to his merits as a person. There are very few people in this country who do not regard with rapture the prospect of being written about or being interviewed on a radio or television program.

Janet Malcolm, *The Journalist and the Murderer*, 1990

In the writing of a biography, it is expedient to approach one's subject from the periphery, from the outside in--to study first the times, then move to the localities and persons of the immediate story.

Catherine Drinker Bowen, *Adventures of a Biographer*, 1959

I was never interested in writing biographies merely to tell the lives of famous men. [Caro is the author of a three volume biography of Lyndon B. Johnson.] I never had the slightest interest in doing that. From the first time I thought of becoming a biographer, I conceived of biography as a means of illuminating the times and the great forces that shape the times--particular political power. A biography will only do that, of course, if the biography is of the right man.

Robert A. Caro in *Extraordinary Lives*, edited by William Zinsser, 1986

In general, a biography has to have a theme, and its subject has to fit into the context of the times the subject lived in. More than that, the subject of a biography should also be a symbol of some sort or the spirit of his or her age. The book should bring out some thematic element of that culture. Broadly, a good biography is one that illuminates and shows the times as much as the person.

Peter Rubie, *Telling the Story*, 2003

I like to think that biographers can sometimes be messengers between past people and the present. What are all these letters and journals there for? Is it possible that when we're dead we have different priorities, that we no longer wish to be silent as it were? I believe there is a case to be made for bringing the dead to life, for a bit, in a way. To be a messenger going backwards and forwards is worthwhile.

Michael Holroyd, "On Writing: Authors Reveal the Secrets of Their Craft," theguardian.com, March 25, 2011

Aspiring writers find biography a less attractive form of creative nonfiction because they like to write about themselves, and unlike memoir, poetry, fiction, and drama, biography offers little chance for self-expression.

Philip Furia in *Writing Creative Nonfiction*, edited by Carolyn Forche and Philip Gerard, 2001

Biography is a vain and foolhardy undertaking. Its essential conceit, that the unimaginable distance between two human beings can be crossed, is unsupportable; each of us is inherently unknowable. The biographer may be able to locate his subject in place and time--to describe the clothes he wore, the food he ate, the jobs he had, the opinions he expressed--but that subject's inner essence is, by its very nature, forever inaccessible.

Jonathan Yardley, *Misfit*, 1997

Picasso was an awful man. I don't think you have to love your subject-- initially you shouldn't--but writing a biography is like picking a roommate. After all you're going to be with that person every day, maybe for years, and why subject yourself to someone you have no respect for, or outright don't like?

David McCullough, *The Paris Review*, Fall, 1999

I think the most biased biography I know of, almost viciously biased against the subject, was Lawrence Thompson's biography of Robert Frost. But Frost did not do the convenient things. Thompson took on the job of being Frost's biographer something like forty years before Frost died, and he was not allowed to publish the book until Frost was gone. That was their agreement. If Frost had died at sixty or seventy, instead of ninety, that would have been much nicer for Thompson. So there's that side of it. And Frost had some pretty unpleasant characteristics, along with tremendous charm. Thompson simply got turned off by him. There was a relationship with a woman that involved them both--they were rivals--there's nothing about that in the biography, of course. Thompson ends by attributing the worst possible motives to anything Frost did. The book is painful to read.

Scott Donaldson, themillions.com, February 27, 2012

The most important thing that you as a biographer can do is to write from the heart. Write only about someone you have deep feelings for. If you care deeply about your subject, either positively or negatively, so will your readers. If you take on a biography about someone you couldn't care less about, possibly for the money, or because you have received a good publishing contract, the readers won't care about your subject either, and probably won't finish reading your book.

Brian Klems, writersdigest.com, December 9, 2013

The biographer's business, like the journalist's, is to satisfy the reader's curiosity, not to place limits on it. He is supposed to go out and bring back the goods--the malevolent secrets that have been quietly burning in archives and libraries and in the minds of contemporaries who have been biding their time, waiting for the biographer's knock on their doors. Some of the secrets are difficult to bring away, and some, jealously guarded by relatives, are even impossible. Relatives are the biographer's natural enemies; they are like the hostile tribes the explorer must ruthlessly subdue to claim his territory.

Janet Malcolm, *The Silent Woman*, 1994

My last biography is no sooner in the stores when the letters start coming suggesting a subject for my next one. The grandmothers of these letter writers are crying from the grave, it seems, for literary recognition. It is bewildering, the number of salty grandfathers, aunts, and uncles that languish unappreciated.

Catherine Drinker Bowen, *Adventures of a Biographer*, 1959

The historian frames a cosmos of happenings in which men are included only as event producers or event sufferers. The biographer explores the cosmos of a single being. History deals in generalizations about a time. Biography deals in the particulars of one person's life.

Paul Murray Kendall in *Biography as High Adventure*, edited by Stephen B. Oates, 1986

As a prism of history, biography attracts and holds the reader's interest in the larger subject. People are interested in other people, in the fortunes of the individual.

Barbara W. Tuchman in *Biography as High Adventure*, edited by Stephen B. Oates, 1986

Research is only research. After all the facts have been marshaled, all the documents studied, all the locales visited, all the survivors interviewed, what then? What do the facts add up to? What did the life mean?

William Zinsser in *Extraordinary Lives*, edited by William Zinsser, 1986

Between history and the novel stands biography, their unwanted offspring, which has brought a great embarrassment to them both. In the historian's view it takes ten thousand biographies to make one small history. To the novelist biographers are simply what Nabokov called, "psycho-plagiarists."

Michael Holroyd, *Works on Paper*, 2002

Biography is not the place for "debunking," although in recent years there has been a trend in that direction. Why would a biographer wish to spend his days of work giving vent to anger or carrying on a literary association with a person he despises? Yet some enjoy this and write bestsellers.

Doris Ricker Marston, *A Guide to Writing History*, 1996

How to begin? I had always shuddered at biographies that began, "It was a clear, cold morning in mid-December 1830, when the cry of a newborn baby broke the winter stillness." And once you begin, how to tell the story of a life that had no story?

Richard B. Sewall in *Extra Ordinary Lives*, edited by William Zinsser, 1986

Considerable commentary focuses on the nexus between biography and fiction. As a narrative genre, biography would seem to have the greatest affinity with the novel, since both excel in the creation of characters and scenes through the sensibility of narrators. And yet the biographer has much in common with the dramatist, since biography is a kind of impersonation and the biographer functions as a kind of actor attempting to represent his subject's sensibility. The greatest biography in the English language, Boswell's *Life of Johnson*, consists mainly of dialogue, with Boswell's own comments serving almost like those of a director's notes.

Carl Rollyson, *Biography*, 2008

The dangers of biography are inaccuracy and hero worship. The biographer needs to cultivate an objective eye that fits his subject into the world with compassion. Most biographers treat their subjects as one of three things: an example, a victim, or a source of wisdom.

Peter Rubie, *Telling the Story*, 2003

One respect in which modern biography resembles fiction is its fascination with its subjects' sexual lives. In the eighteenth and nineteenth centuries the novel was the literary genre above all others to which readers turned for the representation of sexuality. Biography restricted itself to the public lives of its subjects--or, insofar as it dealt with their private lives, did not intrude into the bedroom.

David Lodge, *The Practice of Writing, 1996*

Unauthorized biographies undress their subjects. When John Updike realized that a biographer was on his case, he hurriedly wrote a memoir, *Self-Consciousness,* so that he could forestall the biography. Autobiography and the authorized biography are time-honored methods of attempting to derail independent biographies and make them seem illicit.

Carl Rollyson, *Biography,* 2008

Almost every eminent person leaves behind an abundance of personal data which, skillfully manipulated, can prove him to have been a fool or a knave. Innocuous personal details and casual episodes, if sufficiently emphasized, described with archness and placed in misleading context, can be as damaging in their effect as plain evidence of dim intellect or villainy.

Richard D. Aftick, *Lives and Letters,* 1965

Literary biographers are parasites. They are Fifth Column agents within the ranks of literature, intent on reducing all that is imaginative, all that is creative in literature to pedestrian biography. They are the slaves of their absurd and meager theories. They feed off literature: they attempt to replace it.

Michael Holroyd, *Works on Paper,* 2002

Disagreement over the merits of literary biography will likely subside by default, as the form begins to extinguish itself. Even among those who like it, demand is bound to slacken: Novelists' lives are considerably less interesting than they used to be. Longer, yes, but much drier in every sense; less full of rivalrous brawling, less harrowed by the unemployment that was so often their lot before creative writing programs started offering them day jobs. For another thing, literary biography will be crippled by the absence of many of its old tools. Writers' drafts, those manuscripts that show, line by line, how writers came to do what they did, now disappear with the deleting drag of the mouse; and for all the supposed permanence of tweets and Facebook posts, the deliberate letters that writers used to save and bundle have largely been replaced by emails and texts they don't bother to archive.

Thomas Mallon, *The New York Times Book Review,* June 29, 2014

It is no accident that the popularity of literary biography has increased most notably in the past century and a half, a period which has also been marked by a growing sense that the artist as a person is detached from society, indeed a special kind of person quite apart from the common run of men.

Richard D. Altick, *Lives and Letters,* 1965

Oral biography's biggest problem, of course, is the lack of any controlling intelligence. Recorded interviewees exaggerate and ramble on, often ludicrously.

Thomas Mallon, *In Fact,* 2001

When I'm struggling with my own work I'm often drawn to biographies of writers. Not only do I learn fun facts about prominent figures--Henry James suffered terribly from constipation, Kafka chewed every bite of food 32 times, Flannery O'Conner cared for a flock of around 40 peacocks, Montaigne never saw his wife with her clothes off, Balzac fortified himself with a paste made of unroasted coffee beans--I'm also reminded that there's no single path for living a successful creative or personal life. It's inspiring to read about a flawed human being who struggled with his or her demons and afflictions, experienced paralyzing episodes of failure or self-doubt, but somehow managed to do the work anyway, and produce something that enriched the world. That's my version of self-help.

Tom Perrota in *The New York Times Book Review,* December 1, 2013

Bad books by celebrity authors shouldn't surprise us [Bill O'Reilly's *Killing Kennedy*], even when the subject is an American president. The true mystery in Kennedy's case is why, 50 years after his death, highly accomplished writers seen unable to fix him on the page.

For some, the trouble has been idolatry. Arthur Schlesinger Jr., who wrote three magisterial volumes on Franklin Roosevelt and the new deal, attempted a similar history in *A Thousand Days: John F. Kennedy in The White House.* Published in 1965, it has the virtues of immediacy, since Schlesinger, Kennedy's Harvard contemporary, had been on the White House staff, brought in as court historian. He witnessed many of the events he describes. But in his admiration for Kennedy, he became the chief architect of the Camelot myth and so failed, in the end, to give a persuasive account of the actual presidency.

In 1993, the political journalist Richard Reeves did better. *President Kennedy: Profile of Power* is a minutely detailed chronicle of the Kennedy White House. As a primer on Kennedy's decision-making, like his handling of the Bay of Pigs invasion and the Cuban missile crisis, the book is fascinating. What's missing is a picture of Kennedy's personal life, though Reeves includes a passing mention of Marilyn Monroe being sewn into the $5,000 flesh-colored, skintight dress she wore to celebrate the president's birthday at Madison Square Garden in 1962....

Balancing out, or warring with, the Kennedy claque are the Kennedy haters, like Seymour M. Hersh and Garry Wills. In *The Dark Side of Camelot*, Hersh wildly posits connections between the Kennedys and the mob, while Wills, through he offers any number of brilliant insights into Kennedy and his circle of courtiers, fixates on the Kennedy brothers' (and father's) sexual escapades in *The Kennedy Imprisonment*.

The sum total of this oddly polarized literature is a kind of void. Other presidents, good and bad, have been served well by biographers and historians. We have first-rate books on Jefferson on Lincoln, on Wilson, on both Roosevelts. Even unloved presidents have received major books: Johnson (Caro) and Richard Nixon (Wills, among others). Kennedy, the odd man out, still seeks his true biographer.

Jill Abramson, "The Elusive President," *The New York Times Book Review,* October 27, 2013

20 TRUE CRIME

Crime fiction spends a great deal of time sorting through the chaos to find some order, a sense of resolution for the often inexplicable madness of murder. Real crimes, however, don't work that way. Evidence is misfiled, suspects evade arrest on technicalities, investigations stretch out for years before an end comes in sight--if at all. True crime is a messier affair....

Sarah Wienman, The Daily Beast, May 2010

I define a true crime book as one involving a murder. It's not about art theft or about governmental cover-up. It's really a case involving a murder in which there's an investigation and usually a trial...The best of the true crimes give you some insight into characters, usually the character of the killer, and the situation that produced the crime.

Charles Spicer, crimeculture.com, 2002

What is there to say about true-crime books? They're fun. They can be intellectually compelling, and, like the fictional variety from [crime novelists] Hammett, Cain and that crowd, they're more often than not rooted in the far side of respectability or polite society. Most every writer wants to write one. The trick is to come up with the right crime, the right crook or issue.

Peter Manso, The Huffington Post, July 2011

A number of popular true crime writers today (and yesterday) like to fluff up their narratives with figments from their imaginations, and often sugarcoat the details about a crime for what they think will bring them a wider reading audience. But I don't do that. It's not fair to the memories of the victims, their families, or the cops who worked the cases and brought the killers to justice. I tell it like it is, and I've been told time and time again by victims' families that this is the way they want their loved ones' stories to be told--truthfully, even though it is painful. Seeing things made up, they tell me, is more painful to them because often times the criminals become glamorized in a sense. You won't find glamorized killers in my books.

Gary C. King, allthingscrime.com, July 2013

I prefer an unpublicized case in which I am the only person writing about it because the people involved are so much more willing to cooperate and be interviewed. Publishers, of course, want a story that's been splashed all over television, magazines, and newspapers.

Don Lasseter, crimeculture.com, November 2003

I start every book with the idea that I want to explain how this seven or eight pounds of protoplasm went from his mommy's arms to become a serial rapist or serial killer. I think a crime book that doesn't do this is pure pornography.

Jack Olsen, *Seattle Post-Intelligencer,* July 19, 2002

True crime writing draws upon the methods of nonfiction and fiction, turns the American dream of picket fences and summer picnics into the American nightmare; solicits a particular kind of reader response, and cautiously toes the line between fact and fiction, and the temptation on part of the author to "create and embellish" for the sake of art. True crime writing can be understood as a style, a form, and a genre of universal appeal forever embedded in our popular culture, however sensational and exploitive it has become. Styles of writing and the themes portrayed are often grisly, morbid, and voyeuristic, thus obscuring the work of serious crime historians attempting to establish important links between economic conditions, social mores, and the day-to-day living conditions of people in a given place and time.

Richard Lindberg, richardlindberg.net, 2002

It is generally held that the genre of true crime has been around since the latter part of the 19th century. As a precursor to these nonfiction accounts of crime, writers such as Wilkie Collins, Charles Dickens and William Thackeray borrowed incidents and characters from real crimes for their novels.

Vicky Munro, crimeculture.com, 2001

The tools I have used for my writing career have been my ability to interview people and get them to tell me the truth, and my abilities as an investigative reporter. I might spend weeks verifying some little fact that is just going to be great in my book--it's going to be a little spark. Fiction writers don't need to spend weeks looking for the little spark--they invent it. I write about real people, real Americans getting into trouble, getting out of it, going to the penitentiary, going to the electric chair, being murdered, being saved. And it's all true.

Margaret DiCanio in *The 3rd Degree*, October 1997

Every genre has its own peculiar demands and drawbacks. True crime has more than most. Successful true crime writers have to be self-starters. Many times a week, fledgling authors ask me how they can be crime writers. I tell them as gently as possible that the very nature of the genre requires writers who will find a way themselves. We must not only be writers--but detectives. In researching a crime, we must figure out how to elicit information that seems impossible to get. We have to ask people about pain and horror they would rather forget. We must ask detectives and prosecutors to share their investigations and their findings with us. And it isn't easy.

Ann Rule in *Writing Mysteries*, Sue Grafton, editor, 2002

Occasionally, true crime is where literary writers go to slum and, not coincidentally, make some real money: Truman Capote's *In Cold Blood*, Norman Mailer's *The Executioner's Song*. It's not the Great American Novel, yet somehow such books have a tendency to end up the most admired works of a celebrated author's career. Is it because better writers tease something out of the genre that pulp peddlers can't, or is it just that their blue-chip names give readers a free pass to indulge a guilty pleasure?

True crime labors under the stigma of voyeurism, or worse. It's not just unseemly to linger over the bloodied bodies of the dead and the hideous sufferings inflicted upon them in their final hours, it's also a kind of sickness. Gillian Flynn's novel, *Dark Places*, describes the wincing interactions between the narrator, a survivor of a notorious multiple murder, and a creepy subculture of murder "fans" and collectors. When she's hard for cash, she's forced to auction off family memorabilia at one of their true crime conventions.

The very thing that makes true crime compelling also makes it distasteful: the use of human agony for the purposes of entertainment.

Laura Miller, "Sleazy, Bloody and Surprisingly Smart: In Defense of True Crime," salon.com, May 29, 2014

If you want to be a true crime writer, the best thing you can be is immensely curious. And, you should go to criminal trials. Here are tips and etiquette for trial watching.

1. You can usually get a press pass, but there's often a deluge of writers trying to obtain one. Call the prosecutor's assistant.
2. Study the witnesses, watch the jury, and soak up the entire experience.
3. Try to obtain the court documents from the court reporter or the prosecutor, or purchase them.
4. Observe the other reporters in the room, and analyze what they are doing.
5. If you're sitting out in the hall with potential witnesses, don't ask them about *anything*. Keep our eyes and ears open and your mouth shut.
6. Don't take newspapers into the courtroom.
7. Know what you're getting yourself into. You don't want to start a book unless you're really in love with the story.
8. Absorb detail. When I'm writing a true crime book I want the reader to walk along with me…As far as writing, you can novelize, but keep all of your facts straight.
9. Don't use the real name of a rape or sexual crime victim in your writing.

Ann Rule in "Ann Rule on Breaking Into True Crime," writersdigest.com, by Zachary Petit, July 13, 2012

Why are some true crimes turned into books, while others barely make the national papers? It will hardly come as a staggering surprise to find that publishers choose only those cases that are out of the ordinary: so, while murder is a favorite topic for books, "domestic" murders are not, unless several people in the family are killed. The sort of case that attracts a book publisher is likely to involve a large-scale crime, a mass or serial murder or a murderer who has been freed and has killed again or perhaps a murderer who almost got away with it.

Philip Rawlings, britsoccrim.org, April, 1995

Give me a book that begins with a time and a date and an address, something along the lines of: "At 9:36 on March 24, 1982, Deputy Frank McGruff of the Huntington County Sheriff's Department was dispatched to 234 Maple Street in Pleasantville, North Carolina, a quiet suburb 10 miles west of Raleigh, to follow up on reports of gunshots and screams."

There is nothing more generic that this sort of sentence, and yet there's nothing more seductive, either. The sentence carries promises: the regular-guy lawman, the horrific crime scene, the enigmatic object found lying in the foyer, the minute-by-minute timeline of that fatal half-hour, the witness reports that don't add up, and the multiplication of scenarios and theories and complications.

I've always felt somewhat sheepish about my appetite for true crime narratives, associated as they are with fat, flimsy paperbacks scavenged from the 25-cent box at garage sales, their battered covers branded with screaming two-word titles stamped in silver foil, blood dripping luridly from the last letter. The most famous practitioners of this genre--Joe McGinniss, Ann Rule, Vincent Bugliosi--come coated with a thin, greasy film of dubious repute and poor taste.

True crime is also the mother's milk of tabloid journalism, of endless trashy news cycles in which the same photo of a wide-eyed innocent bride (where is she?); a gap-toothed kindergarten student (who killed him?); a bleary-eyed, stubbled suspect (why did he do it?) appear over and over and over again.

Laura Miller, "Sleazy Bloody and Surprisingly Smart: In Defense of True Crime," salon.com, May 29, 2014

There are many reasons I can't write about a true crime case. Sometimes, (1) there isn't enough there to fill a full-length book; (2) the characters are just not interesting; (3) the case has been over-publicized; (4) the story is too sad; or (5) the timing of a case may be wrong because I am already attending other trials or writing other books...I have to wait until an arrest has been made and a case is headed for trial. From there on it's a gamble; if the defendant should be acquitted, I probably couldn't write the book.

Ann Rule, annrule.com, October 2003

True crime writing really demands that you be honest and back up everything you write with facts. I always keep all my notes, copies of court documents and police reports so that I can verify what I've put into print. True crime is just that--it's the truth. And time after time I've discovered that truth can be stranger than fiction.

Robert Scott, authorsontheweb.com, May 2002

The main audience for true crime works is generally the middle class with more women than men buying the books. There is also a fairly strong teen market, and books of regional interest have specialized markets. For example, both Texas and the Pacific Northwest are strong locales for the true crime market.

Vicky Munro, crimeculture.com, September, 2000

True crime books should be suspenseful. It's easier to create complete suspense in fiction, but it's still possible to hold back the denouement of a real case for a few hundred pages. It's always a temptation for new writers to give the whole thing away in the first chapter, leaning very heavily on verbatim on police files. If you do that, your book will sound stilted *and* will go downhill rather than building tension.

Ann Rule in *Writing Mysteries,* Sue Grafton, editor, 2002

Put simply, adherence to the truth in nonfiction makes a story feel right. Perhaps the most famous compromise of that standard is Truman Capote's imagined graveyard scene at the end of *In Cold Blood,* still considered the benchmark for what he called the "non-fiction novel." A brilliant study of a murdered family and the killers who are eventually hanged, there was no happy ending available to the writer. Capote felt a need to resolve that artificially, blighting his immense achievement in synthesizing research with dramatic storytelling with a dreamy and unconvincing denouement he always regretted.

Mark Mordue, *The Australian,* January 14, 2006

When I'm in a writing mode (eight months of the year), I am at my computer at least six days a week from ten in the morning to about 7:30 in the evening. I require ten pages a day--my personal commitment.

Ann Rule, writersreview.com, July 2002

True crime stories must be post-trial, with the perpetrators convicted and sentenced at the conclusion…Use *active* writing, avoid passive constructions. Remember that detectives probe, dig up, determine, deduce, seek out, ascertain, discover, hunt, root out, delve, uncover, track, trace, and inspect. They also canvass, inquire, question, and quiz.

Jim Thompson in *Savage Art* by Robert Polito, 1995

Writing a true crime book requires the writer to dig into angles not covered in the original rush of publicity and to deeply research the stories of victims, survivors, investigators, attorneys, and others; review all court, prison, psychiatric, medical, police and other documents about the perpetrator and interview people close to him.

Gretchen Brinck, authorsontheweb.com, January 2002

There is nothing like a good murder story to sell newspapers. And a good story needs an eye-catching headline. The Victorians mastered this art and nowhere was the genre better demonstrated than during the 1870s in the *Illustrated Police News.* This was a popular, high-circulation newspaper and a forerunner of the modern tabloids.

The paper reported various types of criminal happenings and bizarre events with arresting headlines and, in an age before press photographs, used graphic artists' illustrations. Headlines contained two essential elements to connect with readers' interests. First was a reference to the nature of the crime and, all importantly, where it had taken place. This was usually preceded by an adjective to stimulate interest and convey a sense of outrage. Thus, in 1873, a "Dreadful Child Murder at Hull" was reported and, in 1876, a "Frightful Wife Murder in Bristol."

Robin Odell, *The Mammoth Book of Bizarre Crimes*, 2010

21 CRITICISM

A "mere book reviewer" writes for newspapers, magazines [and websites and blogs] and is content to treat books as news. He announces their publication, identifies their authors, briefly describes their contents and sometimes renders a verdict. Journalistic critics, who also write for the above media outlets, try whenever possible to climb out of the valley of "mere reviewing" onto the plateau of genuine criticism. The academic critics contribute to popular publications when the chance offers, but most of their work appears in learned journals and in book form. They are usually professors and usually they write for other professors, for serious students and for literary intellectuals. They are enormously influential because they are read in colleges and universities.

Orville Prescott in *Writer's Roundtable,* edited by Helen Hull and Michael Drury, 1959

A good book review should do an evocative job of pointing out quality. "Look at this! Isn't this good?" should be the critic's basic attitude. Occasionally, however, you have to say, "Look at this! Isn't it awful?" In either case, it's important to quote from the book. Criticism has no real power, only influence.

Clive James, poet and author, 2013 interview

Book reviewing in England is and always has been somewhat differently arranged than in the United States. Most often, in the United States, writers review one another's books and there is some sense of generosity born of shared time in the novel-writing trenches. It is more common in England for a novel to be reviewed by what you might call professional book assessors...

It is perfectly acceptable, and even desirable, in England for a reviewer to show off his talent for eloquent invective at the expense of the author-- desirable because it's fun for all, and if a novel is entertainingly killed, that's one less author who will be pulling his chair up to a crowded table.

Jane Smiley, *13 Ways of Looking at The Novel,* 2005

Novelists are not remotely wary of criticizing one another's work in private; they do it all the time. Only when they're asked to commit their shoptalk to print do they grow reticent. A hardy few are prepared to engage tough-mindedly with the works of their peers....

Most fiction writers end up deciding that discretion is the greater part of critical valor. Some recuse themselves from reviewing any contemporary fiction at all. Others review only those novels they can praise in good faith. Still others adopt a tactful, discursive reviewing style that allows them to write about books they don't rate without actually copping to an opinion.

Before we rebuke these writers for their intellectual cowardice, we ought to acknowledge the genuine difficulty of the task they shirk. The literary world is tiny. The subgroup represented by novelists is even tinier. If you're an author who regularly reviews other authors, the chances of running into a person whose novel you have criticized are fairly high....It may not be the worst thing in the world to find yourself side by side at a cocktail party with the angry man whose work you described as mediocre in last Sunday's paper, but the threat of such encounter is not a great spur to critical honesty. [If you're interested in literary courage, read B. R. Myers' book *Reader's Manifesto* where he rips apart several so-called literary giants. A great book and a wonderful read.]

Zoe Heller, *The New York Times Book Review,* September 8, 2013

It is extremely painful to write just what you think about your contemporaries' work, when you are meeting them every day at the club, or at some party. Where personal relations are involved, it is almost impossible to be impartial, because being disagreeably "fair" about the work of a friend does give one a feeling of betrayal. Sooner or later one decides never to review the works of one's friends.

Stephen Spender in *Opinions and Perspectives,* edited by Francis Brown, 1964

The irony is that writers are generally meaner to other writers than critics are. Few critics have anything to gain by penning a bad review...Writers, on the other hand, have everything to gain...It's writers who have personal scores to settle; who drop their professionalism and let it rip. Critics, by and large, say what they think of a book. If they say they don't like it, that usually means they didn't like it, not that they waited for the chance to get back at a bestselling author for the luxury Tuscan villa he owns and they'll never have, or because they have wallpapered their room with rejection slips....

Lesley McDowell, "How Writers Review Their Critics," theguardian.com, September 22, 2010

A lady who was once married to Salman Rushdie had one of her novels published just as the famous *fatwa* was handed down on him. I gave the book a bad review. I was surprised that her pretty awful novel got a solemn, respectful review in *The New York Times* and everywhere else I looked. I was probably the only literate person in America who hadn't heard about the *fatwa*, and when I found out, I was sorry for what I had written. The poor woman had enough to worry about. A few years later, she got hold of one of my novels to review for the *Washington Post* and she *killed* me! She said I wrote "embarrassing surfer prose." Oh, the agony!

Carolyn See, *Making a Literary Life*, 2002

My favorite *Kirkus* review labeled my writing as "awkward and repetitious." I framed that one.

Charles Knief, mysterylinkonline.com, August 29, 2001

Is a reviewer ever justified in attempting to blow a bad book out of the water? I think the answer is yes, but the reviewer must choose his targets with the greatest of care. It's not enough for the book to be bad; other elements must be present: smugness; pretentiousness; and over inflated reputation; clear evidence that a book's badness is not the result of incompetence, but of deliberate design. Such books represent an assault on the republic of letters and should not be ignored.

Peter Prescott, *Never in Doubt*, 1986

People who aren't novelists might think that authors would be well advised to study their negative reviews with care, rather than letting a protective skin form. After all, isn't there something to be learned from the thoughtful analysis of intelligent and knowledgeable critics? Well, maybe, but most of the writers I know don't take them seriously, and neither do I. It's not that I don't respect reviewers. It's that reviewers don't write their columns for writers. They write them with readers in mind, and that's a different thing.

Aaron Elkins, *Mystery Writers Annual,* 2004

I hate orthodox literary criticism, the usual small niggling, fussy-mussy criticism, which thinks it can improve people by telling them where they are wrong, and results only in putting them in straitjackets of hesitancy and self-confidence, and sapping all vision and bravery.

Brenda Ueland, *If You Want to Write,* 1997

Good reviews aren't helpful, and the bad reviews are less. They're not creatively critical. I don't think there's really any point in reading them. You don't learn anything from them.

Thomas Tryon in *Conversations With Writers,* edited by Margaret M. Duggan, 1977

"If you want to be a writer, somewhere along the line you're going to have to hurt somebody. And when that time comes, you go ahead and do it," Charles McGrath said when he was an editor at *The New Yorker.* "If you can't or don't want to tell that truth, you may as well stop now and save yourself a lot of hardship and pain."...

A novelist wrote a withering account of her recent marriage. Soon after the book came out, the author's ex-husband killed himself. Was she correct to write that novel?

Bonnie Friedman, *Writing Past Dark,* 1994

The publishing industry, we hear, is in trouble. So why would a sensible writer tell people not to buy a book? If the novel, as we also hear, is moribund or dead, why drive another nail into its sad little coffin? And lately there seems to be a cultural moratorium on saying something "bad" about anyone or anything, unless you're a politician, in which case that's your job...

There was a time when I wrote negative reviews...I admit it provided a wicked sort of fun, especially when I was writing for an editor-friend who delighted in sending me books that weren't exactly "serious" but got under my skin. Sadly, it's easier to be witty when one is being unkind. Friends would say, "Oh, I just adored your hilarious essay on that celebrity's memoir about her fabulous face-lift." And what would they say when I praised a book? Nothing.

Even so, I stopped. I began returning books I didn't like to editors. I thought, life is short I'd rather spend my time urging people to read things I love. And writing a bad book didn't seem like a crime deserving punitive public humiliation...

But in the last year or so I've found myself again writing negative reviews--as if quitting for three decades I'd suddenly resumed smoking, or something else I'd forsworn. Once more, it's a question of what gets under my skin, and of trying to understand why. I've begun to think, if something bothers me that much, life is too short *not* to say so.

Francine Prose, *The New York Times Book Review*, February 16, 2014

I quit writing after *Publishers Weekly* told me my first novel was "just terrible." Something broke, you see. I was 29 and I'd worked for ten years at that novel, and I didn't see the point of spending another ten years only to be told the same thing again. So I tend bar here in North Plainfield, New Jersey, and try to encourage the other writers who come by now and then. We don't get many writers in North Plainfield.

Luke Walton in *Rotten Reviews and Rejections*, edited by Bill Henderson and Andre Bernards, 1998

There is the critical sin of covetousness, which may cause the book critic to seek fame at the expense of the author whose work he exploits. The closely associated sin of envy leads to the denigration of the work of others for the hidden purpose of self-aggrandizement. To indulge the sin of gluttony is to bite off more than one is prepared to digest, denying others the right to partake. To be lustful is to indulge an inordinate desire for the gratification of one's sense of power. The deadly sin of anger leads to the loss of one's composure and sense of balance during the inevitable exchanges of differing opinion. The deadly sin of sloth is to repeat accepted lies about an author or body of work because the critic is too lazy to dig out the truth.

Carlos Baker in *Opinions and Perspectives From "The New York Times Book Review,"* edited by Francis Brown, 1964

I am never much interested in the effects of what I write. I seldom read with any attention the reviews of my books. Two times out of three I know something about the reviewer, and in very few cases have I any respect for his judgments. Thus his praise, if he praises me, leaves me unmoved. I can't recall any review that has even influenced me in the slightest. I live in sort of a vacuum, and I suspect that most other writers do, too. It is hard to imagine one of the great ones paying any serious attention to contemporary opinion.

H. L. Mencken in *Diary of H. L. Mencken*, edited by Charles A. Fecher, 1989

I think I function in the direct tradition of the early American novel, as a storyteller rather than a philosopher or a teacher; so I'm resented by the school of criticism that rejects storytelling as superficial and looks on the novel as basically as examination of the interior life. The critics don't choose to examine how *well* you tell a story, and that's what I'm interested in.

Howard Fast in *Writing For Your Life*, edited by Sybil Steinberg, 1992

I have never been able to see how the duties of a critic, which consists largely in making painful remarks in public about the most sensitive of his fellow creatures, can be reconciled with the manners of a gentleman. But gentleman or no, a critic is most certainly not bound to perjure himself to shield the reputation of the profession he criticizes.

Bernard Shaw in *Never in Doubt* by Peter S. Prescott, 1986

Most people read books and think them interesting. They don't really reach an intellectual conclusion. They just have an opinion about it, not a judgment. But to reach a judgment about a book is really useful. To have to puzzle it out and then to write out the judgment. So I think that is a function book reviewing performs when it's done well.

Paul Theroux in *Story Story Story*, edited by Jim Schumock, 1999

As for literary criticism in general: I have long felt that any reviewer who expresses rage and loathing for a novel or play or a poem is preposterous. He or she is like a person who has put on full armor and attacked a hot fudge sundae or a banana split.

Kurt Vonnegut, *Palm Sunday*, 1981

The vast academic world exists like everything else, on what it can produce that will secure income. So we have papers on fiction, but they come out of what is largely an industry. In no way does it help those who write fiction or those who love to read fiction.

John Cheever in *Writers at Work, Fifth Series*, edited by George Plimpton, 1981

Criticism and writing are two different talents. I am a good writer but have no critical ability. I can't tell whether something I have written is good or bad, or just why it should be either. I can only say, "I like this story," or "It was easy to read," or other such trivial nonjudgmental remarks.

The critic, if he can't write as I do, can nevertheless analyze what I write and point out flaws and virtues. In this way, he guides the writer and perhaps even helps the writer.

Having said all that, I must remind you that I'm talking about critics of the first caliber. Most critics we encounter, alas, are fly-by-night pipsqueaks without any qualification for the job other than the rudimentary ability to read and write. It is their pleasure sometimes to tear down a book savagely, or to attack the author rather than the book. They use the review, sometimes, as a vehicle for displaying their own erudition or as an opportunity for safe sadism.

Isaac Asimov, *I Asimov: A Memoir*, 1994

[The literary critic's] constant reference to genius is a characteristic of the pseudo-scholar. He loves mentioning genius, because the sound of the word exempts him from trying to discover its meaning. Literature is written by geniuses. Novelists are geniuses. Everything [the critic] says may be accurate but all is useless because he is moving round books instead of through them. He either has not read them or cannot read them properly. Books have to be read...it is the only way of discovering what they contain. The reader must sit down alone and struggle with the writer, and this the pseudo-scholar will not do. He would rather relate a book to the history of its time, to events in the life of its author, or to the events it describes.

E. M. Forster, *Aspects of the Novel*, 1927

Critics are like eunuchs in a harem. They're there every night, they see it done every night, they see how it should be done every night, but they can't do it themselves.

Brendan Behan in *Rotten Reviews & Rejections*, 1998

Academics make careers out of describing who was influenced by whom and how. They collect writers into schools, camps, trends, and tendencies. Novelists of a similar age are also liable to be called a "generation," even if their works have little in common.

Ian Jackman, *The Writer's Mentor*, 2004

In essence, a children's book reviewer reads and writes with two audiences in mind: (1) adults who read reviews to help them select books for children and (2) the children themselves. It is important to remember that most books for children are created with the best intentions in mind. No one sets out to produce a crummy book that kids will hate. If this is your initial assessment of a book you're reviewing, it would be unfair and unwise to let it stand as your final assessment without a great deal of further consideration.

Kathleen T. Horning, *From Cover to Cover*, 1997

ABOUT THE AUTHOR

Jim Fisher is a graduate of Westminster College and Vanderbilt University Law School. He is a Professor Emeritus at Edinboro University of Pennsylvania. In 2004, Southern Illinois University Press published his expose of a bogus literary agent called, *Ten Percent of Nothing*. Rutgers University Press, in 2006, published Fisher's *Writer's Quote Book: 500 Authors on Creativity, Craft, and the Writer's Life*. Jim Fisher is also the author of nine nonfiction books in the true crime and criminal justice genres. Visit Jim's writer's blog, Literary Quotations Collected by Jim Fisher, literaryquotationscollected.blogspot.com.

www.ingramcontent.com/pod-product-compliance
Lightning Source LLC
Chambersburg PA
CBHW070416290526
45791CB00005B/1718